Dialectic of Nihilism

Dialectic of Nihilism

Post-Structuralism and Law

GILLIAN ROSE

BASIL BLACKWELL

© Gillian Rose 1984

First published 1984
Basil Blackwell Publisher Limited
108 Cowley Road, Oxford OX4 1JF, England

Basil Blackwell Inc.
432 Park Avenue South, Suite 1505
New York, NY 10016, USA

British Library Cataloguing in Publication Data

Rose, Gillian
  Dialectic of nihilism.
  1. Law – Philosophy   2. Nihilism
  I. Title
  340'.1   K487.N5

  ISBN 0-631-13191-4
  ISBN 0-631-13708-4 Pbk

Typeset by Katerprint Co Ltd, Oxford
Printed in Great Britain by
Redwood Burn Limited, Trowbridge

For Diana

Contents

Acknowledgements

I would like to thank Jay Bernstein, Greg Bright and Howard Caygill for their works which have supported and sustained mine. I would like to thank, too, Julius Carlebach and Tony Thorlby for strength and good will.

Introduction:
Legalism without Law

This essay is an attempt to retrieve and rediscover a tradition which has been tendentiously and meretriciously 'deconstructed'. The newly vaunted demise of metaphysics has been cast as a theoretical jurisprudence which, nevertheless, leaves law as unknowable as it finds it. The 'deconstruction' of metaphysics involves a reconstruction of the history of law which blinds us to the very tradition which it disowns and repeats. Here the theory and history of law will be addressed as *the question of law*.

The earlier existentialist wave of reception took the thought of Nietzsche and Heidegger to overcome morality; the more recent post-structuralist wave has taken them to overcome legality. Zarathustra's New Law Tables are called upon at critical moments in the work of Deleuze, Derrida and Foucault, who believe themselves to have accepted Nietzsche's challenge to renounce the ambition of previous philosophical labour to overcome the past, and instead to command and legislate the future. The result of this self-denying ordinance is that the world remains not only unchanged, but also unknown. What is more, they invite us to celebrate such impotence at this hecatomb of all previous interpretations.

This destruction of knowledge is justified by its perpetrators as the only way to escape the utopian projections and historicist assumptions of dialectic; 'eternal repetition of the same' is said to be a harder truth than the false and discredited promise of reconciliation. Yet neither the form of this hard truth nor the terms in which it is expressed are neutral: they are always borrowed from some historically identifiable epoch of juridical experience. The terms of this truth may be taken from pre-Homeric religion, Heidegger's Moira or 'the round dance', or feudal warfare, Foucault's 'power'. The invariable form, 'differ-ence' and the recommended *amor fati* have striking affinities with classical natural law. An eternal origin is ascertained indepen-dently both of divine revelation and of positive, human law – but with the crucial difference that it is eternal disorder not order that is perpetuated.

This new location of the origin is sequestered equally from the cunning of dialectical reason (*Vernunft*) and from the courts of critical reason (*Verstand*). Yet its mix of unknowledge and force brings us once again to the mystery of the categorical imperative: inconceivable but absolute. This work will show that the anti-nomy of law, the dual implication of rule and regularity, of force and generality, known to the tradition as *regulae iuris* and to us as 'diachrony' and 'synchrony', is re-exploited as irregularity without a concept (Deleuze's 'repetition') or as multiplicity without a rule (Foucault's 'power').

When the jurisprudential implications are drawn out it becomes possible to achieve an independent perspective on the intrinsically historical claims that metaphysics, dialectics and structuralism have been overcome; for it becomes possible to observe the connections made and reneged between the reconstruction of the history of philosophy and the philosophy of history. The anti-nomy of law, the inscrutable encounter with form in general in Kant's practical philosophy, was expounded by Hegel, and after him by Marx, as the paradox of civil society. The separation in modern states of public from private law, of the realm of needs or economic life from the realm of politics and citizenship, arises from specifically modern forms of private property and formal equality. This separation gives rise to the illusion of sovereign individuality which is represented in the absolute demands of morality and religion, and reproduced and justified in Kant's critical philosophy. The very phase 'civil society', with its implied distinction between society and the state, captures the paradox of life lived in the two apparently different realms of the social and political when both realms are juridical, equally constituted by the civil law. Unaddressable oppositions between morality and legal-ity, autonomy and heteronomy, the good will and natural desire and inclination, force and generality, can be traced to an historically specific legal structure which establishes and protects absolute property by means of the juridical fictions of persons, things, and obligations.

Hegel's *Phenomenology of Spirit* shows how the confrontation between master and slave becomes internalized in the 'person' as the struggle between the good will and natural desire and inclination. Opening up an historical perspective on the development of the idea of 'persons' as the bearers of equal rights and the hypertrophy of their inner life, Hegel expounds the antinomy of law as the characteristic compound in modern states of individual freedom with individual depoliticization. In the *Grundrisse* Marx examines how Capital posits individuals as 'persons', the bearers of rights, and as 'things', the commodity 'labour-power'. The theory of commodity fetishism subsequently developed in the first volume of *Capital* is not simply an account of how material relations between 'persons' are transformed into social relations between 'things'. It is an account of the 'personification' *and* 'reification' intrinsic to the juridical categories of 'commodity', 'capital', and 'money'. Emphasis on the differences between Marx's and Hegel's thinking has obscured the continuity of their preoccupation with the antinomy of law. The juridical opposition of free subjects and subjected things, which characterizes not only relations between different classes but the relation of the individual to itself in modern states, forms the speculative core of Hegel's and of Marx's thinking.

Hegelian and Marxist dialectic does not seek to legitimize the phantasy of historical completion with the imprimatur of supra-historial, absolute method, but focuses relentlessly on the historical production and reproduction of those illusory contraries which other systems of scientific thought naturalize, absolutize or deny. Dialectical history is multiple and complex, not as its critics would have it, unitary and simply progressive; it suspends the history of philosophy within the philosophy of history, and the philosophy of history within the history of philosophy.

The dialectical exposition of the antinomy of law was challenged by legal theorists and *Rechtsphilosophen* in the nineteenth century who sought to solve the mystery of the categorical imperative in a way which would bypass the dissolution of traditional philosophy threatened by the Hegelian system. Instead of suspending the history of philosophy within the philosophy of history as Hegel and Marx had done, Eduard von Hartmann and Adolf Trendelenburg returned to *Kategorienlehre*, the doctrine of categories, as the foundation of *Rechtsphilosophie*, philosophy of right or law. Later neo-Kantian legal theory – for example, Stammler, Cohen, Lask – transferred the antinomy of law to the concept of 'society' which inherits in their work that mysterious combination of unjustifiable force and unconditioned generality originally thought of as the categorical imperative. When the antinomy of law is transferred to the concept of society, and not traced to the paradoxes of civil society, other Kantian contraries are smothered in a similar way. Neo-Kantians resolve the oppositions of autonomy and heteronomy and of morality and legality into a unified legal science by drawing an 'original' category out of the *Critique of Pure Reason*, be it 'mathesis', 'time', or 'power', which serves to reunite the realms of the practical and theoretical, of freedom and necessity. This mode of resolution reveals profound inconsistency in the development of the case for an anti-metaphysical, anti-dialectical, theoretical jurisprudence, since it depends on changing the old sticking point of the unknowable categorical imperative into a new vanishing point, where it remains equally categorical and imperative, unknowable but forceful.

This abstruse story might be considered a mere intellectual curiosity were it not for the way intellectual history repeats itself. The neo-Kantian legal theory of Stammler, Cohen and Lask, was radicalized in its turn by Weber, Lukács, and Heidegger, each of whom in his own way exploded the closed sociological jurisprudence of the neo-Kantian mathesis by opening again the connection between the history of scientific thought and the philosophy of history: rationality, mode of production, Being and time. The inevitable persistence of legal categories throughout their thinking is recognized, and they are not presented as an unproblematic table of categories. For Weber legal-rational authority is the definitive feature of modern, capitalist society, while his distinction between 'formal' (*Zweck*) and 'substantive' (*Wert*) rationality depends on the traditional distinction between the procedures and the substance of the law. Lukács brings Marx and Weber into dialogue by expounding the commodity as a legal–rational category with its juridical correlatives of reification and personification. Heidegger challenges the litigious parameters of modern philosophy by pitting the Kantian form of time against the history of Being so as to permit the laws of temporal calibration to be enjoyed in other settings – where Moira, She-God of time and law, rules, or where Being is danced – prior to the advent of any She-God or He-God.

Ostensibly drawing on Heidegger, post-structuralism de-historicizes his thinking in the very process of appropriating it. Post-structuralism will therefore be considered here with reference also to the case for an anti-metaphysical and anti-dialectical theoretical jurisprudence. For the claims that it has surpassed metaphysics, dialectics and universal history are grounded and presented by reinstating a fundamental category or schema – a mathesis. Eschewing the sociological alternative to metaphysics, post-structuralism nevertheless offers a new mode of address to the same question which originally exercised sociological positivism, namely, the question of law.

In this work Genealogy and Grammatology will be brought back into dialogue both with antecedents which they acknowledge and those which they do not acknowledge. For the reconstruction of post-structuralism requires the more general reassessment of post-Kantian developments – dialectics, genealogy, sociology, structuralism – from the standpoint of their jurisprudential claims and implications.

In turn this is part of a larger endeavour to retrieve the speculative identity of form and history which appears in these most recent works as the opposition of metaphysics and law. Just as I read Hegel's exposition of the antinomy of law as the speculative identity *and* non-identity of the state and religion – of 'politics' and 'ideology', as we have come to call them – so I read the antinomy in the work of our contemporaries as presenting us with a pale cousin: the nihilistic identity and non-identity of law and metaphysics. The case beyond nihilism – from Heidegger's 'magical' version to Foucault's 'administrative' version – will be shown to yield to an historical dialectic which it claims to surpass.

The histrionic design of Hegel's phenomenology was developed in order to gain a purchase on the apparently unassailable authority of reason (*Vernunft*). Natural consciousness is observed in succeeding configurations which culminate for it as individual, rational consciousness in the encounter with law-giving and law-testing Reason. Hegel's text invites us to witness the education of natural consciousness, presented as a series of confrontations set in more and less recognizable historical settings: between two opposed individual consciousnesses, between opposed forces residing within a single consciousness, and between opposed forces belonging to the same communal consciousness. Once natural consciousness has come up against the limits of law-giving and law-testing reason, it is reset as communal consciousness or spirit (*Geist*), and its renewed itinerary passes through the litigious space and time of Greek ethical life to Roman legal status and finally to modern morality.

This text will begin by showing that the drama which Hegel develops as a new philosophical *modus* is the drama of the law itself. The phenomenological experience, where natural consciousness becomes the witness to be investigated by the observing consciousness placed in the position of the judge, re-enacts a trial which has already taken place in the pages of the *Critique of Pure Reason*. For cross-examination reveals the purportedly impersonal authority of Reason to be an ensemble of the three fictitious persons of the law: the judge, the witness and the clerk of the court. The case for scientific method against metaphysics began in this court-room of the *Critique of Pure Reason* and this fact provides the starting-point for the reconsideration of the connection between theoretical innovation and jurisprudence to be tried here.

Since my text is to examine these borders of impersonality and personality, of reason and law, I shall retain gender distinctions as they are found in the tradition. When Philosophy visits Boethius in the imperial prison, when Rousseau brings Sophie along to complete Émile's personality, when Zarathustra goes to visit her with his whip, it is at the crux of gender that philosophy – love of wisdom – , the republic, and the legal fictions of personality explode. This is especially evident in Hegel's exposition of Sophocles' *Antigone* in the *Phenomenology of Spirit*, where the suffering of Antigone, sister and citizen, stands out as the question of the relationship between philosophy, justice and individual identity. To change 'he' to 's/he' would distort all the fundamental oppositions on which the thinking under scrutiny is based, and, in the case of this particular work, would be to assuage a symptom when it might argue instead with a cause.

Here it will not be a matter of fissioning authorial presence into the dual fiction of natural consciousness and abstract, philosophical consciousness – the latter setting out to monitor the less experienced partner but gradually coming to recognize its own story in the culturing of the other. Willing instead to acknowledge that science appeals in the guise of the clerk to the two other legal personae, witness and judge – compacted as that familiar, ungainly 'we' of science – 'we' will seek to re-experience our scientific development without that innocence which unquestioningly accepts the normal, litigious personae and procedures of science, but also without claiming a new, spurious, post-legal authority: the aim is simply to be fully alert, to know the score, when faced with the prospect of newly insinuated law dissembled as a nihilistic break with knowledge and law, with tradition in general.

The speculative identity and non–identity of law and metaphysics is presented here in the form of the chiasmus in which I have found it coiled at the heart of the post-metaphysical tradition: metaphysics is replaced by science; science returns to metaphysics. Each section of the discussion which follows is organized around the twofold jurisprudential transcription of this chiasmus: the move from metaphysics to science will be seen to recapitulate legal argument, while the return from science to metaphysics will be seen to recapitulate legal history.[1]

---

[1] Sources and authorities: for Roman law; Justinian, *The Institutes*, Cicero, and modern commentaries from Gibbon, Maine, to Jolowitz, Stein, Daube; for Greek law: classical philosophy and literature, and modern discussion of law and religion – Vinogradoff, Jones, Daube, MacDowell, and especially the work of Jane Harrison, F. M. Cornford and Gilbert Murray; for Hebrew law: the Cambridge Bible Commentary, Eissfeldt, Daube, Dodd; for Germanic law: from Tacitus to Savigny, Ihering, von Gierke.

Part One

Natural Law and Repetition

1

From Metaphysics to Jurisprudence

Today things will be slightly different. You are on trial. Or, rather, you are to be invited to inspect a court-room in which you have been judge, witness, and clerk for so long that you have ceased to notice its strange *ambiance*. As soon as you arrive each morning you don your gown and wig, check cursorily that the formalities are running their familiar and routine course, and settle down into a profound critical slumber.

Kant's invitation to witness the case for critical philosophy – to learn scientific method in court – takes the reader into a maze of litigation and inquisition during the course of which his status and the nature of the proceedings shift continuously and almost imperceptibly.[1]

[1] See F. D. E. Schleiermacher's discussion of the twofold etymology of *Kritik: Gericht*, court of justice, and *Vergleichung*, comparison, in *Hermeneutik und Kritik mit besonderer Beziehung auf das Neue Testament*, 1838, Friedrich Lucke (ed.), reprinted in Schleiermacher, *Hermeneutik und Kritik*, Manfred Frank (ed.), Frankfurt am Main, Suhrkamp, 1977, p.241f. Compare, too, Schopenhauer's discussion of Kant's doctrine of conscience: 'In the first place, Kant throughout employs *Latin legal expressions*, which surely seem little suited for interpreting the most secret stirrings of the human heart. But from beginning to end he retains this language and juridical presentation, so that they appear to be essential and peculiar to the matter. There is brought to our minds a complete court of justice with trial, proceedings, judge, prosecutor, counsel for the defense, and sentence'. *On the Basis of Morality*, 1841, *Zürcher Ausgabe*, VI, Zürich, Diogenes, 1977, p.211ff, trans. E. F. J. Payne, Indianapolis, Bobbs-Merrill, 1965, p.105ff. Compare Heidegger, 'Nietzsches Wort: "Gott ist tot"', 1943, in *Holzwege*, Frankfurt am Main, Klostermann, 1980, pp.240–41, trans. 'The Word of Nietzsche: "God is dead"' in *The Question concerning Technology and Other Essays*, William Lovitt, New York, Harper and Row, p.90. (To be discussed below, chapter 3, p.54f and note 21.) For a complementary study to this chapter, see Howard Caygill, '*Aesthetics and Civil Society: Theories of Art and Society 1640–1790*', unpublished D.Phil. thesis, University of Sussex, 1982.

At first the setting of the critical project seems metajuridical: a discussion of the legal procedure or 'canon' – the range of available actions (*actiones*), the legal remedy, or the *form* of a possible experience in general, according to which the legal title of concepts in our possession may be deduced and justified.[2] At other times, however, it seems that the substance of the law is at issue; that we are involved in a specific case of unlawful possession: the defence of the 'usurpatory concept' of freedom.[3]

Reason is to be investigated in order to determine what kind of right it can claim to its possessions; but Reason is itself bringing the case. Accordingly, the procedure of this, the highest of courts, is inquisitorial not accusatorial: consciousness, the judge, 'compels the witnesses to answer questions which he himself has formulated'.[4] Appointed by himself, this judge is questioning himself 'after a plan of [his] own'.[5] This solitary task initially involves making an '*inventory* of all [his] possessions through *pure* reason, systematically arranged'.[6] The judge takes up his pen as clerk in addition to his offices as judge and witness.

Once the possessions are systematically arranged, he can run through his claims to legal title. Discovering that he can remember how he acquired most of his possessions, all his theoretical ones, he is able to set about deducing their legal title according to the recognized formal procedures; but in the case of the most prized of them all, 'freedom', he is not able to remember at all how he acquired it. How is he to justify its possession?

With the consternation now of the litigant, he realizes he may have usurped this particular possession and may have to submit to being 'chase[d]' out of his 'supposed property which [he] has no title to hold'.[7] A surge of resistance engulfs him at this prospect,

[2] Kant, *Critique of Pure Reason, Werkausgabe*, III and IV, Wilhelm Weidschel (ed.), Frankfurt am Main, Suhrkamp, 1980, trans. Norman Kemp Smith, New York, St Martin's Press, 1965, A 84–5/B 116–17; and A 796/B 824. For a discussion of 'canon' and 'rules of law', see Peter Stein, *Regulae Iuris From Juristic Rules to Legal Maxims*, Edinburgh, Edinburgh University Press, 1966, p.51ff.

[3] Kant, *Critique of Pure Reason*, A 84–5/B 116–17.

[4] Ibid., B xiii.

[5] Ibid.

[6] Ibid., A xx.

[7] Kant, *Groundwork of the Metaphysics of Morals, Werkausgabe*, VII, trans. H.J. Paton, New York, Harper and Row, 1964, 116. I refer to the marginal pagination identical in the German and in the English translation.

for he has a very strong feeling that the possession is lawful. He makes a decision to fight the action *usurpatio* with which he is contesting his own possession by a defence of *usucapio*: that is, ownership granted by law when a thing has been acquired by quiet possession, *bona fide*, and founded on some mode of acquisition recognized by law which suffices to transfer the *dominium* after a specific period of possession, even though the original acquisition did not take place according to the fully legal form of *mancipatio* (sale).[8]

Our litigant feels confident about the *fact* of possession, and that it occurred in *good faith* (*bona fide*), and that his title is *ex justa causa*, prima facie or apparently right, even though it is not strictly deducible as are the titles of his other possessions.[9] But he still has to argue that the ground of his possession is not merely physical or empirical (*possessio phaenomon*), but intelligible, *de jure* (*possessio noumenon*).[10] He knows that the right to individual property cannot be deduced from a putative original contract, for that would demand from him precisely the historical evidence which is lacking, and which would be mostly empirical were it be found.[11] Such evidence could not be adduced as the intuition underlying the concept to be justified; for in the case of the practical principle of possession it is precisely the difference between merely empirical possession and *de jure* possession which is at issue. Hence all conditions of intuition must be 'removed' in order to 'extend the concept of possession beyond the empirical concept'.[12]

The very meaning of deduction and justification has shifted at this most crucial point. The legalized union of concept and intuition essential to the theoretical deduction of the *Critique of*

---

[8] To elucidate the critical writings I shall use the definitions to be found in the first part of Kant's *Metaphysics of Morals, The Metaphysical Elements of Justice, Werkausgabe*, VIII, abridged trans. John Ladd, Indianapolis, Bobbs-Merrill, 1965, and, where applicable, in *The Institutes of Justinian*, trans. and ed. Thomas Collet Sanders, London, Longmans, Green and Co., 1917. For *usurpatio*, see Justinian, *The Institutes*, Lib.II Tit.VI 13, see Sander's note, p. 146; for *usucapio*, see Kant, *The Metaphysical Elements of Justice*, sec. 33, not translated, and Justinian, *The Institutes*, Lib.II Tit.VI, 'De usucapionibus et Longi Temporis Possessionibus'.

[9] For *ex justa causa*, see Justinian, *The Institutes*, Lib.II Tit.VI 10n.

[10] Kant, *The Metaphysical Elements of Justice*, sec.1 353, tr.p.51.

[11] Ibid., sec.6 369–60, tr.p.58.

[12] Ibid., sec.6 361, tr.p.59.

Pure Reason, 1781–87, where it is expounded by means of the practical ideas of *de jure*, property, possession, justification, turns out, when these ideas are eventually expounded in their own right in the *Metaphysic of Morals*, 1797, to be 'intelligible' but not cognizable. The complex machinery of justification rests on a simple appeal to natural justice: '"Happy is he who is in possesion" . . . is a basic principle of natural justice . . .'[13]

'*Beati possidentes!*' – but our litigant is not at all happy, and that is why he started, and is still attempting, to secure his possession. Equity (*aequitas, die Billigkeit*) has prevailed in this case, the case of the meaning of deduction and justification: a strict application of the letter of the law (*ius strictum*) seems unreasonable and unfair, so a broader sense has been recognized in reaching the verdict in this particular case (*ius latum*).[14] Yet this apparently successful verdict has not really secured the possession at all: for equity is defined by its lack of authorization to employ coercion.[15] There cannot be a 'court of equity',[16] for as soon as one of its decisions were to be enforced a further court of equity would be needed, and so on, *ad infinitum*.[17]

Another disconcerting suspicion creases his critical brow: the case may depend on 'right of necessity [*das Notrecht (ius necessitatis)*]' which, like equity [*die Billigkeit (aequitas)*], lies on the borders of justice and right. These rights are 'equivocal', because 'the authorization to use coercion cannot be stipulated by any law'.[18] Equity 'admits a right without any coercion'; the right of

---

[13] Ibid., sec.6 360, tr.p.59. Compare Durkheim's discussion of Kant's justification of this apostrophe, *Leçons de sociologie*, Paris, Presses Universitaires de France, 1969, pp.163–4.

[14] Kant, *The Metaphysical Elements of Justice*, Introduction, sec.B Appendix I 341, tr.p.39. The English word 'law' tends to elide the distinction between 'right' or 'justice' and positive law which is more clearly marked in other languages: *droit* and *loi; Recht* and *Gesetz; ius* and *lex; dike* and *nomos*. The Latin *aequitas* is the received translation of the Greek *epieikeia*, but it properly translates the Greek *isotes*, equality, see H. F. Jolowicz, *Roman Foundations of Modern Law*, Oxford, Oxford University Press, 1957, p.54.

[15] Kant, *The Metaphysical Elements of Justice*, Introduction, sec.13 Appendix I 341, tr.p.39.

[16] Ibid., 342, tr.p.40. This sounds strange to English ears given our history of the system of equity courts parallel to the system of common law courts; see Radcliffe and Cross, *The English Legal System*, 6th edn, London, Butterworths, 1977, Chapter VIII.

[17] Kant, *The Metaphysical Elements of Justice*, sec.13 Appendix I 342, tr.p.40.

[18] Ibid., 341, tr.p.39.

necessity admits 'coercion without any right'.[19] Each of these equivocal rights (*ius aequivocum*) may be called 'a silent deity who cannot be heard':[20] the words of divine Equity are deliberately muffled snatches of the particular; divine Necessity speaks no words, no law (Greek, *lexis*: way of speaking, word; Latin, *lex*: law) because no words need be spoken while the right of violence is executed. Could this be the 'practical principle' hidden behind the critical cause, a principle which is absolute (categorical) and forceful (imperative) but unnameable? Could it be that this most prized possession, 'freedom', is being held by necessity without any law, and not by equity without any force?

Certainly not! – protests Reason. Coercion is quite unnecessary: everyone will automatically honour this possession because they have the same possession to secure. It is in the interest of every rational being to respect the property of every other rational being. If our litigant believes that his possession is necessary to himself, that he would not exist as a rational being without it, then it must be equally necessary to every other rational being, for otherwise he would not recognize them as rational beings. He can be confident therefore that he is living in a 'kingdom of ends'.

Yet his litigious behaviour indicates that he does not really believe this. He is pretending that he is 'confident', living 'as if' he is a member of a kingdom of ends, but he does not actually 'count on' other rational beings doing so.[21] It is the lack of faith which provoked the crisis of self-justification in the first place.

At the end of this tiresome day our litigant is still in possession of his property; more self-righteous and more sentimental about his claim, more haunted by fear of dispossession. The critical exercise which began by turning authority into jurisdiction has managed in the course of the proceedings to remove it from any jurisdiction: Possession 'is a basic principle of natural justice, for no-one is bound to authenticate his possession'.[22] The recourse to justice has revealed an antinomy in the idea of justice itself: between *the claim to justice* – the *universal* meaning of deduction and justification – first called on, and *the justice claimed*, the demand

---

[19] Ibid.
[20] Ibid., 342, tr. p. 40; Kant refers to 'equity', but *not* to 'right of necessity', as 'eine stumme Gottheit, die nicht gehöret werden kann'.
[21] Kant, *Groundwork of the Metaphysics of Morals*, 84.
[22] Kant, *The Metaphysical Elements of Justice*, sec. 6 360, tr. p. 59.

that this case – the case of justice itself – be treated as a *particular* case.

There is another recourse, not to justice, but to clarification. We do not need, or so it now appears, to try to justify our possession any longer, and we cannot know it, but perhaps we may elucidate further this stubborn intuition of rightful possession which has no concept, this righteousness without a right. As judge and witness, we may retire from the centre of the court-room, and turn, as clerks, to the work of reference on our desk.

The work of reference in question is the *Critique of Judgement*; it is there that the exposition of 'the concept of purposiveness in nature [*in dem Begriffe einer Zweckmässigkeit der Natur*]' is offered as an educative aid in comprehending the idea of 'a kingdom of ends [*ein Reich der Zwecke*]', and hence the idea that freedom (our possession) belongs to us, as beings who can act on ends valid for all rational beings regardless of subjective impulse.[23]

> Teleology considers nature as a kingdom of ends; morality considers a possible kingdom of ends as a kingdom of nature. In the first case the kingdom of ends is a theoretical idea used to explain what exists. In the second case it is a practical idea used to bring into existence what does not exist but can be made actual by our conduct – and indeed to bring it into existence in conformity with this idea.[24]

The idea of a kingdom of ends is 'analogous' to the idea of a *kingdom* of nature, (even though nature 'is regarded as a machine') so far as 'it stands in a relation to rational beings as its ends'. Nature would become a 'kingdom' if all rational beings followed the maxims prescribed by the categorical imperative, since then 'a kingdom of ends would come into existence'.[25] Teleological judgement which 'represents' the product of nature as a 'natural purpose' helps us to form the idea of that realized state.[26] The very difficulty in English of eliding *Zweck* as 'purpose' in nature and *Zweck* as 'end' in morality suggests that this analogy is not as

---

[23] Kant, *Critique of Judgement*, *Werkausgabe*, X, trans. J. H. Bernard, New York, Hafner, 1972, Second Introduction, IX 108, tr. p. 33; *Groundwork of the Metaphysics of Morals*, 80n and 63–4.

[24] Ibid., 80n, translation amended.

[25] Ibid., 84.

[26] Kant, *Critique of Judgement*, Introduction, VIII 103–4, tr. p. 29.

enlightening as it is claimed. The 'definite purpose' which is meant to distinguish freedom as *Endzweck* from nature as *Zweck* is as formal in the latter case as it is in the former. The analogy rests more on the mental operations involved than on connotations of the idea of *Zweck*. For teleological judgement employs understanding and reason, although it does not determine objects.[27]

The analogy between the kingdom of ends and the kingdom of nature draws on two connotations of nature. The first connotation is nature 'as the universal interconnection of existent things in accordance with universal laws – which constitutes the formal aspect of nature as such';[28] this is nature as juridical ('descriptive'), as regulated in the theoretical sense, analogous to the end as realized. The second connotation is nature as 'a purposive order';[29] this is nature as litigious and compelling ('prescriptive'), as regulating in the practical sense which abstracts from material motives, from every 'end that has to be produced', and yet is analogous to the end as goal or purpose.[30] These two connotations of nature are implied both by the teleological judgement which 'represents the product of nature as a natural purpose', and by the aesthetic judgement which presents 'the purposiveness of nature in the form of a thing'.[31]

However, the aesthetic judgement of formal purposiveness, the famous *Zweckmässigkeit ohne Zweck* (purposiveness without a purpose) which is also called *Gesetzmässigkeit ohne Gesetz* (legality without a law), also displays an analogy with the righteousness without a right (*Rechtmässigkeit ohne Recht*, as it were) discerned here.[32] Just as the aesthetic judgement is subjective, when the form of an object harmonizes with the cognitive faculties but without

[27] Ibid., 103–6, tr.pp.29–31.
[28] Kant, *Groundwork of the Metaphysics of Morals*, 81.
[29] Ibid., 84.
[30] Ibid., 82. I shall use the opposition 'juridical/litigious' instead of the standard 'descriptive/prescriptive', because both terms of the former pair are legal and contain the active and passive connotations of regulated and regulating, or (pre-)scripting and what has been (de-)scripted. For a discussion of the opposition between 'description' and 'prescription' which was formulated by Mill to refute Montesquieu, see H. L. A. Hart, *The Concept of Law*, 1961, Oxford, Oxford University Press, 1981, pp.182–3. Compare, too, Hermann Cohen's discussion of the double meaning of law in Kant, *Ethik des reinen Willens*, Berlin, Bruno Cassirer, 1904, p.247. Furthermore, 'prescription' is another word for usucaption; see n.8 above.
[31] Kant, *Critique of Judgement*, Introduction, VIII, 103–4, tr.p.29.
[32] Ibid., sec.5 143, tr.p.62 and sec.22 161, tr.p.78, amended.

any prior concept,[33] so the possession of freedom has a formal harmony with our being, it is *rechtmässig*, but it never comes into existence, *ohne Recht*, never actual and without a concept. The antinomy of freedom and necessity as the antinomy of law itself is captured by this formulation.

The analogy of the two kingdoms does not clarify; it reaffirms what needs to be clarified: not nature, nor the end, but the idea shared by 'the kingdom of nature' and 'the kingdom of ends', that of the *kingdom* itself. A kingdom is 'a systematic union of different rational beings under common laws'.[34] Law is common (*gemeine*) when universal (*allgemeine*) law is the rule: when everyone treats himself and others as an end and not merely as a means, then all laws will be universally valid. This proposition rests on an ellipsis between 'common' and 'universal': the formal universality of treating self and others as an end yields a substantial communality. But laws are either common and not formal (customary), or universal and formal. Can a kingdom be a community, or does the idea of a kingdom not imply an authority or dignitary distinct from each member?

It turns out that the kingdom is in dire need of the distinct authority of a king. For each rational being belongs to this kingdom as 'a *member*, when, although he makes its universal laws, he is himself subject to those laws. He belongs to it as its *head* [*Oberhaupt*], when, as the maker of laws he is himself subject to the will of no other'.[35] Yet this position as head cannot be maintained 'merely through the maxims of the will'; cannot be maintained, that is, merely by virtue of *freedom*.[36] It can only be maintained if the individual 'is a completely independent being, without needs and with an unlimited power adequate to his will'.[37] Even if such a being were conceivable, it is inconceivable that there could be more than one such being: ergo, the kingdom must have a *virtual* king. But if there is an authority distinct from the rest of the members then universal laws are not common laws; people must be subjected to them, not authors of them; and hence

---

[33] Ibid., Introduction, VIII 103, tr.p.29.
[34] Kant, *Groundwork of the Metaphysics of Morals*, 74.
[35] Ibid., 75.
[36] Ibid., translation amended.
[37] Ibid.

they cannot be treated, and cannot treat themselves, as ends in themselves.

The kingdom, 'admittedly only an Ideal', does not sound so ideal.[38] Hidden in the idea of this subjunctive life – to live *as if* one *were* a law-making member – is not solely the 'paradox'[39] of a life lived in one reality 'as if' it were proceeding in a different reality,[40] but the deeper paradox that the split between the ideal and the real itself depends on importing features of the real into the very *form* of the ideal.

This form is conceived by 'abstracting from all subjective ends', all material desire or need, the value of which is merely *relative* to the individual 'subject's power of appetition' and discovering 'something [*etwas*] *whose existence* has in *itself* an absolute value, something which [is] *an end in itself*'.[41] This 'something' can only be man, for 'man, and in general every rational being, exists as an end in himself, not merely as a means for arbitrary use by this or that will: he must in all his actions, whether they are directed to himself or to other rational beings, always be viewed *at the same time as an end*.'[42]

This crucial distinction between ends and means corresponds exactly to the distinction between persons and things:

> The value of all objects that *can be produced* by our action is always conditioned. Beings whose existence depends not on our will but on nature have nonetheless, if they are non-rational beings, only a relative value as means and are consequently called *things* [*Sachen*]. Rational beings, on the other hand, are called *persons* [*Personen*] because their nature already marks them out as ends in themselves – that is, as something which ought not to be used merely as a means . . .[43]

This definition of a person by use of a distinguishing 'ought' indicates the circularity in the exposition of means/things, and

---

[38] Ibid.
[39] Ibid., 85.
[40] Ibid., 84.
[41] Ibid., 64.
[42] Ibid., 64–5.
[43] Ibid., 65.

ends/persons: 'Persons . . . are things [*Dinge*] whose existence is in itself an end . . . such that in its place we can put no other end to which they should serve *simply* as means.'[44] This version of the definition also depends on an insidious *Sollen*.

The idea of rational form itself is constituted by these interlocking sets of oppositions: ends/means; persons/things; absolute/relative; subjective/objective. These distinctions are themselves fundamental juridical distinctions; they are the distinctions on which Roman private law is based: ergo, the form of freedom is the form of private law. This is not to argue that empirical or material assumptions have been 'smuggled in' as intellectual or a priori ones, but to argue that a specific form of legality has been reproduced in the delineation of form as such.[45] Rationality, hedged as it is with protestations as to its essentially negative conception, 'as an end against which we should never act',[46] brings with it the full force and history of the pronouncement in the preliminary remarks on the division of law in the first book of *The Institutes* of Justinian: *Omne autem ius, quo utimur, vel ad personas pertinent vel ad res vel ad actiones* – all our law relates either to persons or to things, or to actions.[47] In the Introduction to *The Metaphysical Elements of Justice* we are told that Ulpian's three famous maxims, to be found at the initial delineation of the scope and form of law in *The Institutes*, are to be redeveloped for the present age: *honeste vive, neminem laede, suum cuique tribue* – live honestly, hurt no-one, give each his due.[48]

Once again it is in the *Metaphysic of Morals* that we find full definitions of the legal terminology employed, this time the distinctions between person, thing and action, even though these terms are essential to the trial of freedom in progress in the three separate courts of criticism.

A *person* is the subject whose actions are susceptible to

---

[44] Ibid., 65–6.
[45] Compare Hegel's argument in 'Natural Law', 1802–3, *Theorie Werkausgabe*, 2, 464, Frankfurt am Main, Suhrkamp, 1977, trans. T.M. Knox, Pennsylvania, University of Pennsylvania Press, 1975, p.79.
[46] Kant, *Groundwork of the Metaphysics of Morals*, 82.
[47] Justinian, *The Institutes*, Lib.I Tit.II 12.
[48] Ibid., Lib.I Tit.I 3, and Kant, *The Metaphysical Elements of Justice*, 'Introduction', 344, tr.pp.42–3.

imputation [*Zurechnung*]. Accordingly moral personality is nothing but the freedom of a rational being under moral laws (whereas psychological personality is merely the capacity to be conscious of the identity of one's self in the various conditions of one's existence) . . .

A *thing* is something that is not susceptible to imputation. Every object of free will that itself lacks freedom is therefore called a thing (*res corporalis*).[49]

Personality, like possession, confers an identity on the noumenal sphere: to consider man from the point of view of his 'capacity for freedom' is to consider him 'from the point of view of his humanity considered as a personality, independently of physical [and of psychological] determinations (*homo noumenon*). In contradiction to this, man can be regarded as a subject affected by these determinations (*homo phaenomenon*).'[50] Accordingly, each man is both a person and a thing (*res corporalis*); and human beings can be conceived without personality: they appear in the 'empty' box of beings with duties but no rights, such as slaves and serfs.[51]

This distinction between persons and things is the basis for distinguishing between rights *in rem* (against everyone) and rights *in personam* (against specific person(s)) which provides the framework for all the general laws subsequently deduced. The crowning achievement of this exposition is that marriage is conceived as a right *in rem* over a person.[52] This right to the 'use' of a person against every other person proves that the definition of individuals as persons, as ends in themselves, presupposes that they be treatable as things, as means. Marriage is assimilated here to Roman *dominium* (absolute property), when in Roman law itself, which did not know rights, it was one of the least formalized relations.[53] This fusing of Roman *dominium*, absolute property, with modern subjective rights may well reveal the

[49] Kant, *The Metaphysical Elements of Justice*, Introduction, IV, 329–30, tr.pp.24–5.
[50] Ibid., 347, tr.p.46.
[51] Ibid., 349, tr.p.47.
[52] The title of this division of *The Metaphysical Elements of Justice* is 'Von den auf dingliche Art persönlichen Recht', 388.
[53] For rights and marriage in Roman law and in modern law, see Jolowicz, *Roman Foundations of Modern Law*, chapters IX and XII.

ambition which has lead reason to appoint itself as judge in the first place.[54] All this rededuction of Roman law is achieved in a 'social [*sic*] state of nature' from the 'pure concepts of reason'.[55]

More disconcerting than this discovery of Roman law in the state of nature is the discovery that it is also present in the kingdom of ends: the realm of 'absolute value'. The kingdom, it will be remembered, was founded after a difficult search for something whose value is not 'conditioned', which cannot 'serve' simply as a means.[56] In order to distinguish this exclusive, absolute value from the host of relative values, a standard of value, of measurement and comparison, is essential. To our surprise we learn that there is money in the kingdom of ends: 'In the kingdom of ends everything has either a price or a dignity.'[57] It is monetary value which distinguishes between persons and things: 'What is relative to universal human inclinations and needs has a market price . . . that which constitutes the sole condition under which anything can be an end in itself has not merely a relative value – that is, a price – but has an intrinsic value – that is, a dignity.'[58]

This is not really so surprising if we recall that in Roman law 'The topic of *Res* or things may be roughly described as the main body of the law: the discussion of all those rights which have a money value, to the exclusion of such rights as liberty, and *patria potestas* which cannot be expressed in terms of money.'[59] The value of liberty and freedom is contrasted with monetary value. In the kingdom of ends where everyone was to treat himself and others as ends in themselves, some must be treating themselves or others as means. One man's dignity, it appears, is another's venality, since the idea of price or relative monetary value is introduced in order to elevate 'the law-making which determines all value' above the market-place, to 'an unconditioned and incomparable worth'.[60]

---

[54] See the translator's Introduction to *The Metaphysical Elements of Justice*, sec. V. E '*Right* in rem *over Persons*', p. xxiv.

[55] Ibid., Introduction, 350, tr. p. 48 and sec. 41 422–3, tr. pp. 70–71.

[56] Kant, *Groundwork of the Metaphysics of Morals*, 65.

[57] Ibid., 77.

[58] Ibid.

[59] This anachronistic formulation is taken from W. W. Buckland, *A Manual of Roman Private Law*, 1st edn, Cambridge, Cambridge University Press, 1928, p. 31.

[60] Kant, *Groundwork of the Metaphysics of Morals*, 79.

Who is this dignitary? When the intelligible concept of the standard of value is distinguished from the empirical fact of money as a medium of exchange, value is derived from the industry incorporated in an exchangeable product by the subjects of a lord, and eventually bought by them again: 'How is it possible that what was originally a commodity finally becomes money? . . . When a ruler demands duties from his dependants in this material (as a commodity), and repays them – whose industry is to be mobilized in the production of those commodities – in the same kind, according to the generally prevailing . . . commercial conventions (in a market or bourse).'[61]

The dignitary is coming into focus. For a community of beings 'completely independent', 'without needs and with unlimited power adequate to the will' was inconceivable.[62] But a being of unlimited power *with* needs, and a being with needs but *no power*, are definitely conceivable. For a 'person' can have power adequate to his will if there are things which he can use as means, and a 'person' who has needs but limited power may treat himself as a means. There is only one full bearer of personality in the kingdom of ends: the lord or king.

The kingdom of ends is, of course, strictly speaking, inconceivable: for it is intelligible, a practical principle, (an ought) not a theoretical concept. This inconceivability itself arises from the attempt to make persons and things, conditioned by each other, into unconditioned values – from the attempt to idealize them. A life based on persons and things cannot be idealized, cannot be made into an Ideal of Reason, or the form of the intelligible, since the basic opposition which is thereby formalized is that of the bearers of the substance of Roman private law.[63]

There is heteronomy at the heart of autonomy: the *hetero – nomos* – the other, unknowable, law – is precisely the *auto nomos* –

[61] Kant, *The Metaphysical Elements of Justice*, 402–3. Compare Hermann Cohen's questioning of Kant's analogy: 'The absolute mean produces the thing. The thing has value, that is market price; for the value is the value of exchange. The person has no value; the person has dignity. Is the market price of the value of labour compatible with dignity? That becomes the great question of modern politics and consequently of modern ethics'. *Ethik des reinen Willens*, p.305.

[62] Kant, *Groundwork of the Metaphysics of Morals*, 75 and see above, p.18.

[63] Compare Otto von Gierke's criticism of Kant's concept of personality in *Natural Law and the Theory of Society 1500–1800*, trans. Ernest Barker, Cambridge, Cambridge University Press, 1934, vol. I, pp.134–5.

the law of the person. The formal law, 'necessary' to our self-consciousness, yet with which we have not 'the slightest acquaintance',[64] utterly intimate and utterly remote, is the 'noumenal realm' of persons and property (things).

This formal law which we 'revere', obeying it from no material or interested motive but sheerly because of its universal practical validity, turns out to serve a formal interest: consciousness and its law are so defined that the semi-rational being can have a perfectly good conscience in its noumenal life, as it strives to enjoy without the obligation to know the 'right of necessity' which guarantees its personality and its property.

Theoretical reason is thereby silenced, and Practical Reason strides out of court with the 'peace and security from external attacks capable of bringing into dispute the territory it seeks to cultivate'[65] inscribed on a scroll tucked under its arm.

Was it a good move to transfer the inscription from the boundary stone to the scroll, from *imperium* to *dominium*? As in Roman law the complexity and refinement of private law which protects absolute property – by contrast, for instance, to the relative property of the Greek *kleros* – went together with the public *imperium* of the magistrate who was not accountable at law;[66] so the transformation of philosophy and science into critical jurisdiction draws attention to its basis in absolute property or *dominium*, which is unjustifiable and ultimately shored up by a categorical imperative, an unconditioned *imperium* which cannot be called to account.

[64] Kant, *Groundwork of the Metaphysics of Morals*, 125.
[65] Ibid., 116.
[66] For discussion of the 'unfettered quality of the governor's *imperium*', see A. N. Sherwin-White, *Roman Society and Roman Law in the New Testament*, Oxford, Oxford University Press, 1963, 1981, pp.3–5. Jolowicz points out that there is no source connecting this immunity with a definition of public law, *The Roman Foundation of Modern Law*, p.50. See, too, the discussion in G. E. M. de Ste Croix, *The Class Struggle in the Ancient Greek World from the Archaic Age to the Arab Conquests*, London, Duckworth, 1981, p.328f. The development of usucaption in the transition of land tenure from *modus* to *locus* and the historically-changing distinction between *possessio* and *dominium* are the focus of Max Weber's *Die Römische Agrargeschichte in ihrer Bedeutung für das Staats- und Privatrecht*, 1981, Amsterdam, P. Schippers NV, 1966, and see the brief summary in *The Agrarian Sociology of Ancient Civilizations*, 1908, trans. R. I. Frank, London, New Left Books, 1976, pp.300–302.

2

Law and the Categories

No peace and security from external attacks ever resulted from this freshly validated right. The infelicitous decision of the court has been quashed, and the case repeatedly reopened as the jurisdiction of each rival court turns to be as contestable as that of the original one.

The attacks, however, have not come from outside. As long as theoretical reason conceives itself as a court, and addresses to itself the *quaestio quid juris*, the question of right, distinguishing this question from the *quaestio quid facti*, the question of fact, it is liable to engender the objection that there are no separate realms corresponding to the two distinct questions, and the objection that the very 'question of right' reveals a practical interest in the ostensibly neutral form of *soi-disant* theoretical reason.

New claimants to the heritage keep appearing, brandishing their own special right, and intent on compounding the matter – on settling out of court. Yet each attempt to fight consciousness and its possessions on non-litigious terrain does not dissolve but reinforces the antinomy of law, the battle over jurisdiction, and ends up back in court.

The two forms of law, theoretical and practical, involved in the hopeless attempt to conceptualize the inconceivable categorical imperative were reconciled in the idea of purpose and in the idea of a person:

> The thought of purpose, together with the thought of order is inherent in the concept of law; hence not only the means–end relation, but also the thought of an end of ends, an ultimate and self-sufficient purpose, is involved in the very concept of law, as an indispensable form of legal

thinking. If this is so, the concept of the person, the subject of the law,[a] must be deemed a category of legal thought which is not based upon nor confined to legal experience but is of conceptual necessity and universal validity. For 'the subject of the law is a being that is considered by a certain historically given law in the sense of an end unto himself, while the object of the law is one that in the same situation is treated as a mere means to conditioned ends.'[1]

This profound equivocation between purpose as the end of ends, as *Endzweck*, and purposiveness as means to an end, as *Zweckmässigkeit*, results in the hundred flowers blooming from the question of law. Some of the new claimants give priority to the 'end of ends', the imperative, normative, evaluating aspect of the categorical imperative; while others give priority to the 'means to an end', purposiveness, the formal, unconditioned, categorical aspect of the categorical imperative.

Whether stressing value in the former case, or validity in the latter, these challengers seem determined to settle out of court. The first set of challengers appear to be prepared to admit that the inconceivability of law derives from its hidden origin in force or in value. Both sets of challengers seek to exploit the connotations of 'purpose' in order to naturalize the question of law. In place of an inconceivable causality, 'purpose', qua value, can serve to identify a realm of norms or functions *sui generis*; while 'purpose', qua validity, becomes efficient, itself 'producing the actuality to which [it] refer[s] . . . immediately becoming cognemes [*Erkenntnisse*], not needing to wait upon intuitions in order to acquire a meaning'.[2]

---

[1] Gustave Radbruch, 'Legal Philosophy', 1932, in *The Legal Philosophy of Lask, Radbruch and Dabin*, trans. Kurt Wiek, Cambridge, Mass., Harvard University Press, 1950, p.156, quoting R. Stammler, *Unbestimmtheit des Rechts-subjekts* (1907), 28–9, *Theorie der Rechtwissenschaft* (1911), 194ff. The translator explains note (a): 'In German legal terminology, "subject of the law" is synonymous with "legal person" and "object of the law" has the meaning of "property".'

[2] 'die praktischen Begriffe a priori in Beziehung auf des oberste Prinzip der Freiheit sogleich Erkenntnisse werden und nicht auf Anschauungen warten dürfen, um Bedeutung zu bekommen, und zwar aus diesen merkwürdigen Gründe, weil sie die Wirklichkeit dessen, worauf sie sich beziehen (die Willensgesinnung), selbst hervorbringen, welches gar nicht die Sache theoretischer Begriffe ist.' Kant, *Critique of Practical Reason, Werkausgabe*, VII, Wilhelm

However, the scene of action has not changed at all: we are still inside the court-room of the civil law. In both kinds of suits the question of the concept of law remains quite distinct from, and anterior to, the question of its force or compulsive power. Law, understood as purpose or as purposiveness, as values or as validity, remains the question of law as concept, as rule or canon, the standard of judgement, a question which can only arise from within its authoritative domain. For if it is nonsensical to ask why a standard is valid, because it is like asking why a ruler is twelve inches long, then it is equally nonsensical to ask why a value is valued, because it is like asking why twelve inches are ruling. In this way, law understood as purpose, whether as values or as validity, shares the conceptual immunity of any answer to the *quaestio quid juris*, the question of the practical, of the categorical imperative. It elides the original abyss between the city of God and the city of man without conferring any new conceptual clarity on it. 'Purpose' recombines these realms by drawing attention to the moment of combination itself – over the instant it is achieved – a never-ending task which has to be repeated time and time again.

Now as before it is the status which we call 'a person' which is called upon to continue living this essentially subjunctive life.[3] The place occupied by 'cause and effect' under the 'categories of relation' in the 'Table of Categories' of theoretical reason is occupied by 'the state of a person' in the 'Table of Categories of Freedom'.[4] The transformation of law into purpose requires 'persons', and the state of these persons reveals the tension in the newly-erected concept of law: if law is a value, its persons are natural; if law, qua validity, is a form, its persons are part fiction,

---

Weischedel (ed.), Frankfurt am Main, Suhrkamp, 1980, 184, trans. Lewis White Beck, Indianapolis, Bobbs-Merrill, 1956, p.68 amended. I have translated *Wirklichkeit* as 'actuality'; *Erkenntnisse* as 'cognemes', because this term becomes the pivot of the neo-Kantian revision of Kant. See the discussion of translating *Erkenntnis(se)* as 'cognition(s)' as opposed to Kemp Smith's 'knowledge', in Wolfgang Schwarz, 'Introduction' and 'Glossary' to *Critique of Pure Reason Concise Text*, Aalen, Scientia, 1982, pp.xvii and 263.
[3] For example see 'Critical Resolution of the Antinomy of Practical Reason', Kant, *Critique of Practical Reason*, 253–9, tr.pp.118–24.
[4] Ibid., 185, tr.pp.68–9; the table is set out on the pattern of the Table of Categories in the *Critique of Pure Reason*, but this is not reproduced in the translation.

part natural; if law, qua validity, is a category, personal life is abolished, and persons, like all other determinations, are subjected to the law, but are not subjects of the law; finally, if law, qua validity, is a concept of reflection, persons become pure fictions, bearers (*Träger*), of the law, without any 'natural' residue, their life spun within the meshes of the 'teleological web'.[5]

Once again you are called upon to act as judge, witness and clerk in these succeeding pleas of *Ignorabimus* – 'we shall not know'.[6] Four typical litigants have been invited to present their suits for transforming the question of law; and they have each agreed to do so under the five familiar headings: the concept of law, the method of law, the categories of law, the persons of the law, and natural law.[7] The plaintiffs are: Emile Lask, associate of the Heidelberg School of neo-Kantians, who will bring a case for purpose qua value;[8] Rudolf Stammler, associate of the Marburg School of neo-Kantians, who will bring a case for purpose as the form or validity of law;[9] Rudolf von Ihering, formal critic of the historical school of jurisprudence and renowned for his work on the forms of Roman law, who will bring a case for purposiveness as the category of law;[10] and Hermann Cohen, founder of the

[5] See Emil Lask, 1875–1915, 'Rechtsphilosophie', 1905, *Gesammelte Schriften*, Eugen Herrigel (ed.), Tübingen, J. C. B. Mohr, 1923, vol. I, p.316, trans. 'Legal philosophy', in Wiek, *The Legal Philosophy of Lask, Radbruch and Dabin*, p.31. The difference between 'categories' and 'concepts of reflection' will be discussed below p.32.

[6] See Radbruch, 'Legal Philosophy', in Wiek, *The Legal Philosophy of Lask, Radbruch and Dabin*, p.57 and n.8 where *Ignorabimus* is seen as the stance of 'relativist legal philosophy' with its refusal to countenance 'ultimate value judgements'.

[7] Some of these headings are drawn from Stammler's mode of presentation, see François Geny, 'The Critical System of Stammler, in Stammler, *Die Lehre von dem richtigen Rechte*, Berlin, J. Guttentag, 1902, trans. *The Theory of Justice*, Issaac Husik, New York, Augustus M. Kelly, 1925, Appendix, pp.501,507 n.5, 'Der Begriff des Rechtes', 'Die Kategorien des Rechts', 'Die Methodik des Rechts'.

[8] The four are arranged in logical not chronological order.

[9] Rudolf Stammler, 1856–1938: *Wirtschaft und Recht nach der materialistischen Gesichtsauffassung*, Leipzig, Veit und Comp, 1896, was the subject of Weber's essay 'R. Stammlers "Überwindung" der materialistischen Geschichtsauffassung', 1907, in *Gesammelte Aufsätze zur Wissenschaftslehre*, Tübingen, J.C.B. Mohr, 1973, trans. *Critique of Stammler*, Guy Oakes, New York, The Free Press, 1977.

[10] Rudolf von Ihering, 1818–92, *Geist des römischen Rechts*, 1852–58, 3 parts, Aalen, Scientia, 1968.

Marburg School, who will bring a case for purpose as the 'matheme' of law – as the reflected concept of time.[11]

Emile Lask claims that the 'two worlds' of the Kantian legal philosophy, formal and empirical, the inner, moral world and the outer, legal world are bridged by 'purposes' understood as a teleological system of 'typical values'. Law, as a typical value, is itself that concept-forming spirit which transforms its pre-legal substratum into legal values.

> The specifically juridical attitude towards reality is made up of two mutually pervading elements. The real substratum is transformed into a spiritual world of pure meanings, under the guidance of teleological relationships; at the same time the totality of what may be experienced is unravelled into mere partial contents.[12]

According to this perspective, to raise the question of law is to raise the question of experience as such, for the 'relations of life are formed typically'. The typical value, comprising ideal postulates, for 'which validity is claimed in any conceivable community life', defines the social, and it is this social value which establishes the law itself in the sphere of values.[13]

Typical values are introduced to distinguish the reality of 'social' phenomena, among them law, but law is then seen as the value which itself delineates the 'social'. Law is like the social in being a typical value, and it is like science in being concept-forming. The idea of law is bordered, on the one side, by the formal idea of the social as a 'system of values compared with any individual value',[14] and, on the other side, by the teleological doctrine of categories, as the method of jurisprudence.[15] In this way, the 'social', although introduced as a 'value', inherits the formal and inconceivable status of the legal, which is, in turn,

---

[11] Hermann Cohen, 1842–1918, the second of his three-part *System der Philsophie, Ethik des reinen Willens*, 1904, is the focus of attention here. The first part, *Logik der reinen Erkenntnis*, 1902, is discussed in G. Rose, *Hegel Contra Sociology*, London, Athlone, 1981, pp.10–11.

[12] Lask, 'Rechtsphilosophie', p.317, tr.p.361.

[13] Ibid., pp.22,17, tr.pp.304–5,298, 'systemic' and 'typical' are used interchangeably in the original.

[14] Ibid., p.305, tr.p.22, amended.

[15] Ibid., pp.325–6, tr.pp.37–8.

restricted to the question of its method, of the serious business of forming its concepts.

> These teleological formations of pre-legal realities are properly adopted by the law, which in the same sense, in the realm of legal meanings, coins the concepts of individual and of collective personality.[16]

The 'old problem of the legal person', with which Lask's discussion reaches its conclusion, reopens all the issues of the nature of law which the discussion has sought to transfer to the seamless realm of the teleological.[17] 'Persons' are not psychological but juridical creations;[18] yet the juridical may be more or less 'adapted' to the teleologically shaped realities of life and culture, and even 'retain' a certain nucleus of 'what is psychophysically given'.[19]

Initially law was introduced by analogy with the social as a typical value, as the teleological forming-principle itself, which could not subsequently be considered as more or less formal. Now, however, the old question of the degree of formality is raised in relation to a 'substratum'. All the legal questions are thereby transferred to the problem of this 'living substratum': is it itself inherently law-like, can it be conceived independently of legal categories? Lask has to concede that the choice is between two different concepts of law which carry with them two different concepts of society drawn from Romanist and Germanist jurisprudence: between the Latin word, *sozial*, implying unconnected and merely coordinated individuals, and the Germanic word, *Genossenschaft*, implying pre-legal personalities of associated individuals.[20] Lask still posits legal personality equivocally as *universitas post rem* and *extra res* – universality after the thing and outside of things – even though *res*, 'thing', is itself a legal category.[21] The theory of law as a typical value breaks down at this point because the choice between a natural or psychological and a fictional view

---

[16] Ibid., p.323, tr.p.35.
[17] Ibid., p.322, tr.p.35.
[18] Ibid., p.321, tr.p.34.
[19] Ibid., p.324, tr.p.36.
[20] Ibid.
[21] Ibid., p.302, tr.p.20 and note h.

of the person should disappear once personality, society and law are understood teleologically.

Lask's case started from the postulate that to understand law as a typical value avoids both the error of formal natural law, which is to hypostatize legal validity into absolute normativeness, and the error of material natural law, which is to hypostatize positive legal norms into absolute values.[22] Instead of resolving the antinomy of formal versus material natural law by defining law as a typical 'social' value, the antinomy is merely transferred to the idea of the social. According to Lask's value perspective, the questions of absolute legal validity and of the cleavage between the meaning of the legal norm and its existence become irrelevant because law is understood simply as the most formal structure within the teleological web of the typical, social value or cultural meaning.[23] Law is renamed but it is not redefined: the 'social' as a value is still confronted with 'persons' whose status is as shaky as it was when determined by formal or material law, for the *quaestio quid juris* remains unanswered.

The plaintiff lost his case, but, learning from this experience, he concentrated subsequently on the categorial side not on the social side of his redefinition of law. In spite of his reservations, Lask left 'the entanglement of the concretized world of law with living reality . . . of being and validity',[24] and devoted himself to 'the realm of pure meanings'[25] in which jurisprudence, a practical enterprise, nevertheless, 'creates everything necessary to fulfill its practical task in a peculiar world of concepts all its own.'[26] He answered his own call for a 'methodology of the future' which would distinguish the teleological and juridical concept of the will, and the juridical elaboration of concepts from the psychological and naturalistic approach by writing a doctrine of categories.[27]

This doctrine of categories is Lask's attempt to justify his earlier preference for a Fichtean view of law as midway between Kant's conception of law as heteronomous and external, and the

[22] Ibid., pp.280–87, tr.pp.6–8.
[23] Ibid., p.299, tr.p.18.
[24] Ibid., p.320, tr.p.33.
[25] Ibid., p.318, tr.p.32.
[26] Ibid., p.326, tr.p.37.
[27] Ibid., p.321, tr.p.34.

sensuous world as irrational, and Hegel's conception of law as the emanation of absolute spirit.[28] He rededuces this Fichtean position by developing a theory of categories which incorporates, and then gives priority to, Kant's 'concepts of reflection'.[29] Kant argues that there are four sets of 'concepts of comparison': identity and difference, agreement and opposition, inner and outer, matter and form, which concern the outer relations of things already constituted or intuitions prior to any conceptual apprehension.[30] The use of these oppositions, however, indicates a prior, distinguishing *reflexio* and does not arise from mere comparison.[31]

By drawing attention to the centrality of these primary oppositions in the whole of the Kantian deduction, Lask tries to solve the antinomy of law, to rid jurisprudence and philosophy of the 'misology' which considers 'form' as timelessly valid, but matter as existing and temporal.[32] The opposition between form and matter – which is also the opposition on which natural law is based – is an 'abbreviation for the relation of *Hingelten*'.[33] Kant's *reflexio* is redefined as intentional or valued validity, using the verb *hingelten*, where *gelten* means 'to be valid' or 'to hold', and where *hin*, which means 'there' as in 'there and back', expresses the purposive connotation. The question of law, first defined as a value, becomes the investigation into the mode by which it intends its validity; natural law becomes a call for a *Bedeutungsdifferenzlehre*, a doctrine of the differentiation of meaning, 'a postulate for the future, an enormous task for which up to now not the slightest inclination is to be found anywhere'.[34] As we shall see, Lask's call was to be answered: his methodology of the future became the methodology of the present, the 'inclination' dominant everywhere.

The second plaintiff, Rudolf Stammler, has stepped into the

---

[28] Lask, 'Fichtes Idealismus und die Geschichte', 1902, in *Gesammelte Schriften*, vol. I, pp.1–274.

[29] 'Die Logik der Philosophie und die Kategorienlehre', 1910, *Gesammelte Schriften*, vol. II, pp.133–179.

[30] Kant, *Critique of Pure Reason*, A 269/B 325, A 280/B 336.

[31] Ibid., A 262/B 318.

[32] Lask, 'Die Logik der Philosophie und die Kategorienlehre', *Gesammelte Schriften*, p.45.

[33] Ibid., p.174; for a discussion of *gelten*, see Rose, *Hegel Contra Sociology*, p.6.

[34] Lask, ibid., pp.169–70.

witness box. He is to bring a case for 'purposiveness' as the form
or validity of the law; but, unlike the other parties, he will seek to
exploit the litigious setting, until he comes to clinch his case by
arguing that the venue has mutated into an 'orthosophical' clinic,
dispensing 'just law'.[35]

Stammler embraces the *quaestio quid juris* as the question of 'a
critique of juristic judgement'. When we judge a given, positive
law to be just or unjust, we relate in the same way to the existence
of that law as we do to any object of perception which we judge as
an object of knowledge: we assess its 'striving' for truth or
rightness.[36] The judgement of 'just law', like any other judgement, presupposes and 'strives' for the unity of nature, which is,
equally, the criterion of a just social life. This striving for justice is
derived from the form of consciousness as such by defining its
principle as systematic regularity.[37] 'Law is a condition and not a
goal; a means, not an ultimate end/a right means for a right
purpose.'[38] Purposiveness (*Zweckmässigkeit*), however, is not a
Sollen, an abstract right, a practical judgement, but a judgement of
existence, of law-likeness (*Gesetzmässigkeit*), of regularity.[39]

The form of consciousness is purposiveness: it intends uniformity and regularity, which is equally to intend 'a community
of free men.'[40] These ideas or ideals of consciousness are not
themselves legal propositions: they are propositions of justice,
derived from the unity of consciousness. Hence the question of
law becomes solely the question of method, since the form, or
judgement, or concept, of justice is always the same:

> Our purpose [*sic*] . . . is to find merely a universally valid
> formal method, by means of which the necessarily changing
> material of empirically conditioned legal rules may be so

---

[35] See note 7 above. Stammler's title *Die Lehre von dem richtigen Rechte*: 'The
Theory of Correct or Just Law' is not conveyed in the English title. 'Venue' –
county within which jury must be gathered and cause tried, originally in the
neighbourhood of the crime; 'change of venue' – to avoid a prejudiced jury.
'Ortho' – 'straight', 'right', 'correct', as in 'orthopaedic'.
[36] Stammler, *The Theory of Justice*, pp.32, tr.p.5.
[37] Ibid., p.201, tr.p.156.
[38] Ibid., p.34, tr.p.26.
[39] Ibid., p.202, tr.pp.156–7.
[40] Ibid.

worked out, judged, and determined that it should have the quality of objective justice.[41]

The law of purposes 'means the establishment of a universal method' for judging particular purposes as just or unjust.[42] This 'law of purposes' provides the criterion and content of social life, and all positive law is derived from it; 'law is the necessary condition for organizing uniformly the social life of men'.[43]

Social life is not conceived as governed by legal propositions, or conventional norms, but by 'right intention', by a claim to validity, not an actual effect. A community or society exists not by virtue of the force of law, for that would be an external and general criterion, nor by virtue of the intentions of individuals, for that would be an internal and ethical criterion, but by virtue of a command which 'possesses the quality of *sovereign* validity. It determines by itself the extent of its domain as well as the class of persons subject to it'.[44] This command is 'legal'. The slipperiness of this argument is instructive: law is not sovereignty, that is, force; nor is it validity, that is, reduced to what people accept. It is '*sovereign* validity', and this means 'that there is a power which has the formal quality of essential inviolability',[45] which has, in short, both sovereignty and validity.

Once again the question of law becomes the concept of the social: the form of judgement itself becomes the form of the social, which inherits inconceivable 'sovereign validity' from the question of law. However, Stammler reveals that the common source of both questions is the question of justice and hence of persons. The 'absolutely unitary method of consciousness' has to incorporate the life of 'persons' into its ideals of uniformity and regularity, although the life of 'persons' has a habit of resisting 'absolute unity' of a formal kind.[46]

The 'life and work of men in common' are the 'matter' of social life or social economy, but this substratum can only be apprehended because it 'is carried on under the condition of a

[41] Ibid., pp.116–17, tr.pp.89–90.
[42] Ibid., p.189, tr.p.141.
[43] Ibid., p.29, tr.p.23.
[44] Ibid., p.236, tr.p.181, emphasis in original.
[45] Ibid.
[46] Ibid., p.182, tr.p.141.

positive law,'[47] which is, in turn, submitted to 'an objective rectification in the sense of its own regularity', its own 'form'.[48] These 'men' who live and work 'in common' are persons, and 'person' is a legal category. But is it a just one? Stammler has to reconcile the conventional notion of person as 'end in himself' with his social ideal of 'participant in a community', and this is where the equation of judgement and justice is most strained. He tries to make the individuality of the person 'meet' the community of work by the concept of the 'neighbour', since this concept embraces respect for the individual as an end in himself, and inclusion in a community. The consolation of any exclusion will be that one 'remains one's own neighbour', a community of one.[49] However, it is quite clear that 'neighbour' is a concept of exclusion, not everyone can be one's neighbour, so these 'neighbours' are arranged in concentric circles of nearer and remoter kin. Uniformity and regularity have been bent into a 'method of arranging the persons living under the law in *concentric circles*', derived from Justinian's *Digest*.[50]

Once these kinship circles are established, with the person/neighbour at the omphalos of each, all 'the legal relations which centre in a given person' may be regarded 'as his property', and 'the general types of legal conduct' may be divided 'into personal performances and those accomplished by means of the legal relations of property'. Even 'personal' life in the intimate sense becomes a legal category, for 'there is a third division, due to the fact that according to the fiat of the law there are certain ready-made relations, the peculiar characteristic of which is reciprocal devotion . . . such as undivided community of life, protective authority, filial subordination and guiding care . . . a performance *with persons legally entrusted*'.[51]

The claim that this a priori account is generally correct is sealed by the attempt to show that it corresponds in essence to Marx's theory of value. The exposition of exchange-value in the first volume of *Capital* is understood to incorporate a reference to a

[47] Ibid., p.244, tr.p.187.
[48] Ibid.
[49] Ibid., p.285, tr.pp.217–18.
[50] Ibid., pp.289–90, tr.pp. 221–2.
[51] Ibid., p.293, tr.p.224.

relation of measure which would be 'objectively just . . . if business were carred on according to principles of justice'.[52] Exchange-value is the legal form of a legal performance, a 'telic' value, which refers to the just, socially-necessary time of labour, to the value of a performance in a 'justly ordered society'.[53] The interesting feature of this strange attempt to appropriate Marx's theory of value is not only that it deliberately ignores the contrast between use-value and exchange-value, and that it makes socially necessary labour time, the form of an historically specific injustice, into the form of justice itself, but that this is what happens when justice is spun between the poles of purposiveness and persons, when law is defined both as absolute and unified, and as perpetually *unterwegs*, underway, as purposeiveness.

Stammler turns the question of 'just law' into the 'mission' of method, the search for a validity which is everywhere and nowhere.[54] Hence the question of law is answered: natural law is the doctrine of justice which unites 'the two separate kingdoms of cause and purpose'. This is called 'orthosophy': the wisdom of the straight or correct; natural, inherent and accomplished; but, equally, it is a striving, a method, a task, developing, unfinished and unfinishable. In spite of all the disclaimers, this case, based on the absolute primacy of law as form, leaves us face to face with 'a matter existing by itself and its motion appearing as unconditioned twitchings [*als unbedingt aufkommender Zuckungen*]',[55] for if everything is a matter of form, form becomes indistinguishable from matter. These contortions pass under new names: law as justice, as form, as consciousness, as social life, but under no new concept.

The third plaintiff, Rudolf von Ihering, is barely managing to conceal his grim satisfaction at the ultimate weakness of Stammler's case. For Stammler had tried to demolish Ihering's exposition of purpose in law by accusing him of committing, as it were, a 'transcendental amphiboly', that is, 'a confounding of an object of pure understanding with appearance', a confounding of

---

[52] Ibid., p.295, tr.p.225.
[53] Ibid., p.296, tr.p.226.
[54] Ibid., Conclusion 'The Mission of Just Law', pp.601–27, tr.pp.471–90.
[55] Ibid., p.616, tr.p.481.

concrete, material elements of law with its absolute, formal validity.[56]

Ihering protested that his position was far more radical than Stammler's, who merely reiterated Kant's banishment of interest from law, and only understands the moral law as an imperative which excludes 'every admisture of interest as a motive'. Ihering, quoting from Schopenhauer, stresses the paradoxical result of this approach: 'I am only an instrument, a mere tool of the moral law, and not at all an end . . .'[57] Stammler's development of a critique of juristic judgement legitimizes Kant's confession that 'The human reason is altogether unable to explain how pure reason without other motives . . . can be practical for itself'.[58] Ihering bases his idea of purposiveness on self-interest, and derives his concept of law from that. As for Stammler, so for Ihering, 'the law of causality [is]: *no effect without a cause*. The law of purpose is: *no volition*, or which is the same thing, *no action without purpose*'.[59] Purpose in this sense of purposiveness is not the form of judgement, but the form of self-reference, 'the exclusive tendency of the will to one's own self as egoism'.[60]

Now it is no easier to derive law from self-interest or egoism than it is to derive it from utterly disinterested reverence for the law, and Ihering has to devote a whole chapter to 'The Problem of Self-Denial' before he can arrive at any idea of law. By then he has redefined 'interest' so that it means 'satisfaction [which] arises with the success of his deed in the person of another, with complete banishment of thoughts of self . . .' and so that any individual interest is seen as a cog in the giant wheel of human

[56] The order is reversed: Stammler criticizes Ihering in the conclusion, ibid., pp.603–4, tr.p.473. I have extrapolated Ihering's defence since his revision of Kant is more radical than Stammler's. The title of Ihering's work *Der Zweck im Recht*, 1877–81, vol. I 3rd edn, vol. II 2nd edn, Leipzig, Breitkopf und Härtel, 1893, 1886, 'purpose' or 'goal' in law, is translated as *Law as a Means to an End*, Isaac Husik, New York, Augustus Kelley, 1913, vol. I only. For 'transcendental amphiboly', see Kant, *Critique of Pure Reason*, A 270/B 326.

[57] Ihering, *Der Zweck im Recht*, p.50n, tr.p.38 n.3, quoting Schopenhauer's critique of Fichte, *System der Sittenlehre*, from *Die beiden Grundprobleme der Ethik*.

[58] Ihering, ibid., p.51n, tr.p.39 n.4.

[59] Ibid., pp.4–5, tr.p.2.

[60] Ibid., p.32, tr.p.24.

purposes or 'social life'.[61] In short, interest, as in Kant, becomes disinterest, and purposiveness plays a functional rather than a formal role in this exposition of law.

> The *person, i.e.* the purpose of his physical self-preservation produced *property, i.e.* the purpose of the regulated and assured realization of that person. The two lead again to law, *i.e.* to the securing of their mutual purposes, otherwise solely dependent upon the physical strength of the subject by the power of the State.[62]

The form of law as abstract norm is a result of the 'struggle for interests',[63] where the reference to interests does not confuse the material with the formal elements of law, but demonstrates that 'the (practical) motive (impulse) of purpose, not the (logical) motive (implication) of the concept, presses with necessity from one to the other,' that is, from law (form) to the state (coercion).[64] This Ciceronian derivation of law from self-preservation oscillates between form and force, between the derivation of society from self, and the derivation of preservation from society: 'this therefore is society, namely the realization by law of the truth of the principle, "Everyone exists for the world, and the world exists for everyone."'[65]

Once Ihering has rededuced the antinomy of law from the idea of purpose, the overwhelming bulk of the first volume of his book is devoted to the exposition of the first phrase of the chiasmus: 'everyone exists for the world,' under the rubric of 'social mechanics'. How does he elide teleology to mechanics?

> This is the picture of society as life presents it daily to our eyes. Thousands of rollers, wheels, knives, as in a mighty machine, move restlessly, some in one direction some in another, apparently quite independent of one another as if they existed only for themselves, nay in apparent conflict, as if they wanted mutually to annihilate each other – and yet all

---

[61] Ibid., pp.54, 57–8, tr.pp.41,43–4.
[62] Ibid., p.73, tr.pp.55–6.
[63] Ibid., p.257, tr.p.193.
[64] Ibid., p.74, tr.p.56.
[65] Ibid., p.92, tr.p.70.

work ultimately together for *one purpose*, and one *single* plan
rules the whole . . . The machine must obey the master; the
laws of mechanics enable him to *compel* it. But the force
which moves the wheelwork of human society is the human
will; that force which in contrast to the force of nature, boasts
of its freedom; but the will in that function is the will of
thousands and millions of individuals, the struggle of
interests, of the opposition of efforts, egoism, self-will,
insubordination, inertia, weakness, wickedness, crime.
There is no greater miracle in the world than the discipline
and training of the human will, whose actual realization in its
widest scope we embrace in the world society.[66]

This deposition is worth quoting at length because it displays so
clearly how transferring the question of law to the concept of
society produces an admixture of mechanics and mysticism, of
wheelwork and miracle, and, behind it all, 'the master'.

Law as the 'lever' of this 'realization' is divided into reward or
trade, and coercion, 'the realization of a purpose by means of
mastering another's will; the concept of coercion presupposes, in
the agent as well as in the passive object of coercion, a voluntary
subject, a living being.'[67] From its original meaning in Roman law
of a private, self-interested association, 'society' comes to mean a
public, political connection of 'unselfish associates for the common welfare'.[68] Reward is overshadowed by coercion, and law is
derived from the state, 'the only source of law', and defined as 'the
sum of the compulsory rules in a State . . . the two elements . . .
are that of rule and realization of it through coercion.'[69] Coercion
may be negative or positive, propulsive or compulsive, its object
the prevention or the undertaking of a certain act; self-defence is
propulsive, self-help compulsive.[70] As this idea of law is unfolded,
its 'realizing', compulsive, imperative aspect comes increasingly
to the fore: 'Coercion put in execution by the State forms the
absolute criterion of law; a legal rule without legal coercion is a

---

[66] Ibid., pp.93–4, tr.pp.71–2.
[67] Ibid., p.234, tr.p.176.
[68] Ibid., p.302, p.226.
[69] Ibid., p.320, tr.pp.239–40.
[70] Ibid., p.236, tr.p.177.

contradiction in terms, a fire which does not burn, a light which does not shine';[71] and 'Maxims are guidance for *free* conduct . . . that of the norm is not; . . . *i.e.* every norm is an *imperative* (*positive – command, negative – prohibition*). An imperative has meaning only in the mouth of him who has power to impose such limitation upon another's will.'[72]

Ihering has clearly rededuced the concept of law as dependent on a sovereign will which is not itself subjected to it: 'the meaning of Roman "imperium": . . . the government free to do as it pleases; the personality of the magistrate in contradiction to the legislative power of the people'.[73] The legal state, of course, erects '*bilaterally* binding' laws to which it is itself subordinated, just as the sphere of Roman *imperium* becomes constantly smaller and that of *lex* constantly larger.[74] However, to transfer the problem of sovereignty from law to society is to invest society as a 'vital force' with that element of *imperium* which remains even when law is dominant and bilateral.[75]

This was the gravamen of Stammler's charge: that law as a function of the struggle for interests remains brute force, compulsive rather than valid. Ihering's defence rests on turning not to the brute matter of history, but to a natural law of social life, a mechanism of prophylactic and repressive methods for guaranteeing the interests of persons.[76] However, the overpowering personality of the magistrate has gradually reduced his charges, those originally juridically self-asserting persons, to passive but voluntary objects of coercion, of the *imperium* of the law of purposes. Once again we discover a *ratione imperii* behind the *imperio rationis*, a reason of empire behind the imperium of reason.[77] To call this imperium 'social life' in lieu of 'law' is simply to exchange one practical idea for another, a mechanical but

[71] Ibid., p.322, tr.p.241.
[72] Ibid., p.330n, tr.p.247 n.38.
[73] Ibid., pp.345–6, tr.pp.258–9.
[74] Ibid., pp.357,346, tr.pp.267,259.
[75] Ibid., p.95, tr.72.
[76] Ibid., pp.398–9, tr.p.298.
[77] See, for example, René David, John E. C. Brierley, *Major Legal Systems in the World Today*, London, Stevens and Sons, 1978, p.81, and H. F. Jolowicz, *Roman Foundations of Modern Law*, Oxford, Oxford University Press, 1957, p.4.

equally mysterious one, and, accordingly, we return the same verdict: no concept.

The fourth plaintiff, Hermann Cohen, adopts a different forensic strategy. Initially, he stages a battle far away from the courts of consciousness, but, at the moment of apparent victory, he tears the veils away, and reveals the old, familiar, litigious setting.[78]

He begins by establishing that the ethics of the pure will, the second part of his tripartite system, is modelled on jurisprudence, the 'mathematics of the cultural sciences',[79] just as pure knowledge is modelled on mathematics in the first part. Jurisprudence, a 'fact' of scientific consciousness and possessing an ideal precision, stands as the 'mathematics' of the cultural sciences because it produces its objects and transcends the epistemological opposition between ordinary consciousness and its object.[80]

Having staked this claim, the onus now falls on Cohen to explicate the 'logic' of the pure will, its mode of producing its objects, in a way which will justify the analogy with jurisprudence, conceived as the matheme of the cultural sciences. 'Matheme' or 'cogneme' implies both the production and the product of actuality, 'without waiting upon intuitions', a kind of efficient causality, which cannot be justified by a transcendental deduction because it precedes the construction of appearances, the combination of concept and intuition.[81] The principle and the product of this operation are together referred to as the 'matheme', because mathematics offers an exemplar of productive cognition and transcends the dichotomy of theoretical and practical reason. In addition, for Cohen, the 'matheme' offers a close scientific analogy of productive cognition which avoids the Hegelian implication that actuality in general is alienated and recaptured. Similarly, jurisprudence, the science of legal concepts, offers an analogy for the activity of the will, its production of its

---

[78] Cohen, *Ethik des reinen Willens*, 1904.
[79] Ibid., p.V.
[80] Ibid., pp.62–3.
[81] I use 'matheme' to capture the unity on which Cohen's system is based, called 'cogneme' (*Erkenntnis*) in the first part, but established by mathematical analogy in both of the first two parts: compare Cohen, *Logik der reinen Erkenntnis*, p.12. For 'cogneme', to translate *Erkenntnis*, see n.2 above.

objects, without implying that the existing state and law present the actualization of the rational.

Cohen draws the outlines of the operations of the will by taking up terms from the *Critique of Pure Reason* which do essential work in the construction of appearances without themselves falling under the rubric of the combination of concept and intuition. The role played by the judgement of origin in pure knowledge is taken by the 'law of continuity' in the productions of the pure will.[82] 'Continuity' is a mathematical concept; and *quanta continua* also designate time and space as concrete intuitions, not as the empty forms of intuition: 'the property of magnitudes by which no part of them is the smallest possible, that is, by which no part is simple, is called their continuity'.[83] *Quanta continua* depend on the synthesis of productive imagination in time: 'Such magnitudes may be called flowing, since the synthesis of productive imagination involved in their production is a progression in time is ordinarily designated by the term flowing or flowing away'.[84] On this basis Cohen will show that the intelligible realm of purposes to which the moral law refers draws its actuality from the operations of the form of inner experience: time.

Prima facie, it would appear that the realm of purposes (*Endzwecke*) partakes of space and not time.[85] Kant tests maxims of actions by making them into the form of a natural law in general: 'Ask yourself whether if the action which you propose should take place by a law of nature of which you yourself were a part you could regard it as possible through your will'.[86] This exercise is called a 'typic of practical reason', because the natural law is serving as a *type* of the law of freedom, and not as a *schematism*, which would correspond 'to natural laws as laws to which objects of sensuous intuition as such are subject', for there is no intuition in the case of moral law.[87] Cohen draws on this idea of a 'type' of natural law as a cognition which needs no intuition,

[82] Cohen, *Ethik des reinen Willens*, p.97; for 'origin' in Cohen, see Rose, *Hegel Contra Sociology*, p.10.

[83] Kant, *Critique of Pure Reason*, A 169–71/B 211–13.

[84] Ibid.

[85] Cohen, *Ethik des reinen Willens*, p.371.

[86] Kant, *Critique of Practical Reason*, p.188., tr.p.72.

[87] Ibid., p.188, tr.pp.71–2

but, in place of nature conceived as appearances in space, he deduces time as the actuality to which the typic refers.

Space produces the 'outer world', the objective image of nature, while time, on the contrary, produces the 'inner world', the subjective image of nature. Time constitutes the inner condition of thought prior to the outer image of space, and is the origin not only of motion and desire, but also of the will.[88] By making outer and inner, a distinction of reflection, into the fundamental characteristic of space and time, Cohen turns the forms of intuition into producers of intuitions; the forms of finite appearance turn into demiurgoi of infinite capacity.

The infinite progress of time is different from the mere universality of infinite space; and on the basis of this distinction between two connotations of infinity, eternity emerges as the fundament of the moral law.[89] The actuality of the realm of *Endzwecke*, the kingdom of ends, is a law of nature, conceived not as space but as timelessness, the ethical timelessness heralded by the prophets, not the ahistorical and pre-social duration (*durée*) expounded by Bergson. Ethical life is not an infinite moral task, but the task of the eternal. The kingdom of ends lives in the repetition of the unity of the will as it refers continually to the future. The difference between time and space, between inner and outer intuition marks out time as the ultimate producer.[90] Difference and continuity, not difference and identity, act as the most primary of the oppositions of reflection, as the vanishing point of a unity which cannot be conceived. Jurisprudence can only figure as a mathematical analogy of this metaphysics of the pure will, which seems to have rededuced messianic time instead of the validity of law and the state.

Suddenly, however, the mystical and mathematical actuality of the moral law is revealed to be pure 'fiction', and we are brusquely landed down again in the mundane setting of litigious space, where such legal and metaphysical fictions are produced. After more than a thousand pages of cognemes, of mathemes, of pure knowledge and the pure will, of this new dogmatic system laid

[88] Cohen, *Ethik des reinen Willens*, pp.376–7.
[89] Ibid., p.379.
[90] Ibid., p.393; see discussion of Bergson below, chapter 6

out by transforming the oppositions of Kantian critical philosophy into productive unities, established by reference to the certain fact of mathematical thinking, we are now informed that the axiomatic unity of the subject of action has been a fiction, just as science and mathematics itself operate with pure fictions as their fundamental principles.[91]

This unexpected confession has been provoked by a belated consideration of *die Gerechtigkeit*, 'justice', neither in the sense of right (*das Recht*) nor of law (*das Gesetz*), but in the sense of justness, rightness, equity.[92] Cohen has still a lot to tell us. His strategy seems to change as the fiction of unity employed so far is to be tested by the 'control of actuality [*die Kontrolle der Wirklichkeit*]', which is brought to 'enliven and expose the relevance or purpose of fictions [*die Sachgemäßheit der Fiktion*]'. We are in court again: 'the forum of actuality'.[93]

The ethical fiction of action is to be investigated to discover what it is covering up: it does not take much questioning to reveal its roots in the historical division of body and soul attributed to labour, and this throws light on another fiction so far assumed: the unity of mankind. Human activity, split into leisure and business (*die Muße und das Negotium*) – the tasks of culture – splits and destroys the concept of the person.[94] The 'control of actuality', acting here as the discerning power, is the historical actuality of culture. 'Culture' refers both to the history of economic activity and the history of ethical life (*die Sittlichkeit*). The ethical is not the judge we expect to find in this forum of actuality, but the mediator, which once linked custom (ethos, *Sitte*) to the ancient gods and attributed equality to humankind. This mediator or control in modern times is called 'virtue', (*die Tugend*), or justness (*die Gerechtigkeit*).[95]

Die Gerechtigkeit as the criterion of the unity of humankind, obscured in history, does not oppose a natural law to positive law and the state; instead it erects science, method, jurisprudence, in

[91] Ibid., p.559. I have added together the pages of the first two parts of Cohen's system, *Logik der reinen Erkenntnis* and *Ethik des reinen Willens*.
[92] Ibid., ch.15, p.599 *ad fin.*
[93] Ibid., p.560.
[94] Ibid., p.562.
[95] Ibid., pp.565, 447, 450–51.

the place of natural law. It erects all those fictional unities which we found obscuring actuality such a short time ago.[96] But it does not, Hegelian fashion, reconstruct history as the actualization of reason, thereby equating law and right with the logic of reason. Instead science provides a forum of actuality by pitting experience against original unity and ultimate ideal, and this is its virtue. The virtue of history guided by jurisprudence is the right of science and the science of right.[97]

'The connection and the conflict of law [*des Rechts*] with ethics presents the fundamental problem of the entirety of law in its entire history: the relation of persons to things.'[98] Cohen reminds us that *The Institutes* of Justinian divide the civil law into persons, things, and action. Action refers to both persons and things, linking them under the titles of obligation. Obligation is included under 'things' in *The Institutes*, and Cohen shows that this is not a survival of primitive thinking as it often assumed by modern commentators.

The equivocation expressed in the standard formula of 'right to a thing against a person' is instructive, for the equation *obligatio personae* = *obligatio rei* reconciles irreconcilables.[99] The unities of 'action', 'subject of action' and 'person' break down in the face of the unity of the thing.[100] All these unities reveal the true designs of personal right – right of a person – to an alien thing: the producer of a thing and the owner of it are equally 'persons', but the owner has a right to the product, the 'thing'. Domination over the action of an alien person is called 'obligation', right to a thing. In support of this exposition of the main divisions of Roman law, Cohen cites Savigny's definition of modern obligation: 'relations of domination over particular actions of alien persons.'[101]

The history of exchange as the history of the way in which the concrete, specific actions of one individual are isolated and compacted to become the property of another, is traced from slave

[96] Ibid., pp.566–7.
[97] Ibid., pp.567–9,570.
[98] Ibid., p.570.
[99] Ibid., p.591 'Obligation' does not have this centrality in English common law; for a concise statement of its centrality in Romano-Germanic legal systems, see David and Brierley, *Modern Legal Systems in the World Today*, p.80.
[100] Cohen, *Ethik des reinen Willens*, p.591.
[101] Ibid., p.572.

society to the 'modern absolute worker', and modern law of
obligation. This domination of action separated from the actor
leaves the concept of the thing in its integrity while perpetually
tearing apart the integrity of the person: property in persons
becomes right to a thing.[102] The transformation of use-value into
exchange-value is the modern way in which specific actions are
isolated by the law of obligation. The unity of the person – the
true meaning of culture and of value – revolves around the value
of things and of isolated actions. Obligation bestows the unity
which makes these isolated and manifold actions into the unity of
the commodity, idealized as money.[103]

The concept of capital brings the relation of person and thing to
the crunch. Capital acts like a person not a thing: 'interest means
production and capital means substance.'[104] The illusion of natural
personality is destroyed by this personification and so is the
anodyne distinction between persons and things.[105] The difference
in the value of the product as enjoyed by the worker and by capital
is expunged in the legal concepts of the product and of the
contract. This difference in value or 'profit of labour' is buried in
the innermost affairs of the state: the law of obligation is the riddle
of the Sphinx of capital, the secret of commodity fetishism.[106]

Cohen celebrates his solution to the 'riddle' which transforms
'exchange interests into the interests of culture' as the work of
scientific virtue (*die Gerechtigkeit*), which has 'won again' the
connection between law and ethics. The 'mythology of capital'
has itself 'redeemed' the myth of the worker as a person.
'Mythology' means law as historical fiction and as redeeming
virtue. Legal positivity is 'mythological' because it offers both a
'natural' realm of equations of the law, and an immanent test by
the *tertium comparationis*, the third, but excluded, party to the
equation, the product, which emerges from the legal relation of
person to person.[107] The description of such equations dominates
Cohen's exposition in place of any constitutive or dialectical
discourse of appearance, form, illusion.

---

[102] Ibid., pp.572–3.
[103] Ibid., p.575.
[104] Ibid., p.576.
[105] Ibid., p.577.
[106] Ibid., p.578.
[107] Ibid., pp.577–8.

The problem of property is the 'old crux of ethics'. Ethical inquiry reveals that self-consciousness is 'a mode of having as much as a mode of being'. From this Cohen concludes that nothing can be gained by transferring the question of property from the shoulder of the entrepreneur to the shoulder of the wage-labourer. He recommends that the distinction originally drawn by Otto von Gierke between community (*die Genossenschaft*) and association or society (*die Gesellschaft*) be brought into play by the future virtue of scientific jurisprudence (*die Gerechtigkeit*).[108] This opposition of community and society raises the question of the relation between the ethical and juristic person in a way that the concept of society by itself fails to do, and escapes the naturalistic prejudice attaching to the legal concepts of individual, person and property.[109] It pits 'community', the fiction of Germanic law, against 'society', the fiction of Roman law,[110] avoiding both the pitfall of socialism, which erects the fiction of Germanic 'community' in place of the fiction of capitalist 'society',[111] and the weakness of sociology, which fails to distinguish adequately between 'society' meanings *socialitas*, with its economic, Roman, private law connotations, and 'society' meaning *consocialitas* with its moral or ethical connotation, developed by the Stoics.[112] It keeps alive the question of the relation between the social and political as the question of how law is to be conceived.

Cohen thus remains with the virtue of *die Gerechtigkeit*, and its scientific corollary, the matheme of jurisprudence, softened by the recognition that *die Gerechtigkeit* (impartiality, rightness) implies equity (*die Billigkeit*). The universal aspect of justice, equality as humankind's *Selbstzweck*, must always be tempered with equity, with respect for the individual. Equity is not simply a convenience of Roman law, an exception to the universality of just law, but the 'biology' to the mathematics of jurisprudence, analogously ruled by teleology, by purpose not by mechanics.[113]

Here the case rests: the Sphinx of law has acquired the eye of

---

[108] Ibid., p.579.
[109] Ibid., p.580.
[110] Ibid., p.581.
[111] Ibid., pp.580–83, 296–7, 240.
[112] Ibid., pp.224–5. Cohen argues that the German *Genossenschaft* is nearer to Latin *societas* than to Plato's '*Gemeinsame der Freunde*'; see, too, pp.292–3.
[113] Ibid., p.587.

equity. The practical idea of law, its inconceivability, is not fixed in the opposition of person and thing, *als bei Kant*, but traced to a 'difference' which is the origin of both the fictions of law and the *Gerechtigkeit* of history. The opposition between difference and continuity within consciousness adverts to, but cannot know, the fundamental productive unity of time, and to individual ethical life as the life of eternity. The difference between person and thing adverts to the productive unity of ethical life from the 'outside', or, better, from the 'out-time', of consciousness, as it is discerned by the virtue of history. The difference between the inconceivable original unity and the oppositions in which it is experienced – time from the perspective of inner and outer consciousness, history from the perspective of person and thing – is the actuality of *die Gerechtigkeit*, actual as a state and as act or activity. The riddle of the Sphinx is the riddle of the kingdom of ends; jurisprudence, is the path, or, rather, the time of the kingdom.

This reversion to metaphysics which we have witnessed in all of the four cases examined has emerged most clearly in each case in the recourse to the social. In place of the old rule, *ubi societas ibi ius*, we now find its inversion, *ubi ius ibi societas*.[114] The original rule, 'where society, there law', read specifically, tells us that 'society' is a legal category, a technical category of Roman law; read as a generalization, it becomes the principle that law is the criterion of the social. The inversion of this rule, 'where law, there society', tells us that the legal is a social category, and that society is the criterion of law. As the criterion, it inherits the practical and inconceivable status of the standard, of the concept which has no concept.

Cohen's suit, the most interesting and strange of these four suits, made us look deeply into this practical nature of the idea of law: it cannot, strictly speaking, be conceived by theoretical reason. We could only see it, as it were, in the reflections of theoretical consciousness as outer/inner, matter/form. Prized out of consciousness in this way and grafted onto the typic of practical reason, law acts as a schema – the very 'mysticism of practical

---

[114] See Dabin, 'General Theory of Law', 1944, translated from the French in Wiek, *The Legal Philosophy of Lask, Radbruch and Dabin*, pp.235–6.

reason' that the typic was designed to guard against.[115] The form of the law of nature has returned as a 'messianic', natural [*sic*] law of temporal repetition.

Our faith in the naturalness of the features of metaphysics has been lost, but, instead of remaining with this difficulty, we have been distracted by the institution of new natural laws. Law cannot revert to constituting appearances as opposed to things in themselves, because things in themselves have turned out to be – persons. Things are never 'in themselves'; they are actions detached from persons and isolated qua things.[116] Attention to the juridical meanings of metaphysical terms has alerted us to the relation of legal form and legal fictions as a relation between the form of inner consciousness and the out-time of consciousness – between time and history – but this experience has been effaced by the development of new unified and productive principles.[117]

---

[115] Kant, *Critique of Practical Reason*, p.190, tr.p.73.

[116] Compare F. W. J. Schelling, '. . . Ding an sich nur hypostatierte Tätigkeit sei' (. . . thing in itself [is] only hypostatized activity), *System des transzendentalen Idealismus*, 1800, Hamburg, Felix Meiner, 1957, p.129. A thing in itself could only be a *res nullius*, defined by Justinian in *The Institutes*: 'Nullius autem sunt res sacrae et religiosae et sanctae: quod enim divini juris est id nullius in bonis est,' that is, 'Things sacred, religious and hallowed, belong to no one; for that which is under divine law is not the property of anyone.' *Res nullius* were either things unappropriated by anyone, such as things common, unoccupied lands, wild animals; or things which cannot be appropriated: sacred things dedicated to the celestial gods; religious things dedicated to underworld gods; and sanctified things, such as the walls and gates of a city, Lib.II Tit.I 7–10. However, Kant argues that there cannot be a *res nullius*: 'a maxim according to which, if it were made into a law, an object of will would have to be in itself (objectively) ownerless [*herrenlos*] (*res nullius*) is contrary to justice,' *The Metaphysical Elements of Justice*, 354, tr.p.52, slightly amended. Kant considers *res nullius* as an object in one's power which cannot be used, not as a thing in which there can be no *dominium*; this differs from the realm of *res nullius* in *The Institutes* which could be used but in which there was no *dominium*.

[117] For 'fictions', see H. Vaihinger, *The Philosophy of 'As if': A System of the Theoretical, Practical and Religious Fictions of Mankind*, 1911, trans. C. K. Ogden, New York, Harcourt, Brace and Co., 1925; for 'functions', see Ernst Cassirer, *Substance and Function and Einstein's Theory of Relativity*, 1910, trans. William Curtis and Marie Collins Swabey, New York, Dover, 1923; for a discussion of neo-Kantian revival of natural law, see Carl Joachim Friedrich, *The Philosophy of Law in Historical Perspective*, 1958, Chicago, University of Chicago Press, 1963, ch.XIX, pp.178–88.

3

Time or History?

The well-known oppositions between Marburg and Heidelberg, the two major schools of neo-Kantianism, collapse when the work of Hermann Cohen and Emil Lask, the major representatives of each school, is examined from the standpoint of its jurisprudential claims and implications.[1] The common root of those familiar oppositions between validity and values, the natural sciences and the cultural sciences, structure and action, naturalistic method and interpretative understanding, between, in short, neo-Kantian bowdlerized theoretical and practical reason, becomes visible in the ambition shared by Cohen and Lask to dissolve the antinomy of law by developing either a productive logic (Cohen) or an intentional logic (Lask) based on Kant's concepts of reflection.

The pertinent opposition between Cohen and Lask is to be found in their reading of time in Kant. Lask understands the a priori as the realm of timeless validity, and the empirical as the realm of the temporal; he seeks to sublate the distinction by analysis of intentional consciousness.[2] Cohen sublates the opposition of a priori and empirical by suspending the temporal realm of consciousness and its objects within the eternal. For Lask, identity and difference become differentiation of meaning; for Cohen, they become differentiation of time. For Lask, outer and inner become distinctions without a difference, internal to intending consciousness; for Cohen, they are opened out by *die Gerechtigkeit*, and

---

[1] For a discussion of the two schools from the standpoint of their methodological claims and with reference to another common root in the work of Lotze, see Rose, *Hegel Contra Sociology*, pp.2–13.

[2] In this context 'to sublate', the standard translation of Hegel's *aufheben*, implies to carry an opposition back to its source.

philosophy itself is opened up again to history. Lask's thinking turns history into logic while Cohen's turns logic into history.[3]

Lask's call for a *Bedeutungsdifferenzlehre*,[4] a doctrine of the differentiation of meaning, was heard by the young Lukács and the young Heidegger, both of whom produced studies of the differentiation of meaning, *hingelten*, with specific reference to Lask, at the same period:[5] Lukács in his *Heidelberg Aesthetics*, 1912–18;[6] Heidegger in his study of the categories and of meaning in Duns Scotus, 1916.[7] However, it was Cohen's perspective that came to prevail over the work of these two thinkers. In all three of these initiatives the realization that the critical philosophy evolves around a litigious question, the *quaestio quid juris*, and depends on juridical oppositions, such as persons and things, had the result of opening up time, the form of inner tuition, to history; it challenges thereby the mysterious categorical imperative on an even deeper foundation of the philosophy of reflection where the initial *reflexio* and property are first identified.

These three chapters follow the jurisprudential journeyings in

---

[3] See Lask's comparison of the conception of history in Kant, Fichte and Hegel, *Fichtes Idealismus und die Geschichte*, 1902, in *Gesammelte Schriften*, Eugen Herrigel (ed.), Tübingen, J. C. B. Mohr, 1923–24, vol. I, pp.1–274, a work which influenced the development of Max Weber's concept and critique of rationality: see Weber, 'Roscher und Knies und die logischen Probleme der historischen Nationalökonomie', 1903–6, in *Gesammelte Aufsätze zur Wissenschaftslehre*, Tübingen, J. C. B. Mohr, 1973, p.16 n.l, trans. *Roscher and Knies: The Logical Problems of Historical Economics*, Guy Oakes, New York, The Free Press 1975, p.219 n.26.

[4] See chapter 1 above, p.32 n.34.

[5] I suspect that Lucien Goldmann recognized the connections between Lukács and Heidegger because he had also been deeply influenced by Lask; see Goldmann, *Immanuel Kant*, 1945, trans. Robert Black, London, New Left Books, 1971, pp.23n,54–7,123n, and *Lukács and Heidegger: Towards a New Philosophy*, 1973, trans. William Q. Boelhower, London, Routledge and Kegan Paul, 1977.

[6] Georg Lukács, 1885–1971, 'Heidelberger Philosophie der Kunst', 1912–14, and 'Heidelberger Ästhetik', 1916–18, in *Frühe Schriften zur Ästhetik, 1912–16, Gesammelte Werke*, vols 16–17, Darmstadt, Luchterhand, 1979; and see 'Emil Lask', *Kantstudien* XXII (1913), 349–70. For a brief discussion of Lask and Lukács, see Rose, *Hegel Contra Sociology*, pp.27–8.

[7] Martin Heidegger, 1889–1976, *Die Kategorien- und Bedeutungslehre des Duns Scotus*, Freiburg Habilitationschrift, 1915, Tübingen, J. C. B. Mohr, 1916, 'Vorwort', and pp.210–11; and see 'My Way to Phenomenology', 1963, *Zur Sache des Denkens*, Tübingen, Niemeyer, 1969, pp.82–3, trans. in *On Time and Being*, Joan Stanbaugh, New York, Harper and Row, 1972, pp.75–6.

Heidegger's thinking in order to comprehend both its strength and its vulnerability and thereby to provide the perspective from which the appropriations of Heidegger's thinking are reviewed in the second part of this work.

We are called by Heidegger back into court with our status clarified as witness. But this time we are going on a journey through the three inner halls,[8] from the court of the judge of consciousness, to the court on Achilles' shield where the judge is the *history*[9] and, it will emerge, even further back, to the court of the voice – of the judge, unbearable to behold,[10] on Mount Sinai. Time and property brings us to the heart of history and of philosophical discourse.

In 1916 Heidegger published an article in the neo-Kantian journal *Zeitschrift für Philosophie und philosophische Kritik* entitled 'The Concept of Time in the Historical Sciences'.[11] It reads like a typical neo-Kantian manifesto of the Heidelberg kind, a *Differenzschrift*,[12] which seeks to distinguish between the concept of time as employed in the physical sciences and as employed in the historical sciences; between time as quantitative standard of measurement, homogenous, mathematical and functional, and time as qualitative expression of value, heterogenous, eventful and substantial.[13] It can also be read as the beginning of Heidegger's

[8] Franz Kafka, *The Trial*, 1925, Frankfurt am Main, Fischer, 1980, p.182, trans. Willa and Edwin Muir, Harmondsworth, Penguin, 1975, p.235.

[9] Homer, *Iliad*, Book 18, lines 497–508; *histor*, originally, a 'wise man', 'one who knows better than the parties to a dispute', hence 'one who knows law and right, a judge', from the verb *historeo*, 'to learn by inquiry', hence 'to narrate what one has learnt', see Liddell and Scott, *Greek–English Lexicon*.

[10] Compare Kafka, *The Trial*, 'Schon den Anblick des dritten kann nicht einmal ich mehr vertragen,' p.182; tr.p.235 fails to convey that it is the *countenance* of the third doorkeeper that the first cannot bear.

[11] Heidegger, 'Der Zeitbegriff in der Geschichtswissenschaft', *Zeitschrift für Philosophie und philosophische Kritik* 161 (1916), 173–88, trans. 'The Concept of Time in the Science of History', Harry S. Taylor and Hans W. Uffelmann, *Journal of the British Society for Phenomenology, 9/1 (1978)*, 3–10.

[12] '*Differenzschrift*' refers to Hegel's famous early essay 'The Difference between Fichte's and Schelling's System of Philosophy', 1801, *Theorie Werkausgabe*, 2, Frankfurt am Main, Suhrkamp, 1977, 9–138, trans. H. S. Harris and Walter Cerf, Albany, State University of New York Press, 1977.

[13] Heidegger, 'The Concept of Time in the Science of History', 176–82,182–8, tr.4–7,7–10. For 'substance and function', see Ernst Cassirer, *Substance and Function and Einstein's Theory of Relativity*, 1910, trans. William Curtis and Marie Collins Swabey, New York, Dover, 1923.

life-long riposte to Husserl's manifesto 'Philosophy as a Rigorous Science', published in the first edition of *Logos*, 1910–11, which was also organized as a *Differenzschrift*, but which contrasted the naturalism and historicism of the physical and cultural sciences not the physical and historical sciences.[14]

In his essay Husserl also distinguishes between quantitative and qualitative time. Qualitative time is experienced as a flow, 'ordered in an overall connection, in a monadic unity of consciousness, a unity that in itself has nothing to do with nature, with space and time or substantiality and causality, but has its thoroughly peculiar "forms". It is a flow of phenomena, unlimited at both ends, traversed by an intentional line that is, as it were, the index of the all-pervading unity. It is the line of immanent "time", without beginning or end, a time that no chronometers measure.'[15] For Husserl this *durée* is the source of a new validity which will legitimize philosophy again in face of the onslaught from the physical sciences which postulate an external nature of discrete beings subject to the law of causality, and from the cultural sciences which lead inevitably from the study of *Weltanschauungen* to historicist scepticism.[16] Qualitative time remains within consciousness: it strips phenomena of their 'nature' and relocates them within 'the extraordinary wealth of consciousness differences.'[17]

For Heidegger qualitative time is substance not flow. He considers not the scientific aspect of the historical sciences, but the historical, the unit of history as something which happens (*die Geschichte – das Geschehen*), which gives rise to history in the chronological or numerical sense; the example, *par excellence*, is the life of Christ, which is not only the beginning of the reckoning of history – BC/AD –, but also the source of the festivals which mark the reckoning of each year – Christmas/Easter.[18]

In this short and quite pedestrian article, Heidegger, nevertheless, suggests a way in which questioning the concept of time in historical science might take us outside scientific consciousness

[14] Edmund Husserl, *Philosophie als strenge Wissenschaft*, 1910–11, Frankfurt am Main, Klostermann, 1981, trans. Quentin Lauer, in *Phenomenology and the Crisis of Philosophy*, New York, Harper and Row, 1965, pp. 71–192.

[15] Ibid., pp.36–7, tr.pp.107–8.

[16] Ibid., pp.50,34, tr.pp.124, 104.

[17] Ibid., pp.38,25, tr.pp.110,94.

[18] Heidegger, 'The Concept of Time in the Science of History', 188, tr.10.

itself, to some place or some time where the opposition of time as flow and time as measurement, and of outer and inner, has not occurred. History as events (*Ereignisse*) in determinate time (*bestimmte Zeitstelle*) is opposed to the characterless time in general (*Zeit überhaupt*) of the critical philosophy.[19] This distinction furnishes the criterion by which the quantitative time of modern consciousness may be identified; it does not become the occasion to seek richer wealth within those bare walls as they stand.

'The history of Being is never past but stands ever before [. . . *die Wahrheit des Seins. Dessen Geschichte ist nie vergangen, sie steht immer bevor*].'[20] The distinction between qualitative time as an event, and the empty quantitative time of the chronometers becomes the key to Heidegger's defiance of the litigious space of the critical philosophy, where consciousness masochistically challenges its own right, and where a judge ultimately prevails who employs accusations (the Greek word *kategoria* means 'accusation') to partition and dominate reality (the German verb *urteilen*, 'to judge', is composed of *ur* – 'original', and *teilen* – 'to divide').[21] The original procedure of the court, the initial reflection which opens up the litigious space in which a judge rules and in which property of a specific kind is defended and justified, is itself to be questioned – but in a different way. The *quaestio quid juris*, which drew attention to the possession of untitled property and which opened up the space of the court, itself depends on a prior division of time.

[19] Ibid., 182,175, tr.7,4.

[20] Heidegger, 'Letter on Humanism', 1946–47, in *Wegmarken*, 1967, Frankfurt am Main, Klostermann, 1978, p.312, trans. in *Basic Writings*, David Farrell Krell (ed.), London, Routledge and Kegan Paul, 1978, p.194.

[21] The following reconstruction takes *das Ereignis* not *Dasein* as the focus of Heidegger's oeuvre including this early essay. For Kant's *quaestio quid iuris* which Heidegger discusses under the heading of 'The External Form of the Transcendental Deduction', see Heidegger, *Kant and the Problem of Metaphysics*, 1929, 4th edn, Frankfurt am Main, Klostermann, 1973, trans. James S. Churchill, Bloomington, Indiana University Press, 1965, sec.18; for the litigious nature of the critical philosophy, see 'The Word of Nietzsche: "God is Dead"', 1943, in *Holzwege*, 1950, Frankfurt am Main, Klostermann, 1980, pp.293–41, trans. in *The Question concerning Technology and Other Essays*, William Lovitt, New York, Harper, 1977, pp.88–91; for the etymology of 'category', see 'Der europäische Nihilismus', 1940, *Nietzsche*, II, Pfullingen, Neske, 1961, pp.71–80; for 'spatiality', see *Sein und Zeit*, 1927, Tübingen, Niemeyer, 1972, trans. *Being and Time*, John Macquarrie and Edward Robinson, Oxford, Basil Blackwell, 1967, 1.3, para. 24.

The initial reflection separates out the a priori from the empirical: consciousness as such or time as such is distinguished from any particular moment or instance of experience. Then the possibility of any instance of experience is reconstructed as the synthesis of precondition and conditioned. Two 'reflections' are involved, one in time and one in space: the first critical reflection occurs in time when the a priori possibility is separated from any actual instance; the second reflection occurs in space when the actual is then reconstructed in the mirror of the a priori, made present again as a re-presentation or image. The first reflection separates the past from the present; the second reflection re-presents the past in the presence of the a priori as an image.

Heidegger shows us that the first movement of reflection does not involve a change of place in time, from the present to the past, but a change in duration of time, from an incompleted to a completed action. 'To reflect' may mean to look into a mirror or 'to think about something'. When we think about something which has happened, is happening or which happens, we relate to it by fixing both its duration in time and its place in time. For duration in time we employ perfect and imperfect tenses; for place in time we employ past, present and future tenses: 'I am drinking' is an imperfect present, a continuous action; 'I have drunk' is a perfect present, an action completed in the present; 'I drink' is an historic present, an achievement which is not marked by reference to its limitation in time as perfect or imperfect.

When we reflect on something which happens (historic present), we perfect what is present: we consider it as completed in order to examine it by putting it in the present perfect, as something which 'has' happened. This does not necessarily mean that we place the event in past time, for we are able to distinguish between actions completed in the past: 'I had drunk', and actions perfected in the present: 'I have drunk'. We may also refer to an action or state as both continuous and complete: 'I have been drinking' – 'have' indicates perfection, and 'been' indicates continuity. However, perfect tenses tend to carry the connotation of something being over – 'I will have drunk' – of being past in the sense of 'without a presence', where 'presence' sounds like the contrary of physical or spatial absence. Yet the past is not 'absent' as the contrary of physical or spatial presence, but 'perfect', the contrary of the imperfect or continuous present.

In German as in English the verb 'to have' which means 'to possess' is used as the auxiliary to form perfect tenses. When we say something or someone 'has' a characteristic, we distinguish the thing or person and the characteristic from each other, and identify them with each other at the same time. The characteristic is the 'property' of the thing or person; the bearer is identified by possession of the characteristic. Similarly, when we reflect about something, we perfect what is present, putting it in the past, attributing properties to it, and then re-presenting it as an image, as a presence in space. When we reflect on an action as completed we imply that it possesses its characteristics as that kind of ownership where the property is distinct from the bearer and identified with and subordinate to it. In English, but not in German, imperfect or continuous tenses are formed with parts of the verb 'to be': 'I was drinking' is a continuous past tense which employs the past of the verb 'to be' as an auxiliary, implying, as a corollary to this argument, a mode of presence not a mode of possession. German has a special verb form for the imperfect that does not use the verb 'to be', just as there are no special forms in German for distinguishing between the historic and the continuous or imperfect present.

Both Hegel and Nietzsche note this connection between the meaning of 'to have' as possession, and its use in verbal syntax as the auxiliary of temporal completion. Under the heading 'The Thing' in the *Encyclopaedia Logic*, Hegel says: 'These determinations are different from each other; on the part of the thing, not on their own part, they have their reflection [*Reflexion-in-sich*]. They are the *properties* of the thing, and their relation to it is that of *Having*' and he comments: 'As a relation *having* [in the 'Doctrine of Essence'] takes the place of *being* [in the 'Doctrine of Being'] . . . the thing is reflection-into-self, an identity which is also different from the differences, from its determinations. − In many languages "to have" is employed to denote past time − and with reason, for the past is sublated being and *Geist* is its reflection-into-self where it persists, and which differentiates from itself this being sublated in it.'[22] Or, as Nietzsche expresses it in *Daybreak*:

[22] Hegel, *Encyclopaedia of the Philosophical Sciences*, Part I, *Logic*, *Theorie Werkausgabe*, 8, trans. William Wallace, Oxford, Clarendon Press, 1975, para. 125, 'The Thing', translation amended.

'*The ego wants everything.* – It seems that the sole purpose of human action is possession: this idea is, at least, contained in the various languages, which regard all past action as having put us in possession of something ("I *have* spoken, struggled, conquered": that is to say, I am now in possession of my speech, struggle, victory). How greedy man appears here! He does not want to extricate himself even from the past, but wants to continue to *have* it!'[23]

Heidegger's texts are exercises in 'grammatical hermeneutics' – to borrow from Schleiermacher: they take the semantics of verbal syntax as the index of the crux of form and history in the critical philosophy.[24] Heidegger's verb-play opens out the critical court so that it reveals the syntax and semantics of a different time: a time in which consciousness is not divided in the critical way. This different time is not 'conceivable', for the original distinction between concept and intuition is one of the problems; nor is it 'possible' or 'actual', for the divorce of possibility and actuality is another. Yet it is *present*.

Heidegger brings into play other ways of expressing presence and possession (identity) which do not carry the implications of time and property informing critical reflection. *Ereignen*, 'to happen', the verbal form of 'the event', *das Ereignis*, first sketched in the 1916 article; *gehören*, 'to belong' and also an old past participle of *hören*, 'to hear'; and *anwesen*, 'to be present' are seminal in this uncovering of the critical palimpsest.

> Das Zusammen*gehören* von Mensch und Sein in der Weise der Wechselseitigen Herausforderung bringt uns bestürzend näher, da*ß* und wie der Mensch dem Sein vereignet, das Sein aber den Menschenwesen zugeeignet ist. Im Ge-stell waltet ein seltsames Vereignen und Zueignen. Es gilt, dieses

---

[23] Nietzsche, *Daybreak Thoughts on the Prejudices of Morality, Werke*, II, trans. R. J. Hollingdale, Cambridge, Cambridge University Press, 1982, sec. 281.

[24] This is how Schleiermacher describes the connection between grammar and meaning in the comparison of the Greek of the *New Testament* and the *Septuagint* with the Hebrew Scriptures, see *Hermeneutik und Kritik*. Heidegger discusses the meaning of the various parts of speech in Scotus's *Bedeutungslehre, Die Kategorien- und Bedeutungslehre des Duns Scotus*, pp. 164f, and the connection between grammar and etymology in *An Introduction to Metaphysics*, 1953, Tübingen, Niemeyer, 1958, trans. Ralph Mannheim, New York, Doubleday, 1961, ch. 2.

Eignen, vorin Mensch und Sein einander ge-eignet sind, schlicht zu erfahren, d.h. einzukehren in das, was wir das *Ereignis* nennen nommen. Das Wort Ereignis ist der gewachsenen Sprache entnommen. Er-eignen heiβt ursprünglich – er-äugen, d.h. er-blicken, im Blicken zu sich rufen, an-eignen.

This is englished as

The belonging together of man and Being in the manner of mutual challenge drives home to us with startling force that and how man is delivered over to the ownership of Being and Being is appropriate to the essence of man. Within the framework there prevails a strange ownership and a strange appropriation. We must experience simply this owning in which man and Being are delivered over to each other, that is, we must enter into what we call *the event of appropriation.*[25]

The last sentence of the German cited here, crucial to the explication, is omitted without any indication from the translated text. English translations of Heidegger, as evident in the one under consideration, generally render *das Ereignis* as 'the event of appropriation', and put back into the idea the objective, possessive genitive which the word is designed to circumscribe. *Das Ereignis* is the historical event, qualitative time, what happens (historic present), another word for 'happening', *das Geschehen*, which is modified in *die Geschichte*, 'history'. *Das Ereignis* also includes the adjective/verb, *eigen/eignen* – 'own', 'to make one's own'. The prefix *er* transforms the imperfect verb, one that expresses a continuous or lasting state, condition or process, into a perfect one, marked by a beginning and an end. Hence *ereignen* connotes identity without representation, property without having, and completion without reflection of a point in time.

There is no event 'of' appropriation: what happens is qualitative, determinate. Heidegger says that *das Ereignis* like the Greek *logos* cannot be translated;[26] like the Greek *logos* it can only be

---

[25] Heidegger, *Identity and Difference*, 1957, German text and trans. Joan Stanbaugh, New York, Harper and Row, 1969, pp.100–101, tr.p.36, Heidegger's emphasis. See the translator's note on *Ereignis*, p.14 n.1.
[26] Ibid., p.101, tr.p.36.

understood by considering its cognates, verbal and substantive, in the original language, and then by considering all the different ways it has been and may be translated into other languages. The passage cited includes *Vereignen* and *Zueignen* meaning 'disowning' and 'owning' as two ways of being present – the *ver* perfects, the *zu* is imperfect: 'Within what has been placed there prevails a strange disowning and owning.' The gerunds make the infinitive do the work usually accomplished by the finite forms of the verb but without the persons of the verb, without its subjects and without its objects.

The other italicized word in the passage which heralds the *Ereignis* is the first verbal substantive in German, gerund in English: 'Das Zusammen*gehören*' which means 'belonging together' and 'having heard together'. Consider 'Als das hörend dem ein Gehörende ist das Denken was nach seiner Wesensherkunft ist' englished as 'As the belonging to Being that listens, thinking is what it is according to its essential origin'.[27] *Gehören* is both the infinitive 'to belong to' and the old past participle of *hören*, 'to hear'. This connection derives from the use of *hören*, 'to hear', and *horchen*, 'to hearken', for the action of a vassal. *Die Hörigen*, 'those who hear', means 'the bondsmen'; *gehorsam*, 'heard' plus the adjectival suffix, means 'obedient'; *gehorchen*, 'hearkened', means 'to obey'. Transferred from persons to things, *das Gehören*, 'belonging to', means 'the things belonging to me'.[28] *Hörend*, 'hearing', and *Gehörende*, 'belonging to'/'having heard', in the second passage cited are expressed together in the first: *Das Zusammengehören*, an event prior to the separation of the hearer or object possessed from the owner's voice. The sentence omitted from the English translation captures this connection between calling and owning: 'Er-eignen hei*ß*t ursprunglich: er-äugen, d.h. im Blicken zu sich rufen, an-eignen.'

---

[27] Heidegger, 'Letter on Humanism', p.314, tr.p.196.

[28] This discussion is developed from Ihering, *Der Zweck im Recht*, 1877–81, Leipzig, Breitkopf und Härtel, vol. I, 3rd edn, 1893, p.330n., trans. *Law as a Means to an End*, Issac Husik, New York, Augustus Kelley, 1913, p.247 n.38: Latin *obedire*, 'to obey', also comes from *audire*, 'to hear'. Compare 'Hence the listeners of the household (*clientes*) together with the slaves strictly so called formed the "body of servants" (*familia*) dependent on the will of the "burgess" (*patronus*, like *patricius*).' Theodor Mommsen, *History of Rome*, 1854–56, trans. W. P. Dickson, London, Dent, 1868, vol. I, p.61.

In both of the English versions of the two passages *Wesen* has been rendered 'essence': *Wesensherkunft* as 'original essence', *Menschenwesen* as 'essence of man'. The English word 'essence' comes from the Latin *essen-tis*, a participle of *esse*, 'to be', invented to translate the Greek *ousia*, a past participle of the Greek verb 'to be'.²⁹ *Ousia* is also latinized as 'substance'. The German word *Wesen* means 'being' or 'essence'; like the Greek it consists of the past participle of the verb to be: *sein – gewesen*. It means 'what has been', not as past or gone, but as present, together with completed actions or states.³⁰ The English 'essence' has no similar connections with the English 'been', and its use in translations of Heidegger is disastrous. *Wesensherkunft* includes the present *her*, the past *wesen*, and the future *kunft*. *Wesen* is 'the belonging together of man and being': what has been or has happened, expressed without any possessive implication in the verb or any possessive genitive, and this also explains why *Wesen* may be translated into English by both 'being' or by 'essence'. The cognate phrase *das Ereignis der Anwesenheit* involves the same complexity.³¹ *Das Anwesen*, 'presence' like Greek *ousia* and Latin *substantia* – English, 'substance' – also means 'property' or 'estate'. It is translated as 'the event of being present', but it means 'the propriation of presence', a subjective and objective genitive in which both words connote event/occurrence, property/own and presence. Heidegger frequently uses *Wesen* as a verb: *Das Geschehen der Geschichte, west als das . . .*; *west* is translated as 'occurs essentially', but it implies 'is/has been present'.³²

Es gibt anfänglicher gedacht, die Geschichte des Seins, in die

---

²⁹ '. . . essence [*essentia*] [is derived] from "to be [*esse*]". The word is new, not used by the old Latinists, but taken of late into the tongue to serve to explain the Greek οὐσία, which it translates exactly.' Saint Augustine, *The City of God*, trans. John Healey, London, Dent, 1973, vol. I, BK. XII, chapter III, p.346; Mario Puelma, 'Cicero als Platon-Übersetzer', *Museum Helveticum*, 37 (Juli 1980), 137–78, and Roland Poncelet, *Cicero, traducteur de Platon: L'expression de la pensée complexe en latin classique*, Paris, E. de Boccard, 1957.

³⁰ Compare Hegel, 'The German language has preserved essence [*das Wesen*] in the past participle of the verb *to be* [*Sein*]: *gewesen*; for essence is past – but timelessly past – being.' *Science of Logic*, Hamburg, Felix Meiner, 1969, vol. II, p.3, trans. A. V. Millar, London, Allen and Unwin, 1969, p.389, amended.

³¹ Heidegger, *The Question of Being*, 1955, text with translation on facing page, Vision Press, 1959, p.62.

³² Heidegger, 'Letter on Humanism', p.332, tr.p.215.

das Denken als Andenken dieser Geschichte von ihr selbst ereignet, gehört. Das Andenken unterscheidet sich wesentlich von dem nachträgliche Vergegenwärtigen der Geschichte im Sinne des vergangenen Vergehens. Die Geschichte geschieht nicht zuerst als Geschehens. Und dieses ist nicht Vergehen.

This passage is englished as

Thought in a more primordial way, there is the history of Being to which thinking belongs as recollection of this history that unfolds of itself. Such recollective thought differs essentially from the subsequent presentation of history in the sense of an evanescent past. History does not take place primarily as a happening. And its happening is not evanescence.[33]

Thinking, translated into a qualitative event, *An-Denken, von ihr selbst ereignet*, an owning, brings with it all that has happened, all the perfections, and does not represent them as something past and gone. To translate *Andenken* as 'recollection' brings in all the unwanted Hegelian implications of *Erinnerung*. The final sentences of the English imply that the standard distinction is being drawn between the process of history, the events of the past, and history, the discipline which apprehends the past. But Heidegger never uses the latinized Greek word *historia*; he always uses the cognate of *geschehen*, 'to happen': *die Geschichte*. The 'history of being' is an objective and a subjective genitive: the English distinction between the events of history (process) and the history of the events (discipline or apprehension) may clarify the identity intended between Being as what has happened and what happens, and thinking *Andenken*, as owning, as event.

We are now prepared to witness the way the juridical poles of subject and object, subject and thing, which frame the litigious space of the critical court, arise out of the wider space of a different court by following the constructions of the Latin substantives out of the Greek verb *eimi*, 'to be'.[34] These dichotomies, which seem

---

[33] Ibid.
[34] Heidegger, 'The Origin of the Work of Art', 1935/6, in *Holzwege*, p.7, trans. in *Basic Writings*, pp.153–4.

fundamental and natural to us, appear specific and limited when set against the surrounding context out of which they were taken. The opposition of subject to thing, owner to object of possession, has arisen by translating parts of the Greek verb 'to be' into Latin substantives, literally, into things which 'stand under', using parts of the Latin verb 'to stand under' instead of parts of the verb 'to be'.

Aristotle says in the *Categories*, '*ὥστε οὐκ ἂν εἴη ἡ οὐσία τῶν ἐν ὑποκεμένῳ*'. This sentence is traditionally translated into latinized vernaculars as 'therefore, substance is not in a subject'.[35] *Ousia*, a past participle of 'to be', means 'has been'; *hypokeimenon*, 'lain under', includes *hypo*, 'under', and *keimenon*, part of the verb *keimo*, 'I lie'. Read according to these literal elements, the proposition says 'what has been is not lain under', has not been posited or put there. But *hypokeimenon* is translated as 'subject' which is quite anachronistic. Aristotle distinguishes between 'primary *ousia*' and 'secondary *ousia*'; secondary *ousia* is laid down or posited, and defines primary *ousia* by differentiating it into genus and species.[36] Strictly speaking, only secondary *ousia* substands, or is *hypokeimenon*, but, if *ousia* is translated as 'substance', then the distinction between what is, *ousia*, and what is posited or put there, *hypokeimenon*, is lost. Something further is lost: the difference between two ways of differentiating. The difference between primary and secondary substance is assimilated to the difference of species and genus, but secondary substance is not a 'species' of the genus 'substance': it is the difference between *ousia* as what has been, and the positing or differentiating of beings.[37]

Hypokeimenon is translated as 'subject', a Latin substantive constructed out of the past participle of the Latin verb *jacere*, 'to

---

[35] Aristotle, *The Categories*, Loeb Classical Library, trans. Harold P. Cooke, London, Heinemann, 1973, v.3a.20.

[36] Ibid., v.26.30.

[37] The problem of primary and secondary substance and the inadequacy of understanding 'category' as 'predicate' are discussed in Franz Brentano, *Von der mannigfachen Bedeutung des Seienden nach Aristoteles*, 1862, trans. *On the Several Senses of Being in Aristotle*, Rolf George, Berkeley, University of California Press, 1975; and in Adolf Trendelenberg, *Geschichte der Kategorienlehre*, 1846, Hildesheim, Georg Olms, 1963, pp.33–71. For Heidegger's acknowledgement of Brentano, see 'My Way to Phenomenology', p.81, tr.p.74; of Trendelenberg, see *Die Kategorien- und Bedeutungslehre des Duns Scotus*, p.5 n.1.

throw', which in 'subject' does not mean 'lain' or 'stand under' but 'thrown under'. Modern philosophical thinking since Descartes has moved from the Aristotelian position where *every* definition lays down something which stands under, just as every sentence has a 'subject', to the axiom that *one* such lain down has priority: the one which also speaks, which lays the others down or which posits secondary *ousia*. This subject of subjects is the ego, the one positing or throwing who is presupposed in all those thrown under.[38] The translation of Aristotle uses 'subject' in the general sense in which, for example, every sentence has a subject.

The translating of *hypokeimenon* by 'subject' even in the general sense, and the translating of *ousia* by 'substance', when 'substance' is nearer *hypokeimenon*, secondary substance which is lain down or posited, are the source, too, of the idea of 'things' as discrete entities composed of substance which is the bearer of accidents.[39] The latin words 'substance' and 'accident' make us think of an empty container in space with properties distinct from (accidental) and yet identified with the bearer. The Greek word *symbebekos*, which is translated as 'accident', means 'standing together', 'coming together', or 'the coming to pass of events': in German, *die Ereignisse*. Substance and accident, *ousia* and *symbebekos*, are covered jointly by what Heidegger calls *das Ereignis der Anwesenheit: ousia*, 'what has been' and 'property' and *symbebekos*, 'concurring'. Both Greek words and both German words connote Being qua event and property qua characteristic. *Das Ereignis* challenges the traditional latinized reading which exclusively distinguishes primary from accidental being and which considers properties as accidental and external in time and space.

Similarly Latin *res* and German *Ding*, thing, originally mean *das Ereignis der Anwesenheit*: an event or occasion which gathers people together into each other's presence over something (*sic*) which concerns them. 'The Roman word *res* means what concerns

---

[38] Heidegger discusses this in several places: see, 'Descartes: Cogito Sum; "I" as a special subject', in *Die Frage nach dem Ding*, 1935–36, Tübingen, Niemeyer, 1975, pp.76–82, trans. *What is a Thing?* W. B. Barton Jr and Vera Deutsch, Indiana, Regnery, 1967, pp.98–106; and 'Der Wandel des ὑποκείμενον zum subiectum', in 'Die Metaphysik als Geschichte des Seins', 1944, *Nietzsche*, II, pp.429–36.

[39] Heidegger, 'The Origin of the Work of Art', *Holzwege*, p.8, tr.p.154.

people, affairs, the case of dispute,'[40] while *das Ding* means an assembly of people in Germanic law.[41] *Res* and thing originally open up litigious space as what concerns and gathers people; but this meaning changes into what is common to each event which gathers, the principle of law, *causa*, or the object of the dispute – in French *causa* becomes *la chose*.[42] In this way 'the thing' which unites people becomes 'the thing' which divides them. The history of the thing persists in modern usage: we use 'thing' both to cover every*thing* which concerns us, every*thing* which exists for us; and we also use 'thing' in the sense of discrete substances and accidents, or in the Kantian sense of the unity of the manifold given in perception.[43] 'Things' in the Kantian framework of quantitative, mathematical space and time turn out to be the projections of an unknowable subject.

'*Aus dem Dingen des Dinges eignet sich und bestimmt sich auch erst das Anwesen des Anwesenden . . .*'[44] The transcendental circle is here rewritten in terms of the way in which 'the thing' in the sense of a discrete entity is determined by 'the thing' in the sense of 'the event'. *Bedingen*, 'to condition', contains the word *Ding*, 'thing'. *Dingen* as verbal process, the happening, the event, circumscribes the mode of presence of the thing as an object with properties.[45] The thing in quantitative space and time is separated out from the qualitative event. The thing or owning becomes the object, the thing owned, and disowned in the inclusive sense.

The etymological story shows how the development of substantives is the 'fate' of verbs, what has happened to them, and how these substantives come to oppose each other in a litigious space which is both narrower and more abstract than verbal

---

[40] Heidegger, 'The Thing', 1951, in *Vorträge und Aufsätze*, Pfullingen, Neske, 1954, p.167, trans. in *Poetry, Language, Truth*, Albert Hofstadter (ed.), New York, Harper and Row, 1975, p.175, amended.

[41] See Heidegger, *What is a Thing?* tr.n.2 p.5; and see the German translation of Tacitus, *Germania*, Arno Mauersberger, Wiesbaden, V.M.A., n.d., secs. 11,12.

[42] See Heidegger, 'The Thing', pp.167–8, tr.p.175; for further discussion of how *res* becomes *causa*, see Peter Stein, *Regulae Iuris*, Edinburgh, Edinburgh University Press, 1966, pp.139–40.

[43] Heidegger, 'The Origin of the Work of Art', *Holzwege*, p.15, tr.p.160.

[44] Heidegger, 'The Thing', p.170, tr.p.177.

[45] See Heidegger, *What is a Thing?* tr.n.3 p.8.

time.[46] Once one *hypokeimenon* attains that special status of positing or projecting the others, these others become defined by it, as what are thrown up against it, 'object' from 'ject' – thrown, and 'ob' – against. The privileged *hypokeimenon*, detached from the question of primary and secondary *ousia*, bears the marks of its strange formation: what was thrown under, sub-ject, now throws out, pro-jects, or defines what comes against it as its ob-jects or things, not 'in themselves' but as appearances.[47] There exists an agency which knows its objects, natural and moral, as its own projections but does not know itself, or knows itself only as active but not as passive. This combination of activity and passivity arises when one being considers itself the source of all other beings, and does not understand the source of them all to be in something which is not one of these beings, not a 'thing' at all but the medium which encompasses all discrete entities.

The activity and passivity of the subject examined by Heidegger is the antinomy of law: for this dual status is legal status as such, according to which the subject is active, 'the subject of the law', and passive, 'subjected to the law'.[48] The phrase 'subject of the law' expresses this antinomy because it is a subjective and objective genitive: the subjective genitive is 'the subject of the law' as actor, as initiator of legal process; the objective or possessive genitive is 'the law's subject', subjected to the law and belonging to the law.

This antinomical history of the subject is the Event which has led an unknown judge to open proceedings in the critical court: it explains why the judge seems to be witness and clerk as well as judge, why everyone's status is so confused, and why a court establised to clarify a 'matter', to settle the legal title of a 'thing' possessed, cannot reach a conclusion or complete its proceedings.

Only a court which knew the identity of its judges and witnesses, its subjects, and which knew why they had come together, could settle anything. For it would be able to translate the actors back into the verbs, the active infinitives without

---

[46] On the development of nouns from verbs, see David Daube, *Roman Law, Linguistic, Social and Philosophical Aspects*, Edinburgh, Edinburgh University Press, 1969, chapter I, 'Linguistic Aspects'.

[47] See Heidegger *What is a Thing?* pp.81–2, tr.pp.105–6.

[48] *Oxford Companion to Law*: 'subject', q.v.

separation of the persons of the verb, out of which their agency and their suffering has been distilled or de-posited. The 'judgement of Paris', for example, tells us both that Paris judged to which of the three goddesses he would award the apple – a subjective genitive, according to which Paris is the source of the judging; and that Paris is judged by the three goddesses, is the object of their judgement – an objective genitive. The dual meaning in this judgement clarifies and connects what gathers the people concerned and their mutual judging.

The Germanic *Ding* was such a court, an assembly of judges where disputing parties would bring their dispute, their thing, to have it settled. But what exactly happened at such an assembly? One of the oldest Greek accounts of an assembly we have is the court of the *histor* on Achilles' shield:

The people were assembled in the market place, where a quarrel
had arisen, and two men were disputing over the blood price
for a man who had been killed. One man promised full restitution
in a public statement, but the other refused and would accept
nothing.
Both then made for an arbitrator, to have a decision;
and people were speaking up on either side to help both men.
But the heralds kept the people in hand, as meanwhile the elders
were in session on benches of polished stone in the sacred circle
and held in their hands the staves of the heralds who lift their
voices.
The two men rushed before these, and took turns speaking their
cases,
and between them lay on the ground two talents of gold, to be
given
to that judge who in this case spoke the straightest opinion.[49]

The word translated 'arbitrator' is *histor* in the Greek. As with the phrase 'the judgement of Paris' the ambiguity of this judging is instructive. On the one hand, the people appeal to the *histor* for a judgement; on the other hand, they themselves seem to judge

[49] Homer, *Illiad*, trans, Richard Lattimore, Chicago, University of Chicago Press, 1961, Book 18, lines 467–508, p.388.

between the judges.[50] In this court there is no exclusive judge or exclusive witness – no subject and object – to obscure the mutual judging. Only our importing of such concepts obscures what is going on – that both judges and people judge and are judged. This is the historical event: the *Ereignis* of the *histor*, the judgement in which all judge and all are judged, the sacred circle.

---

[50] For a summary of scholarly opinion on this point, see Douglas M. Mac-Dowell, *The Law in Classical Athens*, London, Thames and Hudson, 1978, pp.20–21.

4

Self-Perficient Nihilism

The sacred circle of the *histor* brings together and distinguishes people and judges. A continuous line closing into a circle and opening up space becomes the boundary of a judgement, a thing, which holds equally those within and those without as they alternate their witnessing and their judging, in unique space and unique time: the event concerning ownership – *das Ereignis der Answesenheit*.

In reply to Ernst Jünger's essay on nihilism, written for his sixtieth birthday, in which Jünger asked, in the wake of the Second World War, whether the world had surpassed the 'completed nihilism'[1] which Nietzsche had anticipated for the future some sixty years earlier,[2] Heidegger tried to alter the parameters of the debate:

> Your judgement of the situation follows the signs which indicate whether and to what extent we cross over the line and thereby step out of the zone of complete nihilism (*aus der Zone des vollendeten Nihilismus*). In the title of your essay *Across the Line* [*Über die Linie*], the *über* signifies across, *trans,*

---

[1] See Nietzsche, 'the first perfect nihilist [*der erste vollkommene Nihilist*]', *The Will to Power*, Stuttgart, Kroner, 1969. trans. Walter Kaufmann and R.J. Hollingdale, New York, Vintage, 1968, Preface, secs 3,4. In the title of this chapter I render '*sich vollendenden Nihilismus*' 'self-*completing* Nihilism', as 'self-perficient nihilism' by analogy with Hegel's '*sich vollbringende Skeptizismus*', 'self-*fulfilling* scepticism', rendered as 'self-perficient scepticism' in Rose, *Hegel Contra Sociology*, p.153, from Hegel, *Phenomenology of Spirit*, *Theorie Werkausgabe*, 3, Frankfurt am Main, Suhrkamp, 72, trans. A.V. Millar, Oxford, Clarendon Press, 1977, tr.para. 78.

[2] Ernst Jünger, 'Über die Linie', 1950, Martin Heidegger zum 60. Geburtstag, *Werke*, 5, Stuttgart, Ernst Klett, 1960, pp.247–89.

meta. However, the following remarks interpret the '*über*' only in the meaning of *de, peri*. They treat 'of' the line itself, of the zone of self-completing nihilism. If we stick to the image of the line, we find it blends a space which is determined by a place. The place assembles. The assembling shelters what is assembled. Out of the place of the line originates the origin of the essence of nihilism and its completion [*Aus dem Ort der Linie ergibt sich die Herkunft des Wesen des Nihilismus und seiner Vollendung*].³

For Heidegger it is not a matter of stepping across the line which divides consciousness from its objects, judge from witness, a nihilistic age from one beyond nihilism – in a future time and a future space. To step over or across this dividing line is merely to change the status of judge into witness or witness into judge, or the status of subject into object or object into subject, while the line which establishes these statuses remains as dominant as ever. If the line delineates a place, zone, meridian⁴ or circle, then the domain of every point is equally an inside or an outside. There is no question of crossing the line, going beyond, *über* or *trans*, but of *trans*-forming it by knowing that the place 'of' (*über*) the line is not an indeterminate and infinite beyond (*über*) but an end in itself [*Endzweck*], a kingdom of ends. In Greek *peri*, 'of', also means 'goal' or 'end'. If it is recognized that the court of consciousness, the court of the line which separates judge and witness, subject and object, has been set up or projected by consciousness itself, this recognition will challenge its jurisdiction more surely than any attempt to flee beyond its walls: it will transform an oppositional jurisdiction of judges and judged into an encompassing one in which all judge and all are judged. This self-perficient nihilism is the event which completes what first occurred by seeing the litigious space of consciousness and its objects as the re-presenting of its own original partitioning, of a disowning (*Vereignen*) which is to be owned.

---

³ Heidegger, *The Question of Being*, German text and translation, London, Vision Press, 1959, pp.35–7, translation amended.
⁴ Ibid., p.35; 'meridian': circle passing through the celestial poles and the zenith of any place on the earth's surface, or a circle of constant longitude passing through a given place and the terrestrial poles.

However, no metacritique of consciousness could bring us to this event because it would still be based on that divisive particle 'of'. For this reason Heidegger's texts defy any metacritical reading. Like Cohen, Heidegger begins by expounding time as the productive unity and difference internal to Kant's transcendental exposition of experience.[5] The emphasis falls on time not Being as the source of unity and difference because 'time' implies incessant differentiation and this precludes turning Being into a metacritical dimension. For if Being-in-general is seen as the precondition of the former precondition which is now seen to be conditioned, it will, in its turn, be thought as another conditioned – as a representation or appearance in quantitative time and space, not as the qualitative event. It will be reconstructed as another ob-ject 'of' consciousness, reflected by a consciousness which represents time as space. 'Accordingly, a thoughtful glance into this realm of "Being" can only write it as ~~Being~~. The drawing of these crossed lines at first only repels, especially the almost ineradicable habit of representing "Being" as something standing by itself and only coming up at times against people'.[6] 'Being' cannot be transcendental or metacritical for 'it' transcends any oppositions between consciousness and its objects, the a priori and the empirical, the precondition and the conditioned.[7]

The last major attempt to 'end metaphysics', to redefine the goal (*Zweck*) as present, by viewing the Kantian antinomies in the context of the circle which includes them, and to eschew the metacritical antinomy of positing another precondition, is Nietzsche's 'will to power'. Nietzsche's texts are designed to reveal willing and disowning as the source of experience without positing or putting the will in the representational space on which a different perspective is to be achieved. This is why willing is

---

[5] For Cohen see chapter 2 above and *Kants Theorie der Erfahrung*, Berlin, Ferd. Dummler, 1871; Heidegger, *Kant and the Problem of Metaphysics*, trans. James S. Churchill, Bloomington, Indiana University Press, 1965, sec.3.C.

[6] Heidegger, *The Question of Being*, p.81, translation slightly amended.

[7] 'Being is the *transcendens* pure and simple', Heidegger, 'Letter on Humanism', 1946–47, in *Wegmarken*, 1967, Frankfurt am Main, Klostermann, 1978, p.333, trans. in *Basic Writings*, David Farrell Krell (ed.), London, Routledge and Kegan Paul, 1978, p.216, quoted from the Introduction of *Sein and Zeit*, 1927, trans. *Being and Time*, John Macquarrie and Edward Robinson, Oxford, Basil Blackwell, 1967.

named 'will to power'.[8] Nevertheless, Nietzsche's will to power either remains as unknowable as the categorical imperative, or, once it is thought, becomes another representation, such as 'force', a new value as arbitrary as the one replaced. This self-perficient nihilism becomes a new moralism: it concerns a conscience which, consciously willing what it previously disowned as its willing, overcomes and absolves what was a bad conscience in willing; but this good conscience still lives in the opposition between will and representation, between denying and affirming values.[9]

> The zone of the critical line, that is the locale of the essence of complete nihilism [*des vollendeten Nihilismus*] would have to be sought where the essence of metaphysics unfolds its utmost possibilities and gathers itself together in them. That takes place where the will to will wills, that is challenges; *places* everything present solely in the general and uniform placeability of its component parts. As the unconditioned gathering together of such placement B̶e̶i̶n̶g̶ does not disappear. It moves off in an unique estrangement.[10]

This self-completing willing is self-defeating; it remains a willing 'of' something, within the opposition of will and things. By reading all genitives as subjective *and* objective, Heidegger shows instead that the event which gives rise to these oppositions, indicated by the partitioning and dividing 'of', can be discerned in language itself, in the medium which holds and separates, the *inclusive* generative ground – *hervorbringende Grund* – which gives rise to the exclusive objective and subjective genitives:[11]

---

[8] For a succinct version of Heidegger's exposition of Nietzsche, see 'Nietzsches Metaphysik', 1940, *Nietzsche II*, Pfullingen, Neske, 1961, 257–333.

[9] See 'The Word of Nietzsche: "God is Dead"', in *Holzwege*, 1950, Frankfurt am Main, Klostermann, 1980, pp.241–3, trans. in *The Question concerning Technology and Other Essays*, William Lovitt, New York, Harper and Row, 1977, pp.91–3; and compare Nietzsche, 'the conscience of method', *Beyond Good and Evil: Prelude to a Philosophy of the Future, Werke*, III, Schlechta, Frankfurt am Main, Ullstein, trans. 1976. Walter Kaufmann, New York, Vintage, 1968, sec.36.

[10] Heidegger, *The Question of Being*, pp.87–9, with reference to Hegel but equally applicable to Nietzsche.

[11] *Identity and Difference*, 1957, German text and translation, Joan Stanbaugh, New York, Harper and Row, 1961, p.129, tr.p.54.

we see that *Being* means always and everywhere: the Being of *beings*. The genitive in this phrase is to be taken as a genitivus objectivus [i.e. source of . . .]. *Beings* means always and everywhere the beings *of Being* [i.e. possessive]; here the genitive is to be taken as a *genitivus subjectivus*. It is, however, with certain reservations that we speak of a genitive in respect to object and subject, because these terms, subject and object in their turn stem from a particular character of Being.[12]

Invited to think of Being in this way as event we are invited to think again of the difference between primary and secondary *ousia*, not as a difference between genus and species, which would be a difference 'reduced to a distinction, something made up by our understanding' and represented. For Being is not a thing, and the Being 'of' beings is not a relationship between things.[13]

We cannot remain on the judgement seat of the *histor*, inside or outside the polished stone of the sacred circle. This cannot be the Event because the judgement of the *histor* is still in the genitive, even when it is thought of as both an objective and a subjective genitive. Heidegger explicitly considers and rejects the idea of Being as *die Gerechtigkeit* in a way which would include this oldest strata of Homeric 'rightness' which assembles people prior to any codified law.[14] To find the time and hence the event prior to Homeric 'rightness' it is necessary to return to an even earlier form of Greek religion and law, earlier than the mature personalities of the Olympic Gods, and long before the arrival of Dionysus, so important for Nietzsche.[15]

Being is not a thing, thus nothing temporal, and yet it is determined by time as presence. Time is not a thing, thus nothing which is, and yet it remains constant in its passing

---

[12] Ibid., p.129, tr.pp.61–2, and compare *The Question of Being*, pp.87,83.

[13] Heidegger, *Identity and Difference*, p.130, tr.p.62.

[14] Compare notes 8 and 9 above, and also Heidegger's *Einführung in die Metaphysik*, 1953, Tübingen, Niemeyer, 1958, pp.116–17, trans. *An Introduction to Metaphysics*, Ralph Mannheim, New York, Doubleday, 1961, p.128.

[15] For the distinctions between archaic, Homeric, Dionysian, and Orphic religion, see Gilbert Murray, *Five Stages of Greek Religion*, 1912, London, Watts and Co., 1943.

away without being something temporal like the beings in time. Being and time determine each other reciprocally, but in such a manner that neither can the former – Being – be addressed as something temporal nor can the latter – time – be addressed as a being.[16]

But there was a time when the unpersonified changes of time, night and day, season to season, were addressed not as things, not as persons, not as gods, not as beings, but as *daimon*, as the law of (*sic*) 'substantial' not functional time, as *ousia* not as the empty form of intuition.[17]

Dike, justice, and *Moira*, fate, were *Horae*, seasons, before they came to be associated exclusively with different aspects of law. *Dike, Eunomia*, lawfulness, and *Eirene*, peace, three seasons, the sisters of the three *Moirae*, fates, are what happens during the changing seasons. The three *Horae* are the three phases of the moon; the *Moirae* are but the 'three *Moirae* or divisions (μέρη) of the moon herself, the three divisions of the Old Year. And these three Moirae or Horae are also Charites,'[18] for they bring the fruits of each season. They are *daimons*, not individual, immortal, remote and personified gods, but communal and mortal forces, living and dying and living again in the cycle of seasons. The change in time reckoning from the content of seasons to the formal divisions of time is the change from *Dike* as 'the way of the world, the way things happen . . . manifest in the changes of the rising and setting of constellations, in the waxing and waning of the moon and in the daily and yearly courses of the sun,' to *Dike* as the goddess of Vengeance.[19] It is the change from a community which celebrates *Dike* magically and mimetically, in the perfect and imperfect tenses of the dance, in the presence 'of' the daimon,

---

[16] Heidegger, 'Time and Being', 1962, in *Zur Sache des Denkens*, Tübingen, Niemeyer, 1969, trans. *On Time and Being*, Joan Stanbaugh, New York, Harper and Row, 1972, p.3, tr.p.3.

[17] Heidegger discusses the word *daimon* in 'Letter on Humanism', p.351, tr.p.233. The difference between *daimon* and 'god' is one of the central themes of Jane Harrison, *Themis: A Study of the Social Origins of Greek Religion*, 1911, London, Merlin, 1977, which draws on Nietzsche, Bergson and Durkheim in the analysis of pre-Homeric religion and which is, in its own way, a great treatise on time and Being.

[18] Harrison, *Themis*, pp.189–90.

[19] Ibid., p.517.

to a community out of which individuals have been distilled, and which project its gods as independent subjectivities, as law: 'Dike who was the *way* of the world, becomes in Orphic hands Vengeance on the wrongdoer, on him who overstepped the *way*.'[20]

Heidegger considers *Dike* as the verb *dikeo*, not as personified justice, or as norm, but as governing order (*fugender Fug*), overpowering and dominating; not as a good, but as *deinotation*, the strangest of the strange, as *dainon*, power.[21] This is man, not in the first person, but as 'the violent one, not aside from and along with other attributes but solely in the sense that in his fundamental violence [*Gewalttätigkeit*] he uses power [*Gewalt*] against the overpowering [*Überwaltigende*].'[22] *Dike* as this *daimon* is the character of man – *Ethos anthropoi daimon* – and the life of the cosmos and the community, its law.[23] Heidegger finds this character in Greek tragedy and in poetic fragments of Parmenides and Heraklitus, but not in Homer or in classical philosophy. *Dike*, justice, for Heidegger, violence sublimated into governing order, may also be found guarding the wheel of fortune. As such she is the 'Goddess who brings forth, brings to accomplishment', completes or perfects continously.[24] But fortune is also *Moira*, who sends too, but who judges, whose wheel moves in space, litigious space not time.[25] Heidegger captures these two aspectes of *Moira* in his commentary on Parmenides fragment: Moira who sends time and Moira who divides space: Parmenides *'nennt die Moira, die Zuteilung, die gewährend verteilt und so die Zwiefalt entfaltet. Die Zuteilung beschickt (versieht and beschenkt) mit der Zweifalt. Sie ist die in sich gesammelte und also entfaltende Schickung des Anwesens als*

---

20 Ibid., p.527; for 'magic' and 'mimetic', see p.330. Heidegger: 'Man is never first and foremost man on the hither side of the world, as a "subject", whether this is taken as "I" or "We".' 'Letter on Humanism', p.346, tr.p.229.

21 Heidegger, *An Introduction to Metaphysics*, pp.122–3,4, tr.pp.134–5,6.

22 Ibid., p.115, tr.p.126.

23 'Letter on Humanism', p.351, tr.p.233.

24 Harrison, *Themis*, p.523.

25 Ibid., p.477: 'The wheel of Dike moves through time, Moira operates in space'. For Moira, see, too, F. M. Cornford, 'The Origin of *Moira*', chapter II, in *From Religion to Philosophy: A Study in the Origins of Western Speculation*, 1912, Brighton, Harvester, 1980.

Anwesen von Anwesendem.'[26] *Moira,* 'fate', *das Schicksal,* 'sends', *schicken,* 'to send', and 'presents', in the sense of giving presents, *das Geschenk,* 'a present', *schenken,* 'to give a present'; *die Moira schickend verteilt*[27] might be englished as 'fate fating' or 'present presenting misdivides'. *Moira* or *Schicksal* is not the personified Olympian Goddess, but the event *das Ereignis.*[28] *Sich schicken,* 'to send oneself', means 'to happen', the event which sends or presents character to the world by dividing it. The divisions of the moon year are no longer parts of the moon herself but division as such, – *nemein,* 'to divide', *nomos,* 'law': *'Nomos* is not only law but more originally the assignment contained in the dispensation of Being [*ursprünglicher die in der Schickung des Seins geborgene Zuweisung*].'[29]

The event of events, the event which is present in this story of time as substance, the content of the seasons, qualitative time, changing into time as function, as division, quantitative time or law, is light: 'the lighting of being: Being's light [*die Lichtung des Seins*],' for light is common to and present in time and space, whether measured by day and night, the moon or the sun, it illuminates space and alternates time. 'Only so long as the lighting of Being comes to pass does Being convey itself to man [*Nur solange die Lichtung des Seins sich eignet, übereignet sich Seinden Menschen*].[30] Lighting is the dispensation of Being – *die Schickung/ Moira* – and the destiny of the lighting – *das Geschick* – *nomos;*[31] not the narrow light of enlightened reason.[32]

Heidegger's writing prevents us from reading these genitives as

---

[26] Heidegger, 'Moira', 1954, in *Vorträge und Aufsätze*, 1954, Pfullingen, Neske, 1978, pp.243–4, trans. in *Early Greek Thinking*, David Farrell Krell and Frank A. Capuzzi, New York, Harper and Row, 1975, p.97: 'He names the Moira, the apportionment, which allots by bestowing and so unfolds the twofold. The apportionment dispenses (provides and presents) through the duality. Apportionment is the dispensation of presencing, as the presencing of what is present, which is gathered in itself and therefore unfolds of itself'.

[27] Ibid., p.245, tr.p.98.

[28] Ibid., p.240, tr.pp.93–4: 'Moira in its dispensing metes out . . .'

[29] 'Letter on Humanism', p.357, tr.p.238.

[30] Ibid., p.333, tr.p.216.

[31] Ibid.

[32] Compare *'lumen naturale'* – the light of reason, in 'The End of Philosophy and the Task of Thinking', 1964, in *On Time and Being*, p.73, tr.p.66.

subjective and objective genitives: the 'of' works as *peri* indicating the goal, the end or *telos*. *Telos* originally meant the 'place of initiation' and initiation is still the 'end' or 'goal' of philosophy:[33] 'a day when . . . pure space and ecstatic time, and everything present and absent in them have the place which gathers and protects everything'.[34] This place is the opening, *lict*, which in old German meant 'open' as well as 'light'.[35] 'Open' is a dimensional and spatial word, but it is understood here as temporal: 'prior to all calculation of time . . . true time consists in the mutual reaching out and opening up of future, past and present . . . what we call dimension belongs to true time and to it alone[36]/The unity of time's three dimensions consists in the interplay of each towards each. This interplay proves to be the true extending, playing in the heart of time, the fourth dimension . . .'[37] This 'fourth dimension', equally that of four beings, 'earth and sky, divinities and mortals', is historic time, the historic present, the Event, which includes 'everything absent' – perfect – and 'everything present' – imperfect – and thus unites past, present and future.[38] This *telos* of philosophy is the first *telos*, 'the round dance is the ring that joins while it plays as mirroring. Appropriating it lightens the four into the radiance of their simple oneness'.[39] This must be the dance and hymn of the *kouretes*,[40] the youths initiated into the mystery of time not yet divided into nature and law; this end is perfect, completely realized at every point in time.[41] The 'Thing' or assembly has become 'the round dance of appropriation [*der Reigen des Ereignens*]' – the kingdom of ends, redivivus.[42]

[33] Ibid., pp.62–3, tr.p.56. For *telos*, see Liddell and Scott, *Greek–English Lexicon*, q.v., and Harrison, Themis, ch.1.
[34] Heidegger, 'The End of Philosophy', *On Time and Being*, pp.72–3, tr.p.66.
[35] Ibid., pp.71–2, tr.p.65.
[36] 'Time and Being', ibid., p.15, tr.p.14.
[37] Ibid., pp.15–16, tr.p.15.
[38] 'The End of Philosophy', ibid., p.73, tr.p.66.
[39] Heidegger, 'The Thing', in *Vorträge und Aufsätze*, p.173, trans. in Albert Hofstadter (ed.), *Poetry, Language, Thought*, New York, Harper and Row, 1977, p.180.
[40] For the dance and hymn of the *kouretes*, see Harrison, *Themis*, chapter 1.
[41] 'The End of Philosophy', *On Time and Being*, pp.62–3, tr.p.56.
[42] 'The Thing', *Vorträge und Aufsätze*, p.173, tr.pp.180–81.

5

Natural Law and Repetition

The invocation of the *daimons* of earliest Greek memory and the dance of the four have opened out the court of consciousness into the celebration of 'magical nihilism'; where 'magic' is meant in the original sense of an event occurring in an historic present which includes past and future equally as perfect or completed states.[1] This 'self-perficient nihilism' is more literally perfecting than the Nietzschean, for it perfects time not the will; and more literally 'nihilism', for it perfects nothing, no things but 'thinging'. In moving from the perfect will to perfect time, Heidegger moves from a legalism without law, to a law without legalism, from *Dike* as goddess of law, to *Dike* as the original 'way'. History does not begin with *die Gerechtigkeit* (Nietzsche)[2] nor does it begin with the *polis* or state (Hegel).[3] Heidegger suggests that there may be another place/time where history beings and ends, completes itself beyond the 'Western languages' of metaphysical thinking and their onto-theo-logical coinage.[4]

The location of this locution emerges in the essay *Identity and*

---

[1] See F. M. Cornford, 'From Primary Magic to Religion', in *From Religion to Philosophy*, 1912, Brighton, Harvester, 1980, secs 47,48; and Jane Harrison, *Themis*, 1911, London, Merlin, 1977, chapter IV a, and p.330.

[2] See Heidegger, 'The Word of Nietzsche: "God is Dead"', in *Holzwege*, 1950, Frankfurt am Main, Klostermann, 1980, pp.241–3, trans. in *The Question concerning Technology and Other Essays*, William Lovitt, New York, Harper and Row, 1977, pp.91–3.

[3] Heidegger, *Einführung in die Metaphysik*, 1953, Tübingen, Niemeyer, 1958, pp.116–17, trans. *Introduction to Metaphysics*, Ralph Mannheim, New York, Doubleday, 1961, p.128.

[4] Heidegger, *Identity and Difference*, 1957, German text and translation, Joan Stanbaugh, New York, Harper and Row, 1969, p.142, tr.p.73.

Difference: 'The god-less thinking which must abandon the god of philosophy, god as *causa sui*, is thus perhaps closer to the divine God. Here this means only: god-less thinking is more open to Him than onto-theo-logic would like to admit' – 'here' refers to Greek (*theos*) and Latin (*causa sui*).[5]

> We attain to the nearness of the historic only in that sudden movement of a recall in thinking . . . [this] holds true also for our attempt in the step back out of the oblivion of the difference as such, to think this difference as the perdurance of unconcealing overcoming and of self-keeping arrival . . . it may be that this discussion which assigns the difference of Being and beings to perdurance as the approach to their essence, even brings to light something all-pervading which pervades Being's destiny from its beginning to its completion [*Vielleicht kommt sogar diese Erörterung der Differenz von Sein und Seiendem in den Austrag als den Vorort ihr Wesen etwas Durchgängiges zum Vorschein was das Geschick des Seins von Anfang bis in seine Vollendung durchgeht*].[6]

We are invited to a closer listening – *einem genaueren Hinhören* – to witness an advent or presence which is perfect and transitive, which moves from Being to beings, and which 'assigns' (*nomos*, law) the difference of Being and beings to 'perdurance'. This word 'perdurance', which captures the idea of perfect duration, is a felicitous but strange translation of *Austrag* which means 'arrangement' or 'settlement' in the litigious sense of settling something in court.

It seems that, perhaps unknown to himself, Heidegger has brought us into the orbit of Biblical Hebrew: a language which has imperfect and perfect tenses but not past, present and future tenses, and which has no possessive verb 'to have'; a language of the kind into which Heidegger attempts to transcribe German. Heidegger also brings us to the Event of events: the moment when Being is 'proffered as the highest most significant event of all[7]/a giving of presence that prevails in the present, in the past and in

---

[5] Ibid., p.191, tr.p.72.
[6] Ibid., pp.135–6, tr.p.67.
[7] Compare the phrase '*vor Gericht zum Austrag bringen*' – to settle a thing in court.

the future . . .'.[8] *Yahweh* announces His presence: 'Then Moses said to God, "If I go to the Israelites and tell them that the God of their forefathers has sent me to them and they ask me his name, what shall I say?" Then God answered, "I am; that is who I am. Tell them that I am has sent you to them."'[9] In the Hebrew *Yahweh* speaks in the imperfect tense which announces His perdurance: His presence in the future and past as well as the present. He sends this 'perdurance' from Being to beings; the *Austrag* or settlement is His redeeming of Israel from Egypt in the literal, legal sense of redeeming – buying back one's own from slavery.[10] This 'redeeming' presence is the event of owning – *das Ereignis*.

Yahweh is not 'God', not *theos*, until the Hebrew *Qere*, the marginal reading of *Yahweh* as *Adonai*, was translated into Greek as *theos*.[11] The name *Yahweh*, as announced in *Exodus 3.14* may also be read as the Hebrew causative active tense 'He causes to be'.[12] Heidegger expounds the German phrase *es gibt*, which is translated into English as 'there is' but means literally 'it gives', as 'it gives Being . . . a destiny of presence'.[13] Heidegger tells us that 'nowhere in beings is there an example for the active nature of Being, because the nature of Being is itself the unprecedented exemplar.[14]/The perdurance results in and gives Being as the generative ground [*Der Austrag ergibt und vergibt das Seins als hervor-bringenden Grunde*].'[15] There may be nowhere in Indo-Euro-

---

[8] Heidegger, 'Time and Being', in *Zur Sache des Denkens*, Tübingen, Niemeyer, 1969, trans. in *On Time and Being*, Joan Stanbaugh, New York, Harper and Row, 1972, pp.22,14 tr.pp.21,13. Rudolph Bultmann's *Theology of the New Testament*, 1948, trans. Kendrick Gabel, vols I and II, London, SCM, 1978, is compared to Heidegger's *Sein und Zeit* (*Being and Time* trans. John Macquarrie and Edward Robinson, Oxford, Basil Blackwell, 1967) by John Macquarrie: *An Existentialist Theology: A Comparison of Heidegger and Bultmann*, 1955, Harmondsworth, Penguin, 1973.

[9] Exodus 3:13–24, *New English Bible*; see Alexander Altmann, *Moses Mendelssohn: A Biographical Study*, London, Routledge and Kegan Paul, 1973, for sources discussing the meaning of the tetragrammaton, p.408 and n.

[10] See D. Daube, *The Exodus Pattern in the Bible*, 1963, Westport, Connecticut, Greenwood, 1979.

[11] See C.H. Dodd, *The Bible and the Greeks*, 1935, London, Hodder and Stoughton, 1954, p.3.

[12] See the discussion in Ronald E. Clements, *Exodus*, 1972, in the *Cambridge Bible Commentary*, Cambridge, Cambridge University Press, p.23.

[13] Heidegger 'Time and Being', *On Time and Being*, pp.16–20, tr.pp.16–19.

[14] Heidegger, *Identity and Difference*, p.134, tr.p.66.

[15] Ibid., p.140, tr.p.72.

pean languages but there is somewhere in Hebrew, where Being gives itself as 'the unprecendented exemplar', as 'the generative ground' and this may explain why it is unclear whether *Yahweh* says 'I' or 'He' – for no being speaks.[16]

Heidegger seems to give us *Yahweh* without *Torah*: the event seems to include advent and redemption, presence and owning, but not the giving of the law on Mount Sinai, and its repeated disowning.[17] This is evident in the way Heidegger disassociates his position from Hegel's:

> For Hegel the matter [*die Sache*] of thinking is: Being with respect to beings have been thought [*Gedachtheit*] in absolute thinking and as absolute thinking. For us, the matter of thinking is the Same, and thus is Being – but Being with respect to its difference from beings. Put more precisely: for Hegel the matter of thinking is the thought as absolute concept. For us formulated in a preliminary fashion, the matter of thinking is the difference as difference.[18]

With that gerund, *Gedachtheit*, formed from the past participle of *denken*, 'to think', and containing 'memory', *das Gedachtnis*, but which is englished as 'having been thought' (note 'beings having been') Heidegger summarizes accurately his difference from Hegel. In the thinking of Being two ways of expounding history, property and law are at stake. It is not a matter of simply assimilating Heidegger's thinking to the logic of empty, characterless Being with which Hegel begins his *Greater Logic*.[19] For if

---

[16] Since Philo the 'mythological' gods of the Greeks have been compared with the 'historical' God of the Hebrews. Transcribed into verbal form this might be to compare Olympian personalities who live immortally but are distinguished by events completed in time, and *Yahweh*, the living God, occurring in the historic present: an *Ereignis*, an event of ownership, repeated. See the contrast of Greek archetype and Hebrew event in Mircea Eliade, *The Myth of the Eternal Return or, Cosmos and History*, 1949, trans. Willard R. Trask, Princeton, Bollingen, 1974.

[17] For the problem of translating *Torah* as 'law', see Dodd, *The Bible and the Greeks*, pp.40–41.

[18] Heidegger, *Identity and Difference*, pp.112–13, tr.p.47, slightly amended.

[19] Hegel, *Science of Logic*, 1813, Hamburg, Felix Meiner, 1969, trans. A. V. Millar, London, Allen and Unwin, 1969, vol. I, Book I, chapter 1; this is the strategy of Adorno's critique of *Being and Time* in *Negative Dialektik*, 1966, *Gesammelte Schriften*, 6, Frankfurt am Main, Suhrkamp, 1973, p.105, trans.

Heidegger's thinking is considered in its verbal form, then clearly it rewrites Hegel's logic of essence (*ousia*) not the logic of Being.[20]

The difference between Hegel and Heidegger is expressed in this passage as the difference between repetition and recognition. Heidegger transcribes the history of Being into the historic present which is attained, occurs, repeatedly; this is his 'Same': 'the difference as difference'. Hegel reflects the Being of history into a present perfect; he recognizes the historic present as a present with past properties. In Hegel's own words: 'the ground besides being the unity is also the difference of identity and difference.'[21] Heidegger compares his own 'step back [*Schritt zurück*]' with Hegel's 'elevation [*Aufhebung*]'[22] as the difference between pointing 'to a realm which until now has been leapt over', and Hegel's 'heightening and gathering of truth posited as absolute . . . the completely developed certainty of self-knowing knowledge'.[23] From Heidegger's newly discovered 'realm' he can see the dominance of modern technology, 'in all areas of life, . . . functionalization, *Perfektion*, automation, bureaucratization . . .'[24] But what can Hegel see from his 'elevation'? Heidegger does not put Hegel's vision in similar terms: the separation of the modern state and civil society, bureaucracy as the universal class, the distillation of abstract subjectivity from formal law.[25] For Hegel, history begins with the history of states, of the *polis*, of political life;[26] for Heidegger the beginning of history is as much apolitical as political:

Negative Dialectics, E. B. Ashton, London, Routledge and Kegan Paul, 1973, p.98, discussed in G. Rose, *The Melancholy Science: An Introduction to the Thought of Theodor W. Adorno*, London, Macmillan, 1975, pp.70–75.

[20] This challenge to Hegel's *Science of Logic* is most evident in the structure of Heidegger's *Einführung in die Metaphysik*, 1953, Tübingen, Niemeyer, 1958, trans. *An Introduction to Metaphysics*, Ralph Mannheim, New York, Doubleday, 1961.

[21] Hegel, *Encyclopaedia of the Philosophical Sciences*, 1830, Part I *Logic*, sec.121, trans. William Wallace, Oxford, Clarendon Press, 1975.

[22] Heidegger, *Identity and Difference*, p.115, tr.p.49.

[23] Ibid., translation amended.

[24] Ibid., p.118, tr.p.51.

[25] Ibid., see, especially, Hegel, *Philosophy of Right, Theorie Werkausgabe*, 7, Frankfurt am Main, Suhrkamp, 1977, trans. T. M. Knox, Oxford, Oxford University Press, 1967.

[26] See Hegel, *The Philosophy of History, Theorie Werkausgabe*, 12, pp.142, trans. J. Sibree, New York, Dover, 1956, p.111. See, too, chapter 8 below, p.136.

Polis is usually translated as city or city-state. This does not capture the full meaning. *Polis* means, rather, the place, the there, wherein and as which historical being there is. The *polis* is the historical place, the there *in* which, *out* of which, and *for* which history happens . . . Pre-eminent in the historical place, they [violent men] become at the same time *apolis*, without issue amid the essent as a whole [*inmitten des Seienden im Ganzen*], at the same time without statute and limit, without structure and order, because they themselves *as* creators must first create all this.[27]

It seems that Heidegger remains closer to Husserl than the first generation of his students thought and hoped he would be.[28] In *Philosophy as a Rigorous Science* Husserl declared: 'For phenomenology the singular is eternally the *apeiron*.'[29] *Apeiron* is Aristotle's word for the 'infinite', and contains *peri*, 'limit', 'goal', or 'of'.[30] For Husserl consciousness is always consciousness 'of' something, always intentional; for Heidegger the particle 'of' is not intentional, but divisive and proprietal. Heidegger's reply to Jünger shows that *a-peiron*, without a goal, is a bad infinite,[31] whereas he himself takes the *peri*, the *über*, 'goal' or 'of', and shows it to be the whole, the medium common to the apparently exclusive poles of consciousness.[32]

Yet Heidegger's apparent enlarging of rationality so that it includes the oppositions which seem otherwise to establish and limit it, becomes a characterless, empty infinity in its own way. The *Gestell*, the framework, which holds the disowned oppositions of consciousness, is offered as a new way to think of presence without the *vor* or 're' of *Vorstell(ung)*, 're-present(ation)', and the *da* of *Darstell(ung)*, 'present(ation)'. The *ge* in *Gestell*, the particle

---

[27] Heidegger, *An Introduction to Metaphysics*, pp.11–17, tr.p.128.

[28] See the discussion in Elisabeth Young-Bruehl, *Hannah Arendt: For Love of the World*, New Haven, Yale University Press, 1982, pp.45–6.

[29] Husserl, *Philosophie als strenge Wissenschaft*, 1910–11, Frankfurt am Main, Klostermann, 1981, p.43, trans. 'Philosophy as a Rigorous Science' in *Phenomenology and the Crisis of Philosophy*, Quentin Lauer, New York, Harper and Row, 1965, p.116.

[30] Aristotle, *The Physics*, Book III B chapter IV, trans. Philip H. Wickstead and Francis M. Cornford, London, Heinemann, 1970.

[31] Hegel's famous phrase.

[32] For *peri*, see the beginning of chapter 4 above.

which forms the past tense, indicates an event, something which has happened and is present or occurring in what happens, which is not re-presented or presented. But *Ge-Stell* is more revealingly compared with the law which it replaces, *Ge-setz*, 'law', or *gesetzt*, 'posited', of the philosophy of reflection. *Ge-Stell* from *stellen* means, literally, 'put', or 'placed', just like *ge-setzt* from *setzen*, means 'fixed' or 'posited'. If *Gestell* is understood as the dominance of modern technology, this seems as uninformative as the dominance of unknowable law, for all 'technology' means here is an unknown law, although the new word, *Gestell*, may sound as if it tells more about the positing in question.[33]

Heidegger's phenomenology, like Husserl's, is 'eternally *apeiron*', for the *peri, Zweck* or 'goal' of which it treats remains an event within the eternity of language as Husserl's 'singular' is eternally within consciousness. The light of reason, of natural law, has become the blinding light at the end of Dante's *Paradiso*, the form of light itself, which prevents us from seeing anything. Heidegger takes us so far away from the antinomy of law, of theoretical and practical reason, of knowledge and ethics, that this 'place' in which we are de-posited is irrelevant to a life which is lived, understood and transformed in and through that antinomy.[34]

Heidegger proffers a law without legalism, a natural law, which eternally repeats itself. The end of his thinking has as much in common as its beginning with the thinking of Hermann Cohen. Both begin from time and the oppositions of reflection in the *Critique of Pure Reason*, and find eternity in the finite. But Cohen realizes that the prophets who announce *Yahweh*, the event, are implied by his purification of reason.[35] This reason, not purified as in Kant from history, actuality and language, but celebrating Being – after preparatory lustrations and in the vestments of the

---

[33] See translator's note in Heidegger, *The Question concerning Technology*, p.15, and also Rudolph von Ihering, *Der Zweck im Recht*, 1877–81, Leipzig, Breithof und Härtel, vol. I, 3rd edn, 1893, pp.331n, trans. *Law as a Means to an End*, Isaac Husik, New York, Augustus Kelley, 1913, p.247 n.38.

[34] See Heidegger's 'Letter on Humanism' in *Wegmarken*, 1967, Frankfurt am Main, Klostermann, 1978, p.359, trans. in *Basic Writings*, David Farrell Krell (ed.), London, Routledge and Kegan Paul, 1978, p.231, where he reports his rebuffing of a request for ethics.

[35] See the discussion of Cohen in chapter 2 above, p.43.

priest – is disowned by Heidegger. For he shows us 'I am who I am' but keeps the commandments of the *Torah* from us.[36]

This will emerge even more clearly in the way he dissolves the question of Zarathustra's identity.

---

[36] The list of Kant's 'purifications' is that of J. G. Hamann, 'Metakritik über den Purismus der Vernunft', 1784, *Schriften zur Sprache*, Josef Simon (ed.), Frankfurt am Main, Suhrkamp, 1967, pp.219–27.

Part Two

Legalism and Nihilism

6

The New Bergsonism: Deleuze

What has become of the trial of reason, of its personae and its procedures? From out of its midst a prophet has arisen, who, nevertheless, speaks in the future perfect tense and the conditional mood: 'He who will one day teach men to fly will have moved all boundary stones; the boundary stones themselves will fly up into the air before him, and he will rebaptize the earth – "the light one"'.[1] This prophet knows well what has been going on in the critical court-room where we are excruciated by having to bear the multiple and shifting statuses of judge, witness and clerk; 'Yes, even when [a living being] commands itself, it must atone for its commanding. To its own law it must become judge, avenger and sacrifice.'[2]

'Who is Nietzsche's Zarathustra?' asks Heidegger to prompt from us the further question: Who is asking this question – a witness, a judge, a god, a scholar?[3] In posing the question of Zarathustra's identity Heidegger addresses us as a teacher who opens out our perspective by showing us how to 'step back' from the business of the critical court-room. But is this the business of a teacher?

Zarathustra is identified by Heidegger as a mediator and as a teacher; he mediates 'for Dionysus' by speaking for the god in

---

[1] Nietzsche, 'On the Spirit of Gravity', *Thus Spoke Zarathustra: A Book for All and None*, 1883–5, *Werke*, II, Schlechta, Frankfurt am Main, Ullstein, 1979, Part III, sec.II, p.714, trans. Walter Kaufmann, in *The Portable Nietzsche*, Harmondsworth, Penguin, 1981, p.304.

[2] 'On Self-Overcoming', ibid., p.644, tr.p.226, amended.

[3] Heidegger 'Wer ist Nietzsches Zarathustra?' 1953, in *Vorträge und Aufsätze*, 1954, Pfullingen, Neske, 1978, pp.97–122.

three senses: 'of', 'in favour of', and 'in justification of',[4] and in so doing acts as a teacher of the eternal return and of *Übermenschen*.[5] According to Heidegger, Zarathustra teaches not morality but metaphysics: he brings a message of 'redemption' which may release us from 'antipathy' – *Widerwille*, literally, 'against will' – towards the passage of time.[6] This philosophy does not bring release from willing as such. By comprehending willing not as a limited faculty but as the 'Being of beings as a whole', it transfigures antipathy into affirmation.[7] To 'will' time in its modern, Kantian form opens out experience to the history of Being.

In teaching this, Zarathustra does not set himself up as an authority distinct from what he teaches, nor is he installing an *Übermensch* who 'makes naked arbitrariness into a law and a titanic rage into a rule'.[8] He is encouraging us to go over or beyond – *über* – 'a bridge' which we are already traversing.[9] The bridge is time, and we are the people, *Menschen*, who go 'over' or 'beyond' it: *Übermenschen*. The two teachings of the eternal return and of the *Übermensch* require and complete each other but they do not imply any superhuman sovereignty.[10] Furthermore, Heidegger reminds us, 'Nietzsche is not Zarathustra but the questioner' who seeks Zarathustra's identity. Quite consistently Heidegger raises the question of his own status by considering whether his questioning of Nietzsche's thought furthers it or steps back from it: he concludes that it does both of these things.[11] Yet, although the reference to Dionysus as the key to Zarathustra's identity is close to the dénouement offered by Nietzsche himself in *Ecce Homo*,[12] Heidegger's insistence that the meaning of Zarathustra's media-tion of Dionysus is metaphysical respects neither the strange

[4] Ibid., pp.98,119.
[5] Ibid., pp.99,119.
[6] Ibid., p.113.
[7] Ibid., pp.109–10.
[8] Ibid., pp.101–2.
[9] Ibid., p.116, and see, for example, Nietzsche, 'On Redemption', *Thus Spoke Zarathustra*, Part II, sec.20, p.666, tr.p.249.
[10] Heidegger, 'Wer ist Nietzsches Zarathustra?' p.103.
[11] Ibid.
[12] Nietzsche, 'Thus Spoke Zarathustra: A Book for All and None', *Ecce Homo*, 1889, *Werke*, III, pp.574–86, trans. Walter Kaufmann, New York, Vintage, 1969, pp.295–309.

integrity of Nietzsche's text nor the nature of Zarathustra's own enterprise.

Unlike Heidegger, Nietzsche does not attempt to transcribe his discourses into an ametaphysical idiom; and the biblicism in Zarathustra's career is not simply locutionary. Nietzsche keeps the question of Zarathustra's strange identity ever before us: 'Who is Zarathustra to us? What shall we call him? And, like myself [Zarathustra], you replied to yourself with questions. Is he a promiser? or a fulfiller? A conqueror? or an inheritor? An Autumn? or a ploughshare? A physician? or a convalescent? . . .'[13] Zarathustra also describes himself as 'A seer, a willer, a creator, a future himself and a bridge to the future – and alas, also, as it were, a cripple upon this bridge: all this is Zarathustra.'[14] Similarly the question of our identity is repeatedly dramatized as he turns from disciples to cripples and hunchbacks and finds every attempt to address people excruciatingly difficult.[15] Under the heading 'Of redemption' this dramatized difficulty keeps open the question of our reception of Zarathustra's law.[16]

Nietzsche's text explores the possibilities for transcending the Kantian oppositions between morality and legality, between practical and theoretical reason, by making us travel with Zarathustra through fantastical litigious space and time. However, what seems fantastical to us now is a return to the various historical contexts of 'redemption': buying back one's kin from slavery; and of jurisdiction: *ius dicere*, to speak the law;[17] to contexts in which religious, legal, moral and metaphysical discourse are not divorced. 'I draw circles around me and boundaries: fewer and fewer climb with me on ever higher mountains: I am building a mountain range out of holier and holier mountains.'[18]

[13] Nietzsche, 'On Redemption', *Thus Spoke Zarathustra*, Part II, sec. 20, pp. 667–8, tr. p. 251, amended.

[14] Ibid., p. 667, tr. p. 251.

[15] Ibid., p. 670, tr. pp. 253–4.

[16] Consider the 'inverse cripple', ibid., pp. 666–7, tr. p. 250.

[17] For the meaning of 'redemption' see David Daube, *The Exodus Pattern in the Bible*, 1963, Westport, Connecticut, Greenwood, 1979; for 'jurisdiction', see Émile Benveniste, 'ius et le serment à Rome', *le vocabulaire des institutions indo-européenes*, 2, Paris, Les Éditions de Minuit, 1969, pp. 111–22.

[18] Nietzsche, 'Of Old and New Law-Tables, subsection 19, *Thus Spoke Zarathustra*, Part III, sec. 12, p. 728, tr. p. 320 with reference to R. J. Hollingdale's translation, Harmondsworth, Penguin, 1961, p. 225. This passage is repeated

Nietzsche does not hide from us that in 'teaching people to fly' Zarathustra does not just move old boundary stones, he sets up new boundaries; the new law tables are to be seen for what they are: he speaks 'Of Old and New Law Tables'.[19] The overriding aim is to combat the historical and the philosophical effacing of the connections between law and morality.

Within these reinvoked contexts Zarathustra teaches: he offers a Torah;[20] he claims the special status of someone who has eaten of the tree of life as well as of the tree of knowledge and who offers the fruit to others who can only partake of it consecutively: by living, suffering, and labouring in time.[21] Zarathustra admits his claim to a special status, a different perspective, by referring to the holy mountain; but he also knows that the reception of his law will be difficult, and therefore he denies his special status too, and describes himself as well as his listeners as 'cripples'.

In this style Nietzsche avoids erecting a new metaphysics, a new *Logos*, which would replace the opposition of law and morality; or a new morality which would, once again, be exclusively concerned with one pole of the opposition. Instead a text is designed which makes explicit and visible the historical connection between law and morality for the sake of *die Gerechtigkeit*.[22] Zarathustra's discourse is the jurisprudence of this law beyond the opposition of rational versus revealed.

Heidegger, however, treats Nietzsche's strategy as if it were dispensable, and this summary treatment of Nietzsche's drama is deeply allied to Heidegger's repeated denial that Nietzsche's ultimate concern is with *die Gerechtigkeit*.[23] He does not take Nietzsche's thought 'forward' by stepping 'back' and renewing its

---

in *Ecce Homo*, prefaced by 'Zarathustra has an eternal right to say', p.135, tr.p.304.

[19] Nietzsche, ibid., pp. 717–35, Hollingdale tr.pp.214–32.

[20] For 'teachings' as the meaning of Torah, see C.H. Dodd, *The Bible and the Greeks*, 1935, London, Hodder and Stoughton, 1954, pp.40–41.

[21] See, for example, 'The Welcome', *Thus Spoke Zarathustra*, Part IV, sec.11, p.791, Kaufmann tr.pp.392–3.

[22] See, for example, 'On Redemption', ibid., Part II, sec.20, p.669, tr.p.252, where *Gerechtigkeit* is rendered 'justice'.

[23] See, for example, 'The Word of Nietzsche: "God is Dead"' in *Holzwege*, 1950, Frankfurt am Main, Klostermann, 1980, pp.242–3, trans. in *The Question concerning Technology* and *Other Essays*, William Lovitt, New York, Harper and Row, 1977, pp.92–3 and see chapter 4 above, p.72.

erstwhile beginning:[24] he ruins it – by turning the history of the relation between law and morality into the singular Event, *das Ereignis*, and by redesigning metaphysical discourse so that it dissembles its status as the rhetoric of a new law.

The question of *die Gerechtigkeit* has been inherited by those epigoni who, in their turn, 'step back from' and 'further' Heidegger's thinking by transcribing the Kantian antinomy of law into 'productive difference' under the title of abolishing or rewriting metaphysics.[25] These writers also seek to name the singular – beyond the jurisdiction of general and particular – not as the 'Event' of Being, but as differentiation; they inscribe this singular, not as Heidegger does, as 'play in the heart of time', not as perfection or completion of time, but as the movement of duration – *durée* – as imperfect or incomplete time.

The moral and legal ambition served by this transcription is more explicit than it is in the later works of Heidegger. Deleuze, the major philosopher of difference, also asks 'Who is Zarathustra?', but in the name of the 'Third Testament of the future'.[26] The law of this third New Testament is inscribed ironically, for if 'difference' has always been concealed by the logos of representation, then it can only be revealed by a new rhetoric. The tropes of this new rhetoric, like those of the classical one, expound and interpret their law. However, the question of law is not thereby settled: it has come to suffer from *quaternio terminorum*, a multiple ambiguity of terms, as Heidegger's questioning has renewed older French traditions of struggle with the Kantian antinomy also undertaken in the name of the 'end' of metaphysics – from Comte to Bergson, to Deleuze and Derrida. The alleged radical credentials of these recent tentatives warrant re-examination of the original positivist attack on metaphysics in the light of its preoccupation with law.

[24] Heidegger, 'Wer ist Nietzsches Zarathustra?', p.103.

[25] Compare Otto Liebmann's famous defence of Kant against the post-Kantian epigoni, *Kant und die Epigoni*, 1865, Berlin, Reuther und Reichard, 1912.

[26] Gilles Deleuze, *Différence et répétition*, 1968, Paris, Presses Universitaires de France, 1972, p.397; the idea of a 'third' Testament is taken from Joachim of Fiore, c.1132–1202, who divided history into three periods: The Age of the Father (Old Testament), The Age of the Son (New Testament and 42 subsequent generations), and the Age of the Spirit, in which all humanity would be converted. Nietzsche refers to 'Will to Power' as the title of 'this gospel of the future' (*dies Zukunfts-Evangelium*), Preface, sec.4.

Comte distinguished positive philosophy from metaphysics. Positive science does not posit metaphysical entities such as 'soul', 'substance', 'cause'; it considers 'all phenomena as subject to invariable natural laws' and is not concerned with 'things in themselves'.[27] In this way Comte took Kant's theoretical law and applied it to political phenomena as well as natural phenomena to produce a positive science of politics henceforth construed as a realm of 'social' phenomena.[28] Like Kant, however, Comte had to supplement the law of the regularity of appearances by a notion of 'force' in order to provide a detailed account of the natural and social worlds; a notion, which, according to Comte's own rubric, can only be accounted metaphysical.[29] Like Kant, Comte crowns the discovery of invariable natural laws by morals, his seventh and 'master science',[30] and eventually by his 'positive polity'.[31]

Even in principle Comte's 'social physics' fails to replace the feudal and theological politics of the divine will, and the revolutionary and metaphysical politics of popular sovereignty, because it uses 'law' equivocally to mean both the law of these three purportedly succeeding stages of theology, metaphysics and positivism, and also the three different kinds of law characteristic of each stage.[32] Comte's trichotomy draws on the traditional distinctions between revealed law of the Scriptures, the 'theological stage' where reality is seen as the emanation of the divine will; natural right, the 'metaphysical stage' where abstract entities are

---

[27] Auguste Comte, *Introduction to Positive Philosophy*, 1830, trans. Frederick Ferre, Indianapolis, Bobbs-Merrill, 1976, pp.8–9; see John Stuart Mill, *Auguste Comte and Positivism*, 1865, Michigan, Ann Arbor, 1973, p.8.

[28] Ibid., pp.12–13.

[29] Kant, *Metaphysical Foundations of Natural Science*, 1786, *Werkausgabe*, IX, Willhelm Weischedel (ed.), Frankfurt am Main, Suhrkamp, 1980, trans. James Ellington, Indianapolis, Bobbs-Merrill, 1970; and see Jay Bernstein, *Kant and the Problem of Transcendental Realism*, unpublished Ph.d. thesis, University of Edinburgh, 1975; Auguste Comte, *The Foundation of Sociology*, Kenneth Thompson (ed.), London, Nelson, 1976, pp.126–38, especially p.128.

[30] See Comte, *Introduction to Positive Philosophy*, p.57, for five sciences; p.67 for six sciences; and for morals as the seventh 'master science' see Comte, *The Foundation of Sociology*, pp.55–9.

[31] See Mill, *Auguste Comte and Positivism*, Part II.

[32] Compare Georges Davy, 'Durkheim, Montesquieu and Rousseau', 1949, in Émile Durkheim, *Montesquieu and Rousseau: Forerunners of Sociology*, 1892 and c.1901 Michigan, Ann Arbor, 1965, p.148.

posited as the source of law; and positive law, which prior to
Comte, meant the law of human societies, more or less derived
from divine law as apprehended by the light of human reason,
based, that is, on natural law. The natural law tradition distinguishes between knowledge dependent on God's revelation and
knowledge attainable by the natural light of reason inherent in
every rational creature, but both kinds of knowledge have a divine
source.[33] Comte's opposition of positive philosophy to theology
and to natural right revives the old argument for natural law, for
knowledge of invariable laws accessible to the light of human
reason. It takes advantage of the human and secular connotations
of 'positive', while avoiding the political individualism, the
'metaphysics' as he calls it, of natural rights.

If Comte's positive philosophy is seen as a renewal of natural
law in opposition to theology and revelation and to natural rights
arguments of the revolutionary or 'metaphysical' period, then his
outlining of new authorities, his church and polity, should come
as no surprise.[34] For if natural right is posited by man in his
'metaphysical' stage, natural law is posited by God or his new
representative, the positivist priest, in the positive age.[35]

The definition of 'metaphysics' is known to be the weakest
aspect of Comte's case for positive philosophy. Since Kant the
meaning of 'metaphysics' has become systematically ambiguous,
for in the critical philosophy 'metaphysics' has both a pre-critical
and a post-critical meaning. Pre-critically, 'metaphysics' means
the dogmatic thinking which illegitimately extends the pure
concepts of reason beyond any possible experience; post-critically,
'metaphysics' means the extension of knowledge according to

---

[33] *Locus classicus* for these distinctions is Aquinas, *Summa Theologica*, Quaestio
XCI, in *Selected Political Writings*, A. P. d'Entrèves (ed.), Oxford, Basil
Blackwell, 1979, pp.113–17.

[34] Saint-Simon, from whom Comte adapted his law, called the second stage
'metaphysical or juridical', and defined it by the work of the revolutionary
lawyers; see Durkheim's account in *Socialism*, c.1895, trans. Alvin W.
Gouldner (ed.), New York, Collier, 1962, p.165; see, too, Mill's criticism,
Auguste Comte and Positivism, p.67f.

[35] See Comte, *Catéchisme Positiviste*, 1852, Paris, Garnier-Flanmerion, 1966. On
the reading developed here, Comte has more in common with radicalism than
with conservatism; compare the contrary argument in R.A. Nisbet, *The
Sociological Tradition*, London, Heinemann, 1967, pp.9–16.

justified and deduced concepts which can be given in experience and principles which can be confirmed by experience.[36]

If Comte attacks metaphysics in the name of the 'invariable natural laws' of positive philosophy, and Bergson attacks the 'invariable natural laws' of positive philosophy as metaphysics, then Comte is using 'metaphysics' in the pre-critical sense, while Bergson is using 'metaphysics' in the post-critical sense.[37] Yet this distinction merely clarifies the terms, it does not clarify the issue. For although Comte and Bergson seem to have diametrically opposed conceptions of metaphysics, it is nevertheless the case that they both come to depend on physiological notions, 'force' as vital 'tissue' in Comte, *durée* as *élan vital* in Bergson, notions which are metaphysical in the sense of providing the transcendent principle of the physical, a sense indicted by them both.[38]

Comte and Bergson share the same ultimate ambition: to demonstrate that moral experience is continuous with natural experience – Comte from the perspective of the unity of science; Bergson from the perspective of the multiplicity suppressed by science. To quote Spencer, to whom Bergson acknowledged a great debt:[39] '*morality* is essentially one with physical truth – is, in fact, a species of transcendental physiology.'[40] What Comte and Bergson achieve is not the destruction or circumvention of 'metaphysics', but a redrafting of the antinomy of law. Comte,

[36] See Kant, *Prolegomena to any Future Metaphysics that will be able to present itself as a Science, Werkausgabe*, V, trans. Peter G. Lucas, Manchester, Manchester University Press, 1971.

[37] See H. Stuart Hughes's discussion of 'Bergson's aggressive anti-positivism' in *consciousness and society: the reorientation of European social thought 1890–1930*, London MacGibbon & Kee, 1967, p.115f.

[38] 'Physiology' has multiple meanings in Comte ranging from a mechanical notion, implying movement, to a vitalist notion implying life or growth, see *Introduction to Positive Philosophy*, p.32: compare Aristotle's discussion of the etymology and meaning of *physis: Metaphysics*, The Loeb Classical Library, trans. Hugh Tredennick, London, Heinemann, 1980, Book V IV 1014b 16 – 1015a 19.

[39] 'Some fifty years ago I was very much attached to the philosophy of Spencer. I perceived one fine day that, in it, time serve no purpose, did nothing.' Bergson, 'The Possible and the Real', n.d. in *The Creative Mind*, c.1903–1923, trans. Mabelle L. Andison, New Jersey, Littlefield, Adams and Co., 1975, p.93.

[40] *Social Statics*, 1851, extract in Herbert Spencer, *On Social Evolution*, J.D.Y. Peel (ed.), London, University of Chicago Press, 1972, p.24.

who seeks to keep descriptive and normative law distinct, and to restrict science to the former, ends up drafting an external, 'moral' law;[41] Bergson, who wishes to disband the antinomy, drafts a new natural law: 'Let us then give the word biology the very wide meaning it should have, and will perhaps have one day, and let us say in conclusion that all morality, be it pressure or aspiration, is in essence biological.'[42] If metaphysics is a predicament not a choice, its vaunted demise will always issue in bad metaphysics.

Heidegger's questioning of Being has turned the French tradition of surpassing metaphysics into an historical questioning of metaphysics. The quest is no longer to overthrow metaphysical thinking by classifying it as pre-modern (Comte) or as the principle of quantitative classification (Bergson), but to complete and perfect it by tracing the antinomy of law to ontological difference, to open up the antinomy to the history of Being. The Bergsonian heritage has been ostensibly radicalized by this new kind of attention. Bergson's *durée*, intensive time, is taken back to the difference of Being, *das Ereignis*, as it were, and re-emerges in spatial dress: as *spatium intensif* in Deleuze, as *grapheme* in Derrida. These new principles of differentiation are not developed into a 'biological morality' as in Bergson. Instead the suppositious contamination of language by metaphysics is met by a new rhetoric which completes and perfects that history. Difference is developed into a morality or conscience of discourse, an active nihilism, which subverts the tropes of the old law.[43] However, the points of continuity between Bergson and this new metaphysics of difference suggest that the current international appeal of the latter has something in common with the immense international appeal of Bergson to an earlier generation.[44]

In Bergson's earliest and greatest work, *Essai sur les données*

[41] See Mill, *Auguste Comte and Positivism*, Part II.
[42] Bergson, *The Two Sources of Morality and Religion*, 1932, trans. R. Ashley Audra and Cloudesley Brereton, New York, Doubleday Anchor, 1954, p.101.
[43] The French *morale* has a wider meaning than the English 'moral' and the German *Moralität*: it cuts across the Kantian contraries morality/legality and the Hegelian distinction between *Moralität* and *Sittlichkeit*, morality and ethical life.
[44] Henri Bergson, 1859–1941, won the Nobel Prize for Literature in 1927; his early works were translated into English and known in the English-speaking world before the First World War.

immédiates de la conscience, translated with the title *Time and Free Will*,[45] we find ourselves collaborators in a Rousseauian critique of the Kantian court of consciousness, understood as an impersonal, public realm, 'prepared' for language and social life out of pre-social, intense, immediate and somehow 'personal' sensations.[46] For Bergson moral experience is continuous with natural experience not because nature is conceived as geometrical and spatial as in Spinoza,[47] but because experience is initially discontinuity in time, intensity from the perspective of consciousness, and, in later works, *élan vital* from beyond the perspective of consciousness.[48]

In this early work Bergson does not deny the Kantian antinomy of law, he rededuces it as the form of the external, homogenous, social world, and sublates it by carrying that form to the underlying heterogenous reality out of which it has been constructed. He does not seek to abolish but to preserve the 'kingdom within a kingdom', the 'two aspects of the self [*moi*],'[49] one belonging to the intensive realm, the other dressed, whether as judge or witness, for the court of social life. The moral law can only appear in this world as an invisible 'revealer of duty', an inexplicable fact of consciousness; the 'free' act is seen as a contravention of this conventional, public space.[50]

---

[45] Bergson, *Essai sur les données immédiates de la conscience*, 1889, Paris, Presses Universitaires de France, 1976, authorized trans. *Time and Free Will*, F. L. Pogson, London, George Allen and Company, 1912, with a multilingual bibliography of works on Bergson, pp.xi–xviii.

[46] 'Les Deux Aspects du moi', ibid., pp.95–104, tr.pp.128–39. Compare Rousseau, 'A Discourse on the Origin of Inequality', 1755, trans. G. D. H. Cole, *The Social Contract and Discourses*, London, Dent, 1973, The First Part; and Durkheim's discussion of Rousseau on language and society in *Montesquieu and Rousseau*, pp.66–75.

[47] Spinoza treated of 'human vice and folly geometrically . . . Nothing comes to pass in nature which can be set down to a flaw therein; for nature is always the same, and everywhere one and the same in her efficacy and power of action . . .' *Ethics*, 1674, trans. and ed. R. H. M. Elwes, *Works of Spinoza*, vol. II, New York, Dover, 1955, p.129.

[48] See Heidegger's discussion of Bergson in *Sein und Zeit*, 1927, Tübingen, Niemeyer, 1972, trans. *Being and Time*, John Macquarrie and Edward Robinson, Oxford, Basil Blackwell, 1967, H.18,26,432 n.xxx.

[49] Bergson, *Time and Free Will*, p.103, tr.p.139; the phrase 'un empire dans un empire', in quotation marks in the original and translated as 'a kingdom within a kingdom', emphasizes Bergson's opposition to Spinoza who rejected the view of human conduct whereby man is conceived as 'situated in nature as a kingdom within a kingdom', *Ethics*, p.128.

[50] Bergson, *Time and Free Will*, p.176, tr.p.234.

Primary immediate experience is characterized as a quality, not as a medium, so that the Kantian exposition of the possibility of experience can be seen to pertain to a secondary experience which re-presents the first in artificial, homogenous time and space: 'Kant's mistake was to take time as a homogenous medium.'[51] Bergson tries to correct this mistake by developing an account of a prior intuition, heterogenous and immediate, which would be given 'by a being, ever the same and ever changing, and which has no idea of space'.[52] We are asked to 'penetrate into the depths [*sic*] of consciousness', and intuit the 'intensity' of our states of consciousness.[53] We cannot describe this experience directly, for, as soon as we try, we inevitably re-present it as consisting of discrete, mutually external and extended spatial elements.

Instead the contrast built up between immediate or present intuition, *durée*, and the media of re-presentation – space, language and law – is presented as corresponding to two kinds of difference: inner multiplicity, discontinuous and qualitative, versus a symbolic medium of continuous, distinct, numerical units. Duration, once it is conceived, appears in spatial dress: 'Outside us mutual externality without succession; within us succession without mutual externality.'[54] The latter is the homogenous, successive time described by Kant, as opposed to 'real' duration, described by Bergson as qualitative 'permeation' of states of consciousness with no resemblance to number. Bergson concedes that his attempts to describe *durée* have to fail, because 'by the very language which I was compelled to use, I betrayed the deeply ingrained habit of setting out time in space';[55] 'we project time into space' to 'prepare' ourselves for language, for social life and for science.[56]

The wonderful result of this tantalizing and elusive phenomenology of *durée* is that Bergson exactly reproduces the Kantian antinomy. He claims that we have access to *durée*, and hence 'absolute knowledge of ourselves';[57] but the inevitable

---

[51] Ibid., p.174, tr.p.232, amended.
[52] Ibid., p.75, tr.p.101, amended.
[53] Ibid., p.6, tr.p.8.
[54] Ibid., p.171, tr.p.227.
[55] Ibid., p.91, tr.p.122.
[56] Ibid., p.75, tr.p.101.
[57] Ibid., p.177, tr.p.235.

betrayal of pure *durée* once we name it leaves it as unknowable, 'invisible and present' as Kant's moral law. Like the moral law, *durée* is described as a dynamic 'fact' of consciousness, 'time flowing', in opposition to the mechanical laws of knowable, spatial phenomena, 'time flown'.[58] It plays the same role as the noumenal self, the transcendental unity of apperception, which turns into the empirical self once we attempt to cognize it. Bergson can only explain the free act from the perspective of *durée* by depicting a fork in its path,[59] by the metaphor of an 'over-ripe fruit',[60] dropping from a living and developing creature, or as a moment of crisis, a 'thrust' which breaks through the 'crust' of the ego's 'surface'.[61] In short, the weakness of these attempts to translate free action into the medium of spatial intuition has the opposite effect to that intended: it lends support to the Kantian account of the *sui generis* status of the moral realm – which the typic of practical reason may clarify by borrowing the form of a law of nature, but not, as Bergson attempts, by translating moral experience into a species of natural intuition or *durée*.[62]

By his own admission and in opposition to Spinoza whose coinage he borrows, Bergson seeks to defend not abolish the idea of the individual as a 'kingdom within a kingdom', that is, as a kingdom of *durée* within a kingdom of mathematical space.[63] But instead of showing how the laws of the scientific kingdom derive from the laws of the inner kingdom, Bergson shows that the inner kingdom obeys no law: it displays the sublime anarchy of a pulsating heart the rhythm of whose beat depends solely on its sovereign passions.[64] Bergson produced a 'sentimental physics' for his generation as Mill said Comte did for his:[65] based on a

---

[58] Ibid.: for 'dynamic' versus 'mechanical' and 'facts' versus 'laws' see the first few pages of chapter III; for 'time flowing' versus 'time flown' see the last page of chapter III.

[59] Ibid., p.133, tr.p.176.

[60] Ibid., p.132, tr.p.176.

[61] Ibid., p.127, tr.p.167.

[62] For the 'typic of practical reason', see Kant, *Critique of Practical Reason, Werkausgabe*, VII, p.188, trans. Lewis White Beck, Indianapolis, Bobbs-Merrill, 1956, pp.71–2, and chapter Two above, notes 86 and 87.

[63] Bergson, *Time and Free Will*, p.103, tr.p.139, and see note 49 above.

[64] Ibid., chapter I, *passim*, where Bergson draws on various emotions to capture 'qualitative intensity'.

[65] I refer to Mill's comment on Comte: 'It is not sufficient to have made physics

moving but unmathematical principle, renamed *élan vital* when Bergson subsequently apperceived *durée* outside the limits of consciousness.[66]

'Univocal Being is both nomadic distribution [*nomos*] and crowned anarchy' is how Deleuze reformulates Bergson's antinomy: law for the public realm of representation; anarchy for the realm of *durée*.[67] The new Bergsonism no longer seeks a rival account of moral experience: it seeks to open up ontological injustice itself. The appropriation of Being, *das Ereignis*, as it were, is seen as the truth of Bergson's intuition of an intense, heterogenous differentiation, distinct from the homogenous, juridical world. The new metaphysics of difference seeks to make us face our experience squarely as this legalism without law.

Deleuze takes up the paradox noted by Bergson himself that every attempt he made to describe or locate *durée* lapsed into spatial and quantitative metaphors.[68] If the 'multiplicity' of *durée*, its qualitative difference from space, is said to be found in the 'depths' of consciousness, or to be a 'permeation' of states of consciousness, then it becomes a difference of degree not a difference of kind in relation to space.[69] Language, which cannot know *durée*, establishes the idea by drawing on the very metaphysical dichotomies which *durée* is designed to replace: time/space; quality/quantity; inner/outer. If Bergson had intuited *durée* beyond these oppositions, it would be no more within consciousness than without; no less extended in space than in time; for 'real' time could equally well be called 'real' space. Bergson's failure adequately to conceive of the difference between the two realms of the heterogenous and homogenous is also the source of the unsatisfactory account of their relation to each other. *Durée* is both opposed to space as a difference in kind, and presented as the principle itself of difference in kind (quality) versus space as mere

---

sentimental, mathematics must be made so too.' *Auguste Comte and Positivism*, p.193.
[66] See Bergson, *Creative Evolution*, 1907, authorized trans. Arthur Mitchell, London, Macmillan and Co. Ltd., 1911, chapter 1.
[67] Deleuze, *Différence et répétition*, p.55 and p.54 where it is argued that *nomos* qua distribution implies occupied but not divided space: '*un nomos nomade*', p.54.
[68] Bergson, *Time and Free Will*, p.91, tr.p.122.
[69] Deleuze, *Le Bergsonisme*, Paris, Presses Universitaires de France, 1966, pp.23–8.

difference of degree (quantity); if the latter holds, space would be within *durée* not without it.[70]

Deleuze readdresses the question of the intuition of *durée* as the question of how metaphysics might be more consistently and radically circumvented, and how the connections between the two realms might be described once they become distinct; 'what is essential in Bergson's project is to think differences in kind independently of all form of negation: there are differences in being and yet there is nothing negative.'[71] Bergson's ambition according to Deleuze, is to eschew the language of generality: to oppose *durée* to homogenous time, to the order of beings, without assimilating it to an equally general concept of non-being or disorder.[72] From the perspective of this common root of difference in Being, space must be as original as time.

'Psychological *durée* has to be only a well-determined case, an opening into ontological *durée*'.[73] Whether described as *durée*, as *matière et mémoire*, or as *élan vital*, Deleuze considers that to pass through this ontological opening involves 'a veritable leap/the leap into the ontological': a leap beyond the metaphysical and juridical opposition of order and disorder to the realm of intensity.[74] According to Deleuze, Bergson's 'method' of intuition[75] is a kind of mental wager designed to bring us into the presence of this intense, creative principle 'which will perish to be reborn in the next instant, in a twinkling or a shudder, ever renewed.'[76] This pure energy of movement and differentiation, *l'élan vital*, is Being, not according to the negative difference of species and genus, differences of degree, of generality, but according to the positive and creative difference of potential and actual Being.[77]

Durée is the movement from 'virtuality' to actuality which is not the formal Kantian separation of actuality and possibility, nor

[70] Deleuze, *Différence et répétition*, p.308 n.1.
[71] Deleuze, *Le Bergsonisme*, p.41.
[72] Ibid., pp.41–2.
[73] Ibid., p.44.
[74] Ibid., pp.51–2, Deleuze's emphasis.
[75] Deleuze organizes his first chapter around three rules of 'L'intuition comme methode'.
[76] Ibid., p.89.
[77] Ibid., p.105.

does it involve a mathematical notion of extension or space. 'Virtuality' is an alternative translation of the Greek *dynamis* to the conventional Latinized 'possibility' or 'potentiality'.[78] According to Deleuze 'virtuality' is Bergson's answer to the *quaestio quid juris*: 'By right [*En droit*] means virtually';[79] while the *quaestio quid facti* becomes the question of how life 'accedes *actually*' to the freedom of the principle; how conscious life becomes of itself as that movement.[80] On Deleuze's reading Bergson produced a *Naturphilosophie* which culminates at the point when the *élan vital* 'becomes conscious of itself' in the memory of 'man'.[81] The initial difficulty in depicting *durée* within consciousness without implying negation and disorder is overcome once intensity is seen instead as the movement of acutality, 'the virtuality which actualizes itself . . .' a differentiation which is 'never negative but essentially positive and creative'.[82]

Deleuze has repeated for a later generation the 'leap' from the metaphysical order to the realm of intensity, by entering further into the history of the appropriation of Being, *das Ereignis*, as it were, for the sake of a morality which will reclaim the future, 'The Third Testament'.[83] Under the title of *Différence et Répétition* Deleuze rehearses the topoi of the attack on metaphysics by opposing two kinds of generality or order: a quantitative order of equivalence to a qualitative order of resemblances; exchangeable equivalence to inexchangeable singularity.[84] The second order is best understood as a 'miracle' or 'transgression' by contrast to the order of law or regularity, for it perpetually 'puts law into question'.[85] From this perspective the moral law also belongs to an order of uniformity and generality; obligation involves merely the repetition of an habit but no genuine innovation.[86]

---

[78] Compare Heidegger's discussion of this terminology, 'On the Being and Conception of *Physis* in Aristotle's *Physics*, B,1' in *Wegmarken*, 1967, Frankfurt am Main, Klostermann, 1978, pp.237–99, trans. Thomas J. Sheeham in *Man and World* 9/3 (1976) 219–70.

[79] Deleuze, *Le Bergsonisme*, p.111.

[80] Ibid., Deleuze's emphasis.

[81] Ibid., p.119.

[82] Ibid., p.105.

[83] See note 26 above.

[84] Deleuze, *Différence et répétition*, pp.8–9.

[85] Ibid., p.9.

[86] Ibid., p.12.

Like Bergson, Deleuze seeks to describe the principle of the 'second' order – second in thought but primary in its movement – without negation or mediation.[87] The *quaestio quid juris* belongs to the order of equivalence: it commissions an inquiry into concepts whose repeated use constrains and delimits, like a play rehearsed again and again, while discounting repetition in the sense of each unique and singular playing: 'a difference without a concept'.[88] This difference may be discerned between the equalized, causally distinct concepts: 'a dissymmetry, a sort of gaping which will only be fused in the total effect . . . which glows across the gap'.[89]

In spite of his critique of Bergson's divagations within the depths of consciousness, Deleuze, like Cohen and Heidegger, finds his own 'principle' in Kant's discussion of an intuition of 'inner difference'. In section 13 of the *Prolegomena* Kant has to defy his own distinction between space, the medium of mutually external and simultaneous relations, and time, the medium of internal and successive relations. Kant gives the example of seeing a reflection of one's hand or ear in a mirror: the object and its reflection are mutually equal and similar 'in all points that can be known about each separately (in all determinations belonging to quantity and quality)',[90] yet one is aware that the one cannot be substituted for the other: that there is an 'inner difference . . . which no understanding can show to be inner and which only reveals itself through the outer relation in space.'[91] The inner determination of any space can only be known by determining its outer relation to space as a whole of which it is a part. For Kant the difference is intuitable because we can relate it to other parts of space – left and right for the object and its image – but it is not intelligible by any single concept which would name the difference directly, as would be possible if we knew things in themselves and not merely their relations in sensible intuition.[92] Deleuze, following Cohen, takes Kant's distinction as evidence of 'quantitative intensity', of an internal dynamic of space which

---

[87] Ibid., p.16.
[88] Ibid., pp.23–4,26; *répéter*: 'to rehearse'; *répétition*: 'rehearsal'.
[89] Ibid., p.31.
[90] Kant, *Prolegomena*, sec.13.
[91] Ibid.
[92] Ibid.

precedes representation.[93] 'Inner difference' in Kant is a residual term for an intuition which falls short of knowable outer relations, but in Deleuze it provides evidence for a realm of intuition defined as positive and creative, as setting the limits of outer relations.

This distinction between intense, inner space, and represented, outer space, becomes Deleuze's *ouverture ontologique, das Ereignis*, as it were. Aristotle, he reminds us, argued that Being cannot be 'one genus of existing things. For there must *be* differentiae of each genus . . . but it is impossible either for the species of the genus to be predicated of the specific differentiae, or for the genus to be predicated without its species . . . Hence if . . . Being is a genus, there will be no differentiae Being . . .'[94] There must be two kinds of difference corresponding to the two orders identified by Deleuze, and to the two *logoi* in Aristotle: the difference of species depending on uniform concepts, and the difference of genus which speaks through the logic of species, but not according to its principle of differentiation.[95]

According to Deleuze, Being has two characteristics: it is 'communal' and 'collective' as the Being of genus and species; but 'distributive' and 'hierarchical' as the Being prior to the distinction of genus and species.[96] 'Being' seems equivocal in Aristotle's sense of things which 'have the name only in common, the definition (or statement of essence) corresponding with the name being different' as opposed to univocal things which not only have 'the same name but the name means the same in each case – has the same definition corresponding.'[97] According to Deleuze 'Being' is equivocal because it covers both 'specific difference' and 'generic difference'.[98]

In the tradition which stems from Aquinas the dual meaning of Being is bridged by knowledge based on analogy: the Being of

---

[93] Deleuze, *Différence et répétition*, pp.39–40,298 and note, with reference to sec.428, 2nd edn, Hermann Cohen, *Kants Theorie der Erfahrung*, Berlin, Ferd. Dummler, 1871.

[94] Aristotle, *Metaphysics*, Book III. III, 998b 20–27, referred to by Deleuze, *Différence et répétition*, p.49n.

[95] Ibid., p.49.

[96] Ibid.

[97] Aristotle, *The Categories*, The Loeb Classical Library, trans. Harold P. Cooke, London, Heinemann, 1973, Book I 1a 1–6.

[98] Deleuze, *Différence et répétition*, p.51.

God is said to be 'analogous' to the being of creatures.[99] This kind of prediction falls between univocal and equivocal predication: it predicates simultaneously similarity and dissimilarity. According to Deleuze, however, analogy is the way of representation, identity and uniformity. He finds in Duns Scotus an alternative account of univocity, and, following Heidegger, calls on Scotus as the founder of ontology.[100]

For Duns Scotus, 'before "being" is divided into the ten categories, it is divided into infinite and finite. For the latter, namely finite being, is common to the ten genera. Whatever pertains to "being", then, in so far as it remains indifferent to finite and infinite, or as proper to the Infinite Being, does not belong to it as determined to a genus, but prior to any such determination, and therefore as transcendental and outside any genus.'[101] Scotus is able to say that in '"in being" . . . a twofold primacy concurs, namely a primacy of commonness and of virtuality'; for everything has being in the transcendental and in the generic sense.[102]

This reference to Scotus brings out the hermeneutic circle which links the critical, Kantian meaning of 'transcendental' – commonness of concept in relation to intuition – with the scholastic meaning of 'transcendental': virtuality. 'Being is said in a single and same sense of everything of which it is said, but that of which it is said differs: it is said of difference itself;' this expresses the paradox that 'Being *is* different'; and involves the simultaneous predication of sameness and difference.[103]

Read by Deleuze as an active principle, this paradox opens up ontological injustice itself. The 'common' meaning of Being is the mode of law, of judgement and distribution. Deleuze reminds us that the Greek *nomos*, law, may be traced to 'division' or 'sharing', and he describes this kind of distribution – the establishment of a realm of strict boundaries and limits – as 'the sedentary structures of representation'.[104] It is overshadowed by Being in the transcen-

---

[99] For 'analogy' see Frederick Copleston, *Medieval Philosophy*, Part II *Albert the Great to Duns Scotus*, New York, Image Books, 1962, pp.71–8.

[100] Deleuze, *Différence et répétition*, p.52.

[101] Duns Scotus, 1266–1308, *Philosophical Writings*, trans. Allan Wolter, Indianapolis, Bobbs-Merrill, 1978, p.3.

[102] Ibid., p.5.

[103] Deleuze, *Différence et répétition*, p.53.

[104] Ibid., pp.54–5.

dental or ontological meaning which divides in an hierarchical and nomadic way, wandering with no fixed boundaries, a power which surpasses limits. The equalities of the first hierarchy are suspended unequally within the second, which is univocal only in this ontological boundlessness or 'unmeasure' (*démesure ontologique*), – everything is equally subjected to this inequality: 'Univocal being is at the same time nomadic distribution and crowned anarchy.'[105]

Like Bergson, Deleuze aims to make us acquainted with this sovereign anarchy which is somehow present in our 'asymmetrical synthesis of the sensible' and in 'moral' experience. He seeks to show that the intuition of inner difference found in Kant is a difference of intensity, an experience of energy, 'le pur *spatium*.'[106] It is a movement not a schema; a difference of *quantity* not quality, for it is only possible to say of quantities that they are unequal. It is affirmative and positive, and, finally, it is the principle of change in kind not in degree which is inclusive of the Bergsonian contraries: multiple and single, heterogenous and homogenous.[107]

To define this energy 'in general' would make it into a law of nature, when the ambition is to point to the sovereign anarchy which orders of generality presuppose: 'The transcendental principle rules no domain, but gives the domain to be ruled to the empirical principle; it registers the submission of the domain to the principle. It is difference of intensity which creates the domain and gives it to the empirical principle, in accordance with which it annuls itself.'[108] This vassalage is graphically summarized by '*le concept de differenciation*' where 't' is the realm of virtuality and 'c' the actual, qualitative and extended series.[109]

From the 'civil status' of the Kantian synthesis to the fiefs of 'crowned anarchy', Deleuze apperceives *durée* as *démesure ontologique*.[110] Far from avoiding the implication of disorder, Deleuze seems to dance attendance at the court of sovereign anarchy, taking us behind the concept, the apparently self-validating

---

[105] Ibid., p.55.
[106] Ibid., pp.286,287,296.
[107] Ibid., pp.299–309.
[108] Ibid., p.310.
[109] Ibid., p.316.
[110] Ibid., pp.178–9.

measure, to the intuition of the sovereignty which wills that measure. Who is this sovereign? To penetrate this heavily disguised identity Deleuze reiterates the question 'Who is Zarathustra?'

Difference of intensity, difference 'without a concept', serves to recast the kind of repetition involved in the ordinary idea of law; to see beyond the repeated imposition of artificial equivalence to the unequal, singular repetition presupposed. Zarathustra appears to have formulated a new categorical imperative to rival Kant's: 'Eternal recurrence says to itself: whatever you will, will it in such a manner that you also will its eternal recurrence.'[111] Universalizability becomes repeatability; the law of nature becomes a will to 'dethrone' all law, all uniformity; 'There is a realm beyond the law and a realm before the law, and these are united in the eternal recurrence like the irony and black humour of Zarathustra'.[112]

Unlike Heidegger, Deleuze takes Zarathustra's irony seriously: the message of eternal return is ironically delivered as a categorical ımperative, as a law of the exact kind which is to be subverted. Deleuze's Zarathustra has to work relentlessly to remind us not to read 'the eternal return of the same' according to the dichotomy of order/disorder; not to read it as 'an external order imposed on the chaos of the world as something identical which returns'. For 'The Negative does not return. The Identical does not return. The Same and the Similar, the Analogous and the Opposed do not return. Only the Affirmation returns, that is to say the Different, the Dissimilar.'[113] Eternal return is not cyclical time as opposed to linear time, for both the idea of cyclical time and the idea of linear time presuppose homogeneity and succession. This is why, although he claims he will return exactly as he is, Zarathustra 'dies' and 'convalesces': it is not the 'same' Zarathustra who returns.[114] What is repeated is not 'something which exists prior to the return': what remains the same is only the returning, which is to say, the eternal return of the different, or, it is the repetition of

[111] Ibid., p.15.
[112] Ibid.
[113] Ibid., p.382.
[114] Ibid., see Nietzsche, 'The Convalescent', *Thus Spoke Zarathustra*, Part III, sec.13,2.

the dissimilar which is the same.[115] This is how the equivocal, 'difference', is univocal, 'repetition'.

In other words – words of Duns Scotus with which Deleuze concludes – while from the perspective of representation, of law, specific difference of genus and species is 'univocal', and generic difference, transcendental or ontological difference, is 'equivocal', both concur in the univocity of Being. Everything occurs 'between the two kinds [*sic*] of difference'.[116] Deleuze invokes a pure affirmation of this univocity, its realization 'as repetition in the eternal return'.[117] He reminds us finally that the ontological opening belongs to this univocity, and tempts us to leave the 'sedentary distributions (law) of analogy' and to wander through into the opposed realm of 'nomadic distribution or the crowned anarchy of the univocal'.[118]

Zarathustra, on Deleuze's account, is the intriguer at the court of this absolute monarch. But who is this monarch? We have been delivered into the embrace of the Scotist God. For Scotism represents the main alternative to Thomist natural law: the Scotist God rules – not according to His intellect revealed to the light of our reason by natural laws which He obeys too – but by the dictates of His divine and arbitrary will.[119] The 'Third Testament of repetition' is the repetition of a God who never promised a codified law, the God of the second table of commandments with which He can dispense, and, in Deleuze, this licence undercuts the first table of commandments whose reason conforms to natural law.[120]

'The world "makes itself" while God calculates; there would be no world if the calculation were right.'[121] *Différence* unlike *durée* turns morality into transcendental calculus not into transcendental

---

[115] Deleuze, *Différence et répétition*, p.384.

[116] Ibid., p.387

[117] Ibid., p.388.

[118] Ibid.

[119] I repeat here the conventional accusation brought against Duns Scotus; for a correction of this view, see Copleston's chapter on Scotus's ethics, *Medieval Philosophy*, Part II, pp.268–74.

[120] For the second table, the secondary precepts of the decalogue, see Copleston, *Medieval Philosophy*, pp.271–2.

[121] Deleuze, *Différence et répétition*, p.286.

physiology.[122] But it is not the geometry of Spinozistic pantheism where one order reigns;[123] it is the *spatium* of quantitative intensity which replaces Bergson's qualitative intensity: the inequality which lurks in the equality of the world, not the Bergsonian *physis*, growth and evolution, *l'élan vital*, which flourishes amidst the homogenous space of the world. Deleuze opposes a 'differential calculus' to the homogenous, numerical order, and leaves open the question of who calculates, the *quaestio quid juris*, where Bergson's biologism closes it.

This opening invites a 'leap', a sheer affirmation: for to hesitate is to remain in the realm of representation, of law, of the univocity of genus and species, from where the equivocity of beyond and before is audible, but where the risk of the leap into the higher univocity is refused. The *quaestio quid juris* has become a paradox: it is open, but only to those who simply accept the antinomy of the two orders by affirming the underlying inequality as nothing negative; *'l'inégal est le plus positif'*.[124]

It is surprising that this leap should appear so irresistible for we are clearly told that difference – and the God who wields it – is characterless, quantitative not qualitative intensity. His only characteristic is His will, which cuts up that intensity differently each time, arbitrarily and unpredictably. The call to affirm such a difference brings out the passivity at the heart of the call to an 'active' nihilism: for this affirmation is a surrender to the absolute injustice of the highest will. Surrender to repetition in the sense celebrated must equally be a surrender to repetition in the sense deplored; a surrender to the eternal return of the difference of genus and species as much as to the repetition of nomadic difference. To say the least – and to say it in Deleuze's own words – this affirmation is clearly 'equivocal'; but, even clearer, this celebration of ontological injustice is quite unequivocal.

---

[122] See above, note 40.
[123] Deleuze, however, links Duns Scotus and Spinoza on the question of the univocity of Being, *Différence et répétition*, pp.387–8.
[124] Ibid., p.33.

7

Structuralism and Law: Saussure and Levi-Strauss

While the personae and procedures of the critical court are founded and undermined by the *usurpatory concept of freedom*, the latter-day critical sciences of structural linguistics and structural anthropology are undermined by the post-structuralist revelation of the *usurpation of Being* at the heart of their brief. But why do the masks of intriguers, prophets and gods need to be invoked in this cause?

'What then is truth? A mobile army of metaphors, metonyms, and anthropomorphisms – in short, a sum of human relations, which have been enhanced, transposed, and embellished poetically and rhetorically, and which after long use seem firm, canonical and obligatory to a people: truths are illusions [*Illusionen*] about which one has forgotten that this is what they are; metaphors which are worn out and without sensuous power [*sinnlich kraftlos*]; coins which have lost their images [*Bild*] and now matter only as metals, no longer as coins.'[1]

Is 'ontological injustice' better addressed not as the multiform voice of Being – equivocal and univocal, the hierarchical, feudal law of one mood issuing in the equivalent, civil status of the other – but as vocables, 'a mobile army of metaphors' settled in to permanent occupation? Does it make injustice more tangible, and

---

[1] Nietzsche, 'Über Wahrheit und Lüge in aussermoralischen Sinn', 1873, *Werke*, III, Schlechta, Frankfurt am Main, Ullstein, 1976, p.314, extract trans. in *The Portable Nietzsche*, Walter Kaufmann, Harmondsworth, Penguin, 1981, pp.46–7. I have changed the translation of *Bild* from 'picture' to 'image'. See the complete translation 'On Truth and lies in a Nonmoral Sense', Daniel Breazeale, in *Philosophy and Truth: Selections from Nietzsche's Notebooks of the early 1870s*, Brighton, Harvester, 1979, pp.79–100.

thereby transformable to locate it in the civil form itself – in the 'army', the 'coinage', in language as such?

That frequently cited passage from an early essay of Nietzsche's does not simply tell us that truth is an illusion which arises from the rhetorical nature of language; nor does it relapse into the idea of truth under challenge, by deriving 'metaphors' from 'human relations', and 'illusions' from the 'senses'.[2] It tells us something about the power and weakness of rhetoric and illusion themselves. The image, the impulse conveyed to the senses, is the imprint of a stamp, which, as on a coin, establishes the measure of value and marks the medium of exchange. The passage reminds us of something we may have forgotten, even though all our exchanges and contracts ('human relations') depend on memory: that the standard or law we implicitly rely on may have lost its authority but nevertheless continues to mediate our innumerable, immediate exchanges. It is not a matter of abolishing the coinage, for that would reduce not increase our power. We need to grasp that the metal is being given a new stamp.

We are to be taken on a linguistic version of the metajuridical journey already undertaken in the name of 'purpose', of the appropriation of Being, *das Ereignis*, and of 'difference'. Once again the antinomy of law is traced to its source, and, once again, this does not make the law conceivable or knowable, but merely leaves us with the suggestion that we might shift our stance towards it: if Deleuze tempted us to opt for the insecurity of the vassal, then the metaphysics of difference in its linguistic version will tempt us to the greater risks which come with the masks of the intriguer.

A critique of pure language, like a critique of pure reason, initially describes what is 'given' to consciousness as independent of the precondition, but ultimately shows that the 'given' is

---

[2] This would seem to be the reason behind Gayatri Chakravorty Spivak's selective quotation of this passage omitting these phrases and using the Levy translation which renders *Bild* as 'obverse', 'Translator's Preface', Jacques Derrida, *Of Grammatology*, Baltimore, The Johns Hopkins University Press, 1976, p.xxii; and Nietzsche, *Early Greek Philosophy and Other Essays*, vol. II, Oskar Levy (ed.), London and Edinburgh, T. N. Foulis, 1911, p.180; see, too, Derrida's citing of this passage, 'White Mythology: Metaphor in the Text of Philosophy', in *Marges de la philosophie*, Paris, Les Editions de Minuit, 1972, p.258, trans. *Margins of Philosophy*, Alan Bass, Brighton, Harvester, 1982.

dependent on the precondition, that it is conditioned.[3] The transcendental deduction will turn on the way this ambiguity in the relation between the conditioned and the precondition is exploited: the meaning of 'representation' shifts from 'given to intuition', independent of thought, to the conditioned, the construct of thought, or, 'object of experience'; while the meaning of the precondition shifts from the unknowable 'condition of possibility' in the case of theoretical reason to the active, creative principle in the case of practical reason.[4]

Although a metajuridical exposition of language, like a metajuridical exposition of thought, claims to overcome the antinomy of theoretical and practical law presupposed in the original procedure, it has the effect of reinforcing the transcendental circularity of precondition and conditioned even while claiming to have stepped outside it. For it weakens the demarcation between the precondition or principle and the conditioned or representation, either as in Cohen, where regional object domains of individual sciences are constituted on the model of the typic of practical causality, or, as in Schopenhauer or Bergson, where representation conforms to the law of causality as a form of the understanding (*Verstand*), while actuality, the will or *durée*, belongs to a different, non-causal, non-juridical order. These kinds of exposition claim to step outside the transcendental circle because they abolish the distinction between appearances and things in themselves, between phenomena and noumena. Yet they retain a transcendental movement, albeit an exposition or laying out of the principle of virtuality instead of the critical deduction of the conditions of possibility.

Whether the procedure is critical deduction or metajuridical exposition it will both presuppose and undermine a connection between the poles of precondition and conditioned. Both the meaning of 'representation' and the meaning of the 'condition',

---

[3] See Klaus Hartmann, 'On Taking the Transcendental Turn', *Review of Metaphysics* XX (1966), 223–49, especially, 242–3: and Émile Benveniste, 'De la subjectivité dans le language', *Problèmes de linguistique générale*, 1. Paris, Éditions Gallimard, 1966, pp.258–66.

[4] See Schopenhauer's dense and devastating 'Criticism of the Kantian Philosophy', Appendix to the first volume of *The World as Will and Representation*, 1819, *Zürcher Ausgabe* II, Zürich, Diogenes, 1977, pp.509–651, trans. E.F.J. Payne, New York, Dover, 1966, vol. 1, pp.413–534.

'principle' or 'law' are inherently unstable: defined, on the one side, by their relation to their common other, the 'thing in itself' or noumenal realm, and, on the other side, by their opposition to each other.

The first critiques of Kant to be entitled 'metacritique' were developed in the name of language by Hamann and Herder.[5] The designation 'metacritique' is misleading, for both Hamann and Herder point out that the inseparability of reason and language makes a critical deduction impossible. They do not attempt a metacritique of signification, which would shift the deduction from experience as such to language as such, since a move of that kind would equally suppose that signification and sense can be distinguished from within the very medium, language, which is under examination. They sought to redescribe the connection of thinking and language without making those initial distinctions between a priori and empirical, and between conditioned and precondition, on which any transcendental deduction depends; in effect such distinctions posit a realm of representation or nature but then present what has been posited or put there as if it were independent of 'purified' thought.[6]

Slightly later critics of Kant sought to make a virtue of the circularity of precondition and conditioned inherent in the transcendental deduction by embracing its necessity. In his exposition of thinking Fichte derived the non-ego from the act of the ego, the posited from the positing, while in his exposition of language Humboldt developed the notion of linguistic 'type' by drawing on the original Greek meaning of *typos*, stamp, imprint, or 'inner form'.[7] This 'organicist' exposition of signification has come to be opposed to the critical or 'intellectual', but they represent two attempts to solve the same problem.[8] The notion of 'inner form'

---

[5] J. G. Hamann, 'Metakritik über den Purismus der Vernunft', 1784, *Schriften zur Sprache*, Joseph Simon (ed.), Frankfurt am Main, Suhrkamp, 1967, pp.219–27; J. G. Herder, 'Verstand und Erfahrung, Vernunft und Sprache, eine Metakritik der reinen Vernunft', 1799, *Werke*, XXI, Hildesheim, Gorge Olms, 1967.

[6] See Henri Lefebvre, *Le Language et la société*, Éditions Gallimard, 1966, pp.138–9.

[7] See Wilhelm von Humboldt, *Scriften zur Sprache*, Michael Böhler (ed.), Stuttgart, Reclam, 1973, Nachwort, pp.248–54.

[8] See Hans Aarsleff, *From Locke to Saussure: Essays on the Study of Language and Intellectual History*, London, Athlone, 1982, Introduction, especially, pp.13–16,

reiterates the familiar move from the condition of possibility to the active principle, with language not thought as the medium of experience. This move is vulnerable to the criticism contrary to that made of the transcendental deduction, that explicitly, not implicitly, it legislates its conditioned.

Language may replace thought as the medium of experience because it also displays the dual aspect of law: on the one hand it is juridical, in the sense of observable regularities; on the other hand it is normative and litigious, an imperative which serves as the standard of value but which may be questioned.[9] To refer the transcendental deduction to language raises the same questions regarding law as the reference to thought, but the reference to language tends to draw out the meaning of law as 'custom' or 'institution', that is, as social. Organicist expositions of language as independent of the human will are as liable to be considered 'social' as are critical deductions of language from human capacities and conventions.[10] Indeed, the history of sociological thought reveals precisely this range of meaning of the 'social', from critical and contractual, to historical and autonomous.[11]

Saussure's *Course in General Linguistics* addresses the *quaestio quid juris* to the 'general faculty which governs signs . . . the linguistic faculty proper', also called 'the faculty of articulating words', which 'gives unity to speech'.[12] The *Course* proceeds on classic transcendental lines: the distinction between *langue* and *langage*, corresponds to the distinction between the a priori and the

31f. An alternative account may be found in Ernst Cassirer, 'Introduction and Presentation of the Problem', and 'The Phenomenology of Linguistic Form', chapter 1 *The Philosophy of Symbolic Forms*, vol. 1 *Language*, 1923, trans. Ralph Mannheim, New Haven, Yale University Press, 1970, pp.73–114,117–76.

[9] Compare the analogy of grammar and legal rule in Peter Stein, *Regulae Iuris*, Edinburgh, Edinburgh University Press, pp.53–64.

[10] See 'Breal vs. Schleicher: Reorientation in Linguistics in the Latter Half of the Nineteenth Century', and 'Wilhelm von Humboldt and the Linguistic Thought of the French Ideologues', in Aarsleff, *From Locke to Saussure*, pp.293–334,335–55.

[11] See Georges Gurvitch, *L'Idée du droit social: Notion et système du droit social, histoire doctrinale depuis le XVIIe siècle jusqu'à la fin du XIXe siècle*, 1932, Aalen, Scientia, 1972.

[12] Ferdinand de Saussure, *Cours de linguistique générale*, 1915, Tullio de Mauro (ed.), Paris, Payot, 1979, p.27, trans. *Course in General Linguistics*, Wade Baskin, Glasgow, Fontana/Collins, 1974, p.11.

empirical; the distinction between 'concept' and 'sound-image' corresponds to the distinction between concept and intuition or representation where 'representation' is 'given'; the exposition of linguistic value corresponds to the move from the introductory 'description' to the transcendental reconstruction where the concept and sound-image as signified and signifier appear as a construct of signification.

The distinction between language as diachronic and as language as synchronic, on which the transition to the reconstruction of linguistic value turns, plays a dual role: diachrony as 'span of time' is first introduced as inseparable from the concept of a language as a combination of social fact and linguistic rule, as a system of values;[13] but it is also defined as the empirical, 'events', in relation to the a priori synchronic 'projection' and relegated to a different order of consideration on pain of transcendental amphiboly – of confusing a fact of language as such with an innovation of speaking which remains individual.[14] This inclusion and exclusion of time from the exposition of linguistic value brings us to the heart of the theory of contract on which the case for a general linguistics rests. A critique of pure signification reveals even more concretely than a critique of pure thought that the connection between linguistic form and legal form is a question which cannot be opened up further by means of criticist, transcendental probing.

The 'Introduction' to the *Course* follows the introductory procedure for a transcendental argument: language is distinguished from speech as the only 'fact' of speech that can 'introduce a natural order into a mass that lends itself to no other classification'.[15] It is then possible to reconstruct the place of language in the facts of speech as an exposition of how language relates a priori to a fact of speech without confusing this with any empirical instance of speaking (*parole*). On this basis a further distinction is made between 'concept' and 'sound-image' where 'sound-image' stands for 'the representation of the linguistic sound'. These 'sound-images' are to be found in 'the brain' where they wait to be

---

[13] Saussure, *Course in General Linguistics*, pp.112–13, tr.p.78.
[14] Ibid., Part One, Chapter III, sec.8.
[15] Ibid., p.25, tr.p.9.

unlocked by 'given concepts' defined independently of sound-images as 'facts of consciousness'.[16]

The initial description of the speaking circuit of concept and sound-image depends on a distinction between the 'executive' or 'active part': '(c → s)', and the 'receptive' or 'passive part': '(s → c)'. Saussure's terminology corresponds to the Kantian separation of receptivity and spontaneity.[17] The phrase 'sound-image' itself – 'sound' and 'image' – encompasses the mix of representation and signification, receptivity and spontaneity, more clearly separated by 'sound-image' and 'concept', and even more by 'signified' and 'signifier' where the implication of active and passive seems reversed.[18] In these initial distinctions which pertain to a description of the speaking-circuit prior to any constitution of significa-tion, the foundations of the later account of linguistic value are being laid.

The further distinction between language as a 'social product/passively assimilated by the individual' and an act of speech which is 'a wilful and intellectual' act of the individual serves the same purpose.[19] For by 'social' Saussure means that it is 'outside the individual who can neither create or modify it by himself; it exists only by virtue of a sort of contract signed by members of a community.'[20] Language is contracted or posited by the commun-ity but its use is not 'affected by the will of the depositaries'.[21] It is the 'most important' of several systems of signs 'within society', that part of social psychology to be called 'semiology' and which 'would show what constitutes signs, what laws govern them'.[22]

A contract in which the terms are independent of the will of the depositaries can only be a will or testament. Of course the distinction between the idea of language as a contract signed by the members of a community as free, conscious, rational beings, and the passivity of those individuals as depositories but not as speakers, is a distinction between general and particular, and

---

[16] Ibid., p.28; tr.p.11 renders *les faits de conscience* as 'mental facts'.
[17] Ibid., p.29, tr.p.13.
[18] Ibid., p.99, tr.p.67, and see notes 133,132,128 in the French edition.
[19] Ibid., p.30, tr.p.14.
[20] Ibid., p.31, tr.p.14.
[21] Ibid., p.38. tr.p.19.
[22] Ibid., p.33, tr.p.16, and see note 51 in the French edition.

general and individual will, which simply sets the level of formalism – that is, determines the kind of generality that is to be examined.[23] But the contract is a strange one: rational – 'signed [*passé*]'; and irrational – independent of the 'will of the depositaries'.[24] The analogy between language and contract involves a vitiating circularity – it refers signification to the 'signing' of a contract.

The 'Introduction' to the *Course* serves the same purpose as the 'Introduction' to the *Critique of Pure Reason*: it establishes the distinction between the a priori and the empirical, and the need for a justification of pure language. Part One of the *Course*, 'General Principles', corresponds to the transcendental aesthetic of the first *Critique*; while Part Two, 'Synchronic Linguistics', corresponds to the deduction. The description of the 'sign' as a combination of 'sound-image' and 'concept' within the medium of 'reception', 'a fact of potential language',[25] in the first part, leads, in the second, to the constitutive level, the deduction of language 'as a system of pure values'.[26] The transition from the first to the second order of exposition is effected by discussion of the 'arbitrary' and contractual nature of the sign, and, consequent on this, the separation of static from evolutionary linguistics. As the justification of pure value takes increasing precedence over the justification of pure signification the spontaneous or 'executive' point of view takes over from the 'receptive' point of view.[27] Part Two concludes with a discussion of 'syntagmatic and associative relations' which, as in the 'Systematic Representation of all the Synthetic Principles of Pure Understanding' of Kant's first critique, expounds the role of reproductive memory – 'rules of all relations of appearance in time'.[28]

In the first part, 'General Principles', the discussion of the linguistic sign is cast from the 'receptive' perspective of the

---

[23] Ibid., p.37, tr.p.18.
[24] Ibid., p.31, tr.p.14.
[25] Ibid., p.98n, tr.p.66n: note provided by the editors of the first edition.
[26] Ibid., p.155, tr.p.111.
[27] Compare Roland Barthes, *Elements of Semiology*, 1964, trans. Annette Lavers and Colin Smith, London, Cape, 1972, pp.54–7.
[28] Kant, *Critique of Pure Reason*, I, Second Part, First Division, Book II, chapter II, sec.3.

speaking circuit, '(s → c)', sound-image to concept.[29] The sound-image is 'the representation given by the testimony of the senses'; it is deposited not posited.[30] The linguistic sign is 'a two-sided psychological entity' consisting of concept and sound-image 'intimately united'; they differ in degree of abstraction, but 'each recalls the other'.[31] Concept and sound-image are thus said, respectively, to differ merely in degree and to differ in kind, and this confusion is not clarified by the drawing.[32] Saussure's substitution of 'signifier' and 'signified' for 'sound-image' and 'concept' is said by the editor of the 1967 French edition of the *Course* to emphasize the arbitrary nature of the sign and to prevent preoccupation with its sensory aspect. Yet this defence remains irrelevant to the issue of its cogent differentiation.[33] For what is interesting is not whether Saussure inconsistently and unnecessarily worries us about the natural, non-arbitrary nature of the sign, but whether the distinctions with which he delineates the idea of the sign recast the problem of signification at all. The ambiguity between difference of degree and difference of kind which dogs the components of the sign indicates that Saussure has merely raised again the *quaestio quid juris* regarding the concept: the problem of its apparently relational nature. To rename the concept 'the signified' is to exchange an active implication – the concept conceives – for a passive one: 'signified'; while the 'signifier' renames the sound-image in a way which makes it sound active. The 'sign' in its entirety includes both active and passive connotations and is held to be differential, relational and formal.

The 'arbitrary' or 'unmotivated' nature of the sign is established by contrast with, *inter alia*, 'spontaneous expressions of reality

---

[29] Saussure, *Course in General Linguistics*, p.29, tr.p.13.

[30] Ibid., p.98; tr.p.66 renders this 'the impression that it makes on our senses'.

[31] Ibid., p.98, tr.p.66.

[32]

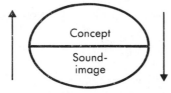

Ibid., p.99, tr.pp.66–7, and see note 132 to the French edition.

[33] Ibid., n.128.

dictated, so to speak, by natural forces'.[34] The astounding example given of a 'natural bond' is the 'symbol of justice, a pair of scales', – the traditional symbol of the social and conventional in opposition to nature.[35] Yet the distinction between 'spontaneous' and 'unmotivated' is intended to draw attention to the kind of social rules and conventions which the concept of a language implies: whether they are rational or irrational; that is, how they are to be justified.[36] Even though he has taken the symbol of law as the exemplar of imitation, by describing signs as 'arbitrary' Saussure means that they are legislated not imitated, and he goes on to specify the kind of legislation. He admits that this idea of language as arbitrary – conventional and social – implies a contract 'between concepts and sound-images' to which all would freely consent, but, since 'the masses have no voice', this indicates that the accepted law of connection between concept and sound-image is merely 'tolerated', and is not 'a rule to which all freely consent'.[37]

Language is said to be more arbitrary than other social institutions 'united by nothing but the choice of means'.[38] Although this comparison leaves it unclear whether the difference is one of degree or one of kind, to say that language is 'more arbitrary' than other social institutions is taken to mean that language is more rational. For, according to Saussure, to say that an institution is 'arbitrary' implies that its conventions have been posited or agreed on.[39] However a perfectly rational 'society' would not need to make contracts between concepts and sound-images, for 'contract' implies that things have been equalized which are otherwise unequal. Saussure acknowledges that if we consider the community of speakers and their language without considering time we would not see the effect of the 'social forces' that influence language; strictly speaking, we would not have a concept of language at all, for 'language' implies a medium of circulation, and 'circulation' implies movement in time.[40]

[34] Ibid., p.102, tr.p.69.
[35] Ibid., p.101, tr.p.68.
[36] Ibid., pp.100–101, tr.p.68.
[37] Ibid., p.104, tr.p.71.
[38] Ibid., p.110, tr.p.76.
[39] Ibid., p.112, tr.p.78.
[40] Ibid., p.111, tr.p.76.

In order for the object under scrutiny to be language we must examine 'everything that deflects reason in practical contacts between individuals'.[41] Saussure argues that this means that language cannot be a pure contract: for if it is to be living the action of time and social force must be considered. Potential life, after all, be it of a language or of a physical being, is not independent life at all. The 'social' cannot be conceived 'as a community of speakers [*masse parlante*]', plus a language, but without time, since a perfect community would not need the contracts which define a society and its language; it would have the 'simple convention that can be modified at the whim of the interested parties', which is to say, that its language would be at one with 'nature' and would not distinguish between 'signifier' and signified'.[42] Without time and social force we have no language – not even as 'rational' contract.

In his 'static' or 'synchronic' linguistics Saussure wishes to examine language as a perfectly arbitrary 'system', and not as a 'living' force, even though it is only as a living force, that is, with reference to time, that we have a concept of language.[43] In effect there are two concepts of the social and language, and two concepts of law at issue: free and rational – 'arbitrary', and tolerated – 'force'. Saussure admits that two ideas of law 'in the legal sense are involved': 'synchronically' or rationally, language rules are general, regular, but not imperative – that is, they are juridical; while 'diachronically', language rules are forceful, but in no way general – that is, they are normative or litigious.[44] Even before Saussure calls for a further non-legal, and scientific sense of law, he has distinguished this third sense by contrasting the law of the projection of an object (synchronic state), with the objects themselves considered individually (diachronic events).[45] This third 'scientific' sense of law refers to the kind of investigation at stake: it is transcendental. It sounds as if diachrony – force and irrationality – has been relegated to a less systematic level of inquiry; but in effect, a distinction has been made between pure

[41] Ibid., p.112; tr.p.78 renders *practiques* as 'actual'.
[42] Ibid., p.113, tr.p.78.
[43] Ibid., pp.115,112, tr.pp.79,77.
[44] Ibid., p.134, tr.p.95. See 'Introduction', above p.2, and note 9, above.
[45] Ibid., pp.124–5, tr.p.87.

time and empirical time. The rejustification of the synchronic study of language as pure or perfect contract sublimates force into value and time into space – implied by the idea of contract when it was first introduced.

There would be no way of conceiving the equation of signifier and signified without the medium of time, yet language is to be considered as 'a system of pure values which are determined by nothing except the momentary arrangement of its terms'.[46] Value is an arrangement of terms on the condition that time has become 'momentary' and spatial, 'a span of time'.[47] The problem of value is said to arise in those sciences in which change over time is intrinsic to their subject matter, and to be an especial problem in linguistics where value is not connected with any 'natural' base.[48] This might equally be said to indicate that 'force' has been turned into the abstract time of the contract as it equates things belonging to different orders, and that this is how value is purified or 'pure'.

Once synchrony and diachrony have been separated as an order of explanation versus an order of description, the contract, that mixture of force and irrationality out of which the problem of value first arose, appears to take second place, as the 'executive' role of value is isolated for further synchronic examination. As the question of value acquires increasing dominance so the question of the articulation of thought itself increasingly replaces the uneasy distinction between concept and sound-image, signified and signifier, in the search for 'a synchronic reality [*une realité synchronique*]'.[49] 'The characteristic role of language is to serve as a link between thought and sound'; 'thought' is here active again, and 'sound' passive. 'The somewhat mysterious fact is rather that "thought-sound [*la pensée-son*]" implies division and that language works out its units while taking shape between two shapeless masses . . . Language might be called the domain of articulations . . . each linguistic term is an *articulus* . . .'[50] According to Saussure this fact is 'mysterious', because, although an idea is fixed in a sound and a sound becomes the sign of an idea, this does

---

[46] Ibid., p.116, tr.p.80.
[47] Ibid., p.142, tr.p.101.
[48] Ibid., p.116, tr.p.80.
[49] Ibid., p.152, tr.p.109.
[50] Ibid., p.156, tr.pp.112–13.

not occur as a 'materialisation of thought' nor as a 'spiritualisation of sound'.[51]

This 'mystery' may be the mystery of what Saussure means by 'thought', which he implies is both prior to and dependent on the division of sounds: 'Thought, chaotic by nature, has to become ordered in the process of its decomposition.'[52] Hence it is not at all clear that 'linguistics works in the borderland [*le terrain limitrophe*] where the elements of sound and thought combine; their combination produces a form not a substance',[53] for the idea of language as articulation seems to apply to thought and to sound quite independently of each other. The connection between thought and sound remains mysterious because we are not told anything about it, and this may be why Saussure's remarks apply to writing as much as to sound.[54]

The real 'mystery' is that of articulation as such, of its law. This is confirmed by the transition which Saussure makes from talking of the sign to talking of 'the linguistic term' and even, simply, of 'words', thereby reversing the earlier emphasis on the passivity of the signified: 'one tends to forget that *arbor* is called a sign only because it carries the concept "tree", with the result that the idea of the sensory part implies the idea of the whole'.[55] According to the synchronic perspective of value 'it is from the independent whole that one must start and through analysis obtain its elements'.[56] Value is subsequently explicated 'from the conceptual viewpoint', that is, from the 'signified', while from 'the material viewpoint', the former 'signifier' is assimilated to the same analysis by simple analogy.[57]

It is only now, in the examination of value, that the paradox of contract which Saussure drew on to develop the concept of a language is itself fully developed. Values, linguistic and non-linguistic, 'are apparently governed by the same paradoxical principle. They are composed (1) of a *dissimilar* thing that can be

---

[51] Ibid., p.156, tr.p.112, amended.
[52] Ibid.
[53] Ibid., p.157, tr.p.113.
[54] Ibid., pp.165–6, tr.pp.119–20.
[55] Ibid., p.99, tr.p.67.
[56] Ibid., p.157, tr.p.113.
[57] Ibid., and compare chapter IV, secs 2,3.

exchanged for the thing of which the value is to be determined' –
this is the exchange of a word for a concept or idea, the question of
'signification' – (2) of *similar* things that can be compared with the
thing of which the value is to be determined' – this is the
comparison of word with word whose value is 'fixed by
everything that exists outside it', the question of value.[58] From the
perspective of value 'concepts are purely differential and defined
not by their positive content but negatively by their relations with
the other terms of the system. Their most precise characteristic is
in being what the others are not.'[59] Saussure concludes that value,
not the connection of signifier and signified, expresses 'the
linguistic fact in its essence and fullness'.[60]

As the examples of exchanging francs with bread (signification)
and comparing francs with more or less francs (value) reveal, the
exchange of dissimilar things is intrinsic to the comparison of the
similar, yet the prior exchange has been defined as extrinsic to
the system of value. This exchange is the form of contract as
employed earlier to define the arbitrary nature of language. Here
the examples reveal that '*dissimilar* things' are made relatively
equal and similar when they are exchanged. Social force is pressed
into the 'rational' equivalence of the contract of exchange. The
value according to which that equalizing occurs is comparable to
other 'similar' things when the measure of value also becomes the
medium of exchange – when there is money. The comparison of
five francs with one franc can occur only because of the exchange
of francs with non-francs. The 'form' of value indeed derives from
the 'substance' in this sense, and this derivation is the 'social fact'
which explains why 'the arbitrary nature of the sign explains in
turn why the social fact alone can create a linguistic system'.[61]

The 'social fact' in Saussure's system is not what he himself calls
the 'paradoxical principle' of value but the paradox of contract:
that value as a differential dervies from value in exchange but
seems to rule per se, as a 'form' not as the transformation of
'substance'. Saussure wants to isolate the measure of value from
the medium of exchange: five to one, not one to bread. Is this

---

[58] Ibid., pp.159–60, tr.p.115.
[59] Ibid., p.162, tr.p.117.
[60] Ibid.
[61] Ibid., p.157, tr.p.113.

conceivable? Yes: it is the simple definition of a rule or convention, namely, a standard of value according to which all 'exchanges' are governed. All that Saussure's 'linguistics' tells us is that language as such is a rule or convention, and, further, that this rule is a regularity without force, 'synchronic'. Yet his explication of value as differentiation, as *articulans*, implies energy or force, and the discarded origin of value in exchange alludes to a law which is rational but not the result of free consent.

The exposition of syntagmatic and associative relations which follows the justification of value, draws on the working of memory. 'Association' or 'memory' was first mentioned in the initial, neutral, preconstitutive description of concept and sound-image, as 'the psychological association' of sound-image and concept, the former 'located in the brain'.[62] We can now see that the initial description of concept and sound-image is not neutral, but is packed with the constitutive or transcendental principle to be deduced. For associative relations are now said to unite 'terms *in absentia* in a virtual mnemonic series'; and once again it it said that 'their seat is in the brain'.[63] This confusion in Saussure between thought and brain may be linked to the confusion of imagination or memory as recollecting or 'associating' images and concepts, and reproductive and retentive memory which creates and retains names or signs, an example of the latter: 'let this be called a mini-floppy disk'.[64] This distinction between imagination and stipulation may clarify the relations in the *Course* between signs, contracts and psychology.

A contract may be considered to be a form not a substance because specific qualitative features of the property exchanged are translated into quantitative terms or 'value': heterogenous property becomes an abstract universal 'thing'.[65] The stipulation of a contract effects this translation; the words of the stipulation are

---

[62] Ibid., p.28, tr.pp.11–12.
[63] Ibid., p.171, tr.p.123, amended.
[64] Compare Hegel, *Encyclopaedia of the Philosophical Sciences*, Part III, *Philosophy of Mind, Theorie Werkausgabe*, 10, Frankfurt am Main, Suhrkamp, 1977, trans. William Wallace, Oxford, Clarendon Press, 1971, secs.461–2,458. For Derrida's discussion of these sections see 'The Pit and the Pyramid: Introduction to Hegel's Semiology', *Margins of Philosophy*, pp.94–101 and n.6, tr.pp.81–95 and n.15; and chapter 8 below, p.167.
[65] Compare Hegel, ibid., sec.494.

both act, or deed, and thing – 'deed' has both this general and legal meaning.[66] It is productive and retentive memory not imaginative association which produces these names or signs by deleting the qualitative associations of an intuition or representation and conferring a new connotation on it arbitrarily connected with the original associations.[67] Productive memory but not thought as such is involved in the formation of linguistic signs. The bestowal of the name effects the transition form qualitative association to quantitative value: it stipulates a juridical 'thing'.

On this account value is not isolated as self-justifying once the analogy of the contract has established the distinction between form and substance. For it is the relation of form and substance which makes it possible to apprehend how 'value', the sign, is both act and thing: Saussure's 'linguistic fact in its essence and fullness', the differential or rule.

This account of signs, contract and language may be drawn out from Saussure's linguistics by taking seriously the 'apparent paradoxes' and 'mysteries' which he admits. Such an approach does not reduce his endeavour to a naturalistic or psychologistic theory of signification, nor does it deconstruct and celebrate the sheer arbitrariness of the uncovered rule. Instead the question of the imperative at the heart of synchrony becomes the question of the historical connection between psychology and objective spirit. In this way its law may become knowable.

This approach holds for structuralist anthropology too, and throws a quite different light on the succeeding project of 'post-structuralism'. Levi-Strauss's case for structuralist science depends on a transcendental argument which he explicitly adapts from Saussure's linguistics in order to turn anthropology into a critique of pure mythology. His justification likewise rests on a theory of contract designed to steal history from its apologists,[68] and it

---

[66] Ibid., sec.493, with reference to sec.462. Hegel calls this '*die vollgültige Tat*'.

[67] Ibid., secs 457 (*Zusatz*),458, 'The sign-creating activity may be distinctively named "productive" memory [*Gedächtnis*] (the primarily abstract "Mnemosyne") since memory which in ordinary life is often used as interchangeable and synonymous with remembrance (recollection) [*Erinnerung*] and even with conception [*Vorstellung*] and imagination [*Einbildungskraft*] has always to do with signs only.'

[68] 'Time Regained' is the title of chapter 8 in Levi-Strauss, *The Savage Mind*, 1962, London, Weidenfeld and Nicolson, 1974, pp.217–44.

employs the terminology of structural linguistics to establish what he calls, borrowing from Kant, anthropology's 'Copernican revolution'.[69]

In Levi-Strauss's hands the critique of scientific thought is changed into a critique of pure mythology. Scientific thought which 'creates events by means of structure' is contrasted with mythological thought or '*bricolage*' which creates structures by means of events.[70] The scientist works with concepts which open up reality; the *bricoleur* with signification which reorganizes it. 'Concepts aim to be wholly transparent with respect to reality, signs allow and even require the interposing and incorporation of a certain amount of human culture into reality.'[71] Signs, 'half-way between concepts and percepts', are the 'link between images and concepts.'[72] The question of the nature of this link is the *quaestio quid juris*, for the 'link' is the rule which the deduction seeks to justify. It is indeed apt that Levi-Strauss should call this rule 'mythical thought' since it is necessary but unknowable: 'Mythical thought [is] imprisoned in the events and experience which it never tires of ordering and re-ordering in its search to find a meaning'.[73] Levi-Strauss's work consists of the attempt to make such structuring knowable by developing what might be called, borrowing from Husserl and with reference to Deleuze's *pur spatium*, a phenomenology of internal space consciousness.[74]

'From words the linguist extracts the phonetic reality of the phoneme: from the phoneme he extracts the logical reality of distinctive features. It is the same phoneme which will show at this new level the basic identity of empirically different entities'.[75] The 'phonetic reality of the phoneme' separates the a priori from the empirical, the 'words'; and the 'new level' distinguishes the

---

[69] See Levi-Strauss, Postscript to chapters III and IV, in *Structural Anthropology*, trans. Claire Jacobson and Brooke Grundfest Schoepf, Harmondsworth, Penguin, 1979, p.83; and Kant, *Critique of Pure Reason*, B xxii a.

[70] Levi-Strauss, 'The Science of the Concrete', in *The Savage Mind*, p.22.

[71] Ibid., p.20.

[72] Ibid., p.18.

[73] Ibid., p.22.

[74] By analogy with Husserl, *Vorlesung zur Phänomenolgie des inneren Zeitbewußtseins*, 1905, edited by Heidegger, 1928, trans. *The Phenomenology of Internal Time Consciousness*, James S. Churchill, The Hague, Nijhoff, 1964.

[75] Levi-Strauss, 'History and Anthropology', 1949, *Structural Anthropology*, p.20.

constitutive or reconstitutive level from the preliminary description, 'the basic identity of empirically different entities'. Levi-
Strauss's transcendental ambition is further revealed when he goes
on to say that in anthropology as in linguistics 'it is not
comparison that supports generalization but the other way
round'.[76]

Accordingly the 'new level' is that of 'the unconscious structure
underlying each institution and each custom', the law or principle
which makes them possible. 'Unconscious' is meant in a transcendental not in a psychological sense: it means the precondition of
consciousness which cannot itself be an object of consciousness;
'the transition from conscious to unconscious is associated with
progression from the specific to the general'.[77] 'Structure' means
both 'forms fundamentally the same for all minds', and 'an
activity which imposes form upon content'.[78]

Levi-Strauss calls this justification of structure 'synchronic',
and, like Saussure, synchrony is distinguished from diachrony, or
history, in two ways: from diachrony as the realm of the 'unique
and dissimilar', whereby the empirical is distinguished from the
constitutive; and from diachrony as part of the constitutive level
itself, 'by showing institutions in the process of transformation
history alone makes it possible to abstract the structure which
underlies the many manifestations and remains permanent
throughout a succession of events.'[79] Elsewhere Levi-Strauss calls
this 'an antinomy of historical knowledge' arguing that quantify-
ing events in history to reach the continuous always involves a
move from individual 'events' to the realm of 'possible pre-
existents'.[80] As a 'temporary internality' history has a 'spurious
intelligibility' which hides the 'abstract schematizing' involved in
all knowledge. Historical consciousness is as spatial and projected,
and hence as 'mythical', as any other.[81]

On the basis of this distinction between empirical history and
the time of the synchronic, Levi-Strauss seeks to reconstruct the

[76] Ibid., p.21.
[77] Ibid., pp.20–21.
[78] Ibid., p.21.
[79] Ibid.; in the Postscript, 1958, Levi-Strauss qualifies the opposition synchronic/
    diachronic, but he continues to offer a transcendental formulation, pp.88–91.
[80] Levi-Strauss, 'History and Dialectic', *The Savage Mind*, p.258n.
[81] Ibid., pp.255,254,259–60.

actual as possible, 'the complete range of unconscious possibilities'.[82] As a result of this 'kind of straining process' in the case of societies with 'dual organization',[83] those structural elements are retained which define a social institution or custom: 'the need for a rule; the concept of reciprocity providing the immediate resolution of the opposition between the self and other; and the synthetic nature of the gift'.[84] These three elements coincide with the features which define both the synthetic, a priori judgement, and the contract: first, both judgement and contract ('gift') imply a rule; secondly, both imply a concept of reciprocity, for determining the relation of agent and patient in the judgement, and of parties and thing in the contract; and, thirdly, both imply the synthetic nature: synthetic a priori judgements are necessary and universal but 'ampliative', that is, they make possible a genuine new addition of knowledge, while the contract makes synthetic exchange possible as qualitatively different things are exchanged under the quantitative rule of exchange or value.[85]

The theory of contract at the heart of Levi-Strauss's critique of pure mythology, its synchronic exposition, is revealed by his argument that anthropology, like linguistics, is susceptible to mathematical analysis.[86] For both sciences rest on knowledge of elements discernible as 'the projection, on the level of conscious and socialized thought, of universal laws'.[87] Hence the 'systems of relations' of these elements may 'be expressed in terms of mathematical functions'.[88] Just as it was argued by Levi-Strauss that the distinction between the availability of written sources and the lack of written sources is the symptom of the distinction between history and anthropology, not its definition,[89] so here the susceptibility of anthropology to mathematical analysis does not refer to mathematics simply as numerical expression but draws

---

[82] Levi-Strauus, 'History and Anthropology', *Structural Anthropology*, p.23.
[83] Ibid., p.22; for 'dual organization', p.10.
[84] Ibid., p.22.
[85] See Kant, *Critique of Pure Reason*, Introduction, secs.I–IV, and 'Table of Categories', A 80/B 106.
[86] Levi-Strauss, 'Language and the Analysis of Social Laws', *Structural Anthropology*, pp.56–8.
[87] Ibid., p.59.
[88] Ibid., pp.58,59.
[89] Levi-Strauss, 'History and Anthropology', ibid., pp.24–5.

attention to anthropology as a *mathesis* in the hermeneutic sense recaptured by Heidegger, in which transcendental arguments relate the conditioned to the precondition which is already known;[90] and it draws attention to the *mathemes* of anthroplogy in the sense employed by Cohen, in which the precondition is not simply the 'condition of possibility' but an active principle or 'value'.[91]

The *gustèmes* or 'constituent elements' of *cuisine* 'which may be organized according to certain structures or oppositions' provide an example of the latter kind of exposition.[92] The first kind of exposition is exemplified by Levi-Strauss's discussion of the mathematical study of marriage 'of every possible type of exchange between partners . . . to arrive at every type of marriage rule actually operating in living societies'.[93] This study treats marriage regulations as modalities of the laws of exchange, which is to say it treats their stipulations as 'signs' or 'values'.[94] Up to now, according to Levi-Strauss, only 'poets' have known that words are values, but henceforth the mathematical anthropologist will know so too.[95]

In Levi-Strauss's thinking, the 'mathematical' and the 'mythical' can be seen as the Janus-faces of the exchange at the heart of human culture. This centrality of contract and exchange, however, is often obscured by Levi-Strauss: structural analysis is sometimes developed from the perspective of contract and exchange which he calls 'communication'; [96] and sometimes from the perspective of 'the time and space modalities of the universal laws which make up the unconscious activity of the human mind'.[97] From the former perspective, exchange itself precedes any distinction between nature and culture which emerges in the

---

[90] Heidegger, *Die Frage nach dem Ding: Zu Kants Lehre von den transcendentalen Grundsätzen*, 1935–36, Tübingen, Niemeyer, 1975, trans. *What is a Thing?* W. B. Barton Jr and Vera Deutsch, Indiana, Regnery 1967, B.5 especially sec.6.

[91] For Cohen see chapter 2 above, p.41.

[92] Levi-Strauss, Postscript, *Structural Anthopology*, p.86.

[93] Levi-Strauss, 'Language and the Analysis of Social Laws', ibid., p.60.

[94] Ibid., p.61.

[95] Ibid.

[96] Postscript, ibid., p.83.

[97] 'Language and the Analysis of Social Laws', ibid., p.65.

move to value from the qualitative to the quantitative view.[98] From the latter perspective, Levi-Strauss seems to fall into the familiar transcendental problem: 'nature' is posited independently of any reconstruction of the cultural,[99] and 'nature' is a construct of culture, dependent on the cultural.[100]

Levi-Strauss's exposition of value links language, kinship and economy more closely and literally than Saussure. For Levi-Strauss's 'Copernican revolution', defined in terms borrowed from linguistics as the detection of 'the universal rules underlying the phonemic patterning of languages', and as 'an intervention of culture in nature, an artefact imposing rules upon the sound continuum', is to 'consist in interpreting society as a whole in terms of communication'.[101] The 'artefact' turns out not to be the imposition of culture on nature, but to be the constitutive rule or law prior to their opposition: 'communication' – by which is meant the law of exchange or contract. The endeavour of understanding society as communication 'is possible on three levels since the rules of kinship and marriage serve to insure the circulation of women between groups, just as economic rules serve to insure the circulation of goods and services, and linguistic rules the circulation of messages'.[102] These three forms of communication are three forms of exchange, and 'it is therefore legitimate to seek homologies between them . . . and the transformations which make the transition possible from one to another'.[103] Yet what has been justified is not three forms of exchange but the form of exchange itself: 'communication' – that trio identified as definitive of social custom or institution – 'rule', 'reciprocity' and 'synthesis'.[104]

Levi-Strauss presents kinship, language and economy as three different forms of this rule, but he neither justifies nor deduces them as distinct and different forms in the way that he justifies rule or 'communication' itself. The idea of kinship is introduced as a

[98] For example, see Levi-Strauss, 'Time Regained', *The Savage Mind*, pp.224–5.
[99] For example, see 'Totem and Caste', ibid., p.124.
[100] For example, 'This mediation between nature and culture . . .', 'Systems of transformation', ibid., p.91.
[101] Levi-Strauss, Postscript, *Structural Anthropology*, p.83.
[102] Ibid.
[103] Ibid.
[104] See above, pp.126–7.

solution to the 'universal' problem of nature and culture.[105] This imbalance between the deduction of 'rule' and the assumption of kinship leaves one unconvinced that there is an independent realm of kinship, unconvinced that there is such a thing as 'kinship', except as a juridical 'thing' derivable from the redescription of the question of value.

In Levi-Strauss's justification of synchrony, thought emerges most clearly as the problem which others claim to solve: as 'myth', unknowable but universal. Levi-Strauss takes the transcendental turn for the science of anthropology, making the 'mystical goals' of his pre-critical colleagues into the mythical object of his science, and making the usual claim for such a criticist deduction that 'a metaphysical view of history' is thereby eschewed.[106] 'Time Regained', the title of one of his pieces, captures the mathematical and mythical metaphysics of history which this scientist believes he has secured.[107]

[105] See Introduction, Levi-Strauss, *The Elementary Structures of Kinship*, 1944, trans. James Harle Bell *et al.*, London, Eyre and Spottiswoode, 1969.
[106] Levi-Strauss, Postscript, *Structural Anthropology*, p.84.
[107] See note 68 above.

8

Law and Writing: Derrida

Alluding to the twelve tables of Roman law, its earliest codification, Derrida calls his interpretation of Rousseau in *Of Grammatology* 'the twelfth table' to the eleven essays collected in *Writing and Difference*.[1] The first table of the twelve, 'Force and Signification', concludes with an evocation of Zarathustra's attempt to descend from the mountain, 'Behold, here is a new law table; but where are my brethren who will carry it with me to the valley and into the hearts of flesh?'[2] Dramatizing the German even further by making it a matter of 'engraving' the law into hearts of flesh, the French translation of the passage from Nietzsche acquires a spurious comparability with Rousseau's law engraved in the heart indicted in the *Grammatology*.[3] Derrida's attempt to replace old law tables with new ones turns on this contrast between the old law engraved in the heart discerned by Rousseau and the new law which Zarathustra is made to want to engrave in the heart.

In order to transform metaphysics into the question of writing Derrida reconstructs while claiming he is deconstructing and closes questions while claiming he is opening them. His identification of 'the question in which *we are posed*',[4] and of the new law

---

[1] Jacques Derrida, *Positions*, Paris, Les Éditions de Minuit, 1972, trans. Alan Bass, London, Athlone, 1981, p.12, tr.p.4; the contents of Derrida, *L'écriture et la différence*, Paris, Éditions du Seuil, 1967, are set out as a table in the English edition: *Writing and Difference*, trans. Alan Bass, London, Routledge and Kegan Paul, 1981.

[2] Derrida, *Writing and Difference*, p.49, tr.p.30.

[3] Nietzsche, *Thus Spoke Zarathustra, Werke*, II, Schlecta, Frankfurt am Main, Ullstein, 1979, p.446; and see *L'écriture et la différence*, p.49, where '*in fleischerne Herzen tragen*' is translated as '*à le graver dans les coeurs de chairs*'.

[4] Derrida, 'La parole soufflée', *Writing and Difference*, p.292, tr.p.194.

table which his rhetoric serves and which he would have us serve must themselves be questioned. It will not be a matter here of 'deconstructing' the 'metaphors' of Derrida's 'discourse', of 'delimiting' its 'fatal complicity' with 'the indestructible desire for full presence',[5] but of arguing that Derrida's 'posing of the net', his 'positions: scenes, acts, figures of dissemination', which he takes care to distinguish from 'positing' in Hegel, revives a Fichtean absolute act of positing.[6]

Derrida assures us that 'in no case is it a question of a *discourse against truth* or science', but he asks why 'when every ethical preoccupation has been suspended' Heidegger qualifies 'temporality as authentic – and proper (*eigentlich*) and inauthentic – or improper'.[7] Derrida's 'deconstruction' of '*the metaphysics of the proper*' (French: *propre*; German: *eigen*, 'own'; *eigentlich*, 'authentic'; *das Ereignis*, 'the event of appropriation')[8] becomes an ethical discourse against ethics, against the ego and its own.[9] If so far in this work the transcendental structure of an argument has been seen to provide a clue to its jurisprudential claims and implications, in this case the reverse is true: Derrida's *Naturrechtlehre*, his philosophy of right or jurisprudence, takes us to the heart of his strange affair with transcendental philosophy which he woos and disdains, coaxing it into and repelling it from his embrace.

The *Grammatology* is introduced as a critique of ancient and modern natural law: 'Arche-speech is writing because it is law. A natural law. The beginning word is understood, in the intimacy of self-presence [*de la présence à soi*] as the voice of the other and as commandment.'[10] Derrida argues that the idea of 'divine' and 'natural' law depends on a metaphorical use of human writing: sensible, finite writing is transformed into the medium in which divine law is revealed and serves as the perfect expression of God's

[5] Ibid., pp.291–2, tr.p.144.
[6] Derrida, *Positions*, pp.132–3, tr.p.96.
[7] Ibid., p.79, n.23, tr.p.105 n.32; and 'Ousia et Grammè', *Marges de la Philosophie*, pp.73–4, trans. in *Positions*, p.102–3 n.25.
[8] Derrida, *De la Grammatologie*, Paris, Les Éditions de Minuit, 1967, p.41, trans. *Of Grammatology*, Gayatri Chakravorty Spivak, Baltimore, The Johns Hopkins University Press, 1976, p.26.
[9] I refer to Max Stirner, *Der Einzige und sein Eigentum*, 1845, trans. *The Ego and his Own*, New York, Dover, 1973, discussed by Derrida in 'White Mythology' *Margins of Philosophy*, pp.257–8, n.9, tr.pp.216–17 n.3; see below, p.166.
[10] Derrida, *Of Grammatology*, p.30, tr.p.17.

breath and voice: His *Logos*.[11] This metaphor of God's writing then 'founds the "literal [*propre*]" meaning given to writing: a sign signifying itself signifying an eternal verity, eternally thought and spoken in the proximity of a present Logos'.[12] It is not a simple matter of transferring the 'literal' meaning of writing as human and sensible to a divine, supersensible and infinite realm. The point is that the initial establishing of what is 'natural' and 'literal' depends on the idea of writing: the literal or proper meaning of writing is 'metaphoricity itself'.[13] 'Metaphor' is the Greek equivalent of the Latin 'difference': Greek *phero* becomes Latin *fero*; Greek *meta* becomes Latin *dis*; hence 'writing is difference'.

Derrida's examples of this transferred use of writing to establish the 'natural' and the 'literal' range from the Talmud to Descartes and Rousseau. In spite of the 'profound differences' (*sic*) the 'same metaphor' is to be found in these treatments: the idea of natural law depends on the equation of voice and writing.[14] Attention to these profound differences reveals, however, the reconstruction of these traditions which Derrida proffers as 'deconstruction'.

For the idea established by the 'metaphor' of writing is that of law not nature. The idea of a 'natural' law was developed in explicit contrast to another kind of divine writing: the law revealed in the Scriptures versus the law discernible to the light of reason, or later, by the heart. The source of the transferred idea of natural law is a known connection between writing and law. The more literal writing of which the Bible is composed, the covenant and law (*Pentateuch*), the history of its unstable reception (*Writings* and *Prophets*), the Gospels and Apostolic Epistles of the *New Testament*, is contrasted with law apprehended directly by the light of reason: natural law. The writing of reason is contestable for it is not written in the same way as revealed law. Moreover the criterion of intelligibility, what it takes to read it, is known to be transferred.[15]

---

[11] Ibid., p.29, tr.p.17.
[12] Ibid., p.27, tr.p.15.
[13] Ibid.
[14] Ibid., pp.28–9, tr.p.16.
[15] See, for example, the controversies whether Jewish or Christian revelation deviates more from natural law discussed in Alexander Altmann, *Moses Mendelssohn: A Biographical Study*, London, Routledge and Kegan Paul, 1973, chapter 6.

The Rabbi, cited by Derrida from the Talmud, who says 'if all the seas were of ink, and all ponds planted with reeds, if the sky and the earth were parchments and if all human beings practised the art of writing – they would not exhaust the Torah I have learned, just as the Torah itself would not be diminished any more than is the sea by the water removed by a paint brush dipped in it' is celebrating the idea of law (Torah) as prior to any other.[16] He is not defining 'nature' by means of a dissembled writing for there is no idea of nature in general in what he says and no word for nature in Biblical Hebrew.[17] The Talmud cannot be used to trace the beginning of the history of natural law: for it concerns the learning or tradition – the passing on – of known law not the realization of law in general.

Nor can Rousseau be used to mark the modern form of natural law when 'the determination of absolute presence is constituted as self-presence, as subjectivity'[18] except by obscuring Rousseau's contention that natural law should be challenged in the name of natural right. Rousseau is quoted by Derrida in such a way that he appears to contrast decadent, dead, human writing with divine, living writing engraved in the heart, so that he appears to oppose the heart to the Bible and to reason: natural law '"is also engraved in the heart of men in ineffacable characters . . . There it cries to him."'[19] But it *cries* to him and this is the issue, for the cry is litigious – a troubled voice, an appeal: will it be answered or not? It is this new status of 'man' in relation to the law that Rousseau seeks to explore in all its precariousness. Derrida attributes new dogmas to Rousseau and turns the latter's questioning of authority into a naturalist eschatology (*sic*).

Derrida draws attention to the paradox of a self-presence in a medium which is distinct from that presence: the *logos* or voice present in writing. According to Derrida the metaphor of writing hides the trouble of the voice. This reconstruction of the contrary *logos/graphos* assimilates *logos* to voice, and obscures the historical

---

[16] Derrida, *Of Grammatology*, pp.27–8, tr.p.16.
[17] See, for example, H. Wheeler Robinson, *Inspiration and Revelation in the Old Testament*, Oxford, Clarendon Press, 1946, p.1ff.
[18] Derrida, *Of Grammatology*, p.29, tr.p.16.
[19] Ibid., p.29, tr.p.17.

connection of *logos* and law, written and unwritten.[20] Greek *logos*, 'word', from the verb *legein*, to say, corresponds to the Latin *legere*, 'to read' or 'declare', from which comes *lex*, the public declaration of *ius*, 'custom' or 'right'.[21] By focusing on the contrary *logos/graphos* Derrida reconstructs the 'history' of the metaphor of writing to produce a tale of misology and misarchism. This tale has the effect of denying that there has been a tradition which has known that the relation between *lex* and *ius*, law and custom, written law and spoken law, writing and voice, is the centre of all signification.[22]

Writing is defined transcendentally by Derrida as 'all that gives rise to inscription in general'; the *grapheme* is defined metacritically as the element which cannot be defined by the system of oppositions of metaphysics – the cybernetic *programme* is said to name such an element.[23] Furthermore just as Levi-Strauss argued that the distinction between history as dependent on written sources and anthropology as dependent on non-written sources betrays a deeper distinction between conscious and unconscious structures, so Derrida's concern with writing is equally a concern to deduce the possibility of history: 'History and knowledge, *istoria* and *episteme* have always been determined . . . as detours *for the purpose of* the reappropriation of presence.'[24]

While 'history' has meant the 'final repression of difference' Derrida makes 'only difference . . . from the outset and in all respects historical'. History as *differance* – spelt with an 'a' – is 'the movement of play that "produces" . . . these effects of difference'.[25] By writing a history of writing Derrida seeks to rewrite history: to 'produce the law' of the relationship of texts to their vanishing point;[26] to produce a 'history of the possibility of

---

[20] See the discussion of the *Logios Aner*, or 'Man of Words', in Gilbert Murray, *The Rise of the Greek Epic*, 1907, Oxford, Oxford University Press, 1934, p.94.

[21] See Peter Stein, *Regulae Iuris*, Edinburgh, Edinburgh University Press, 1966, pp.9–10.

[22] See ibid., 'Declared law and undeclared law', pp.3–25; see, too, 'Ius et le serment à Rome, and 'Le serment en Grèce', in Benveniste, *le vocabulaire des institutions indo-européennes* 2.

[23] Derrida, *Of Grammatology*, p.19, tr.p.9.

[24] Ibid., p.20, tr.p.10.

[25] Derrida, *Positions*, p.78 n.22, tr.p.104 n.31.

[26] Derrida, *Of Grammatology*, p.234, tr.p.163.

history which would no longer be an archeology, a philosophy of history or a history of philosophy'.[27] A grammatology, a science of writing, is a science of history. Writing is the condition of history not because history depends on written sources, but because writing is the precondition of that self-consciousness which becomes the object of an historical science: 'before being the object of a history – of an historical science – writing opens the field of history – of historical becoming. And the former (*Historie* in German) presupposes the latter (*Geschichte*).'[28]

Derrida, by his own admission, rewrites history; he produces a history, a writing, which does not dissemble that it is productive, which does not disguise itself as reappropriation. He makes 'writing' the unaddressable source of history so that it is not possible to consider the transformation of custom into writing which constitutes the beginning of that historical self-consciousness which becomes the reflection of historical science. For if writing 'opens up' history it is because historical reflection begins when the law is written, when sovereignty becomes addressable because the law has been formalized in an inscription.[29] This is exactly how Hegel connected the writing of prose and the origin of 'history': 'In our language the term history [*Geschichte*] unites the objective with the subjective sides, and denotes quite as much the *historia rerum gestarum* as the *res gestae* themselves; it is what has happened no less than the narration of what has happened.'[30] Derrida cites this passage but not Hegel's succeeding explanation for this dual meaning: 'it is the state which first presents subject-matter that is not only adapted to the prose of history but involves the production of such history in the very progress of its own being.'[31] Derrida's equation of writing and history, on the contrary, makes it impossible to raise the question of sovereignty or to question historical self-consciousness except by accusing it of bad faith when it presents its work as immediate and full presence

---

[27] Ibid., p.43, tr.p.28.

[28] Ibid., p.43, tr.p.27.

[29] See Stein, *Regulae Iuris*, p.21.

[30] Hegel, *The Philosophy of History, Theorie Werkausgabe*, 12, Frankfurt am Main, Suhrkamp, 1973, p.83, trans. J. Sibree, New York, Dover, 1956, p.60, amended.

[31] Derrida, 'Violence and Metaphysics', *Writing and Difference*, p.168, tr.p.114; Hegel, *The Philosophy of History*, p.83, tr.p.61, amended.

in the medium of writing. The definition of writing as 'all that gives rise to inscription in general' implies a priori that writing is pre-scription: that is prescribes or commends and that it is the pre-condition of inscription. In this way Derrida closes the question of form itself.

By construing and reconstructing Rousseau's and Levi-Strauss's account of writing as the indicator of their theory of law Derrida reduces their thought to its utopian and anarchist residue. Rousseau's *Essay on the Origin of Languages* is the centre of discussion in the *Grammatology*, but the discussion of language in the first part of Rousseau's *Second Discourse* on the origin of inequality is not set in the context to which it belongs: the exposition in the second part of the discourse of the antinomical relation of law and inequality. Rousseau argues that law relieves *and* reinforces inequality: 'for the flaws which make social institutions necessary are the same as make abuse of them unavoidable.'[32] Derrida justifies what he himself calls an 'ex-orbitant' choice of text, but his choice is truly exorbitant: it permits him to cite Rousseau's remark 'Writing is the origin of inequality', and to reserve for himself all insight into the antinomy of law.[33] In the midst of the discussion of Levi-Strauss he cautions, 'the access to writing is the constitution of a free subject in the violent movement of its own effacement and its own bondage. A movement unthinkable within the classical concepts of ethics, psychology, political philosophy and metaphysics.'[34]

Those classical concepts forged by Kant in his transformation of Rousseau's thought into the three critiques centre on the antinomy of law. Yet Derrida claims it as his discovery and attributes 'an eschatology of the *propre* (*propre, proprius*, self-proximity, self-presence, own-ness)' to everyone else.[35] The final intention of the *Grammatology* is 'to make enigmatic what one thinks one under-stands by the words "proximity", "immediacy", "presence" (the proximate, [*proche*], the own [*propre*], and the pre of presence).'[36]

---

[32] Rousseau, 'A Discourse on the Origin of Inequality', *The Social Contract and Other Discourses*, trans. G. D. H. Cole, London, Dent, 1973, p.99.
[33] Derrida, *Of Grammatology*, p.419, tr.p.297.
[34] Ibid., pp.192–3, tr.p.132.
[35] Ibid., pp.156–7, tr.p.107.
[36] Ibid., p.103, tr.p.70.

Derrida succeeds instead in making the antinomy of law an enigma; for self-reference becomes eschatological and unknowable: 'why *subjects*? Why should writing be another name for the constitution of *subjects* and, so to speak, of *constitution* itself? of a subject, that is to say of an individual held responsible [*tenu de répondre*] (for) himself in front of a law and by the same token subject to that law?'[37]

The enigma or trace is 'the opening of the first exteriority in general, the enigmatic relationship of the living to its other and of an inside to an outside: spacing'. Arche-writing, 'at first the possibility of the spoken word, then of the "*graphie*" in the narrow sense, the birthplace of "usurpation", denounced from Plato to Saussure . . .'[38] takes the place of Kant's 'usurpatory concept of freedom', which gives rise to the *quaestio quid juris*, and establishes the space of the critical court but which prevents the case from ever being closed. Derrida argues that this usurpatory trace is not the Event of appropriation, *das Ereignis*, since Heidegger's 'Being', although it is not a concept nor is it the word 'being', it is still the voice *of* Being: 'the logos *of* being'.[39] The trace is referred instead to Nietzsche's 'originary' writing, which is said to refuse the *Logos* as truth.[40] *Differance* has an '*unheard of* sense'; it is not a voice, but 'an economic concept designating the production of differing/deferring'.[41] Nietzsche and Heidegger must be saved from this reading which simplifies the question of usurpation and is vulnerable to the critique to be found in Nietzsche and in Heidegger of such a Fichtean discourse of positing and production.

The Hegelian critique of positing would offer the most serious challenge to Derrida's *differance* as production; and by concluding his opening chapter with an attempted rebuttal of Hegel, Derrida seems to acknowledge this. Hegel is said to have been 'caught up in this game' of deconstructing from the inside and yet to have debased writing as exteriorization, as 'the contrary of interiorrizing memory . . . that opens up the history of the spirit'.[42]

[37] Ibid., p.399, tr.p.281.
[38] Ibid., p.103, tr.p.70.
[39] Ibid., p.33, tr.p.20.
[40] Ibid., p.32, tr.p.19.
[41] Ibid., p.38, tr.p.23.
[42] Ibid., p.39, tr.p.24.

Hegel's absolute knowledge is said to be 'the effacement of writing in the logos, the retrieval of the trace in parousia, the reappropriation of presence'.[43] This assessment restates in the terminology of the grapheme the standard critique of Hegel: that all externalization is alienation to be reappropriated by the Absolute. Similarly Derrida's acknowledgement that 'within this horizon . . . Hegel is *also* the thinker of irreducible difference', and that 'all, that is, except [his] eschatology, may be reread as a meditation on writing', restates the standard distinction made between the radicality of Hegel's method and the conservation of his system.[44]

The familiarity of Derrida's equivocation regarding Hegel is instructive since it reveals his own dilemma. For *differance*, defined as 'productive', is either the old transcendental enigma, 'scenes', 'acts', renamed 'signification' or 'discourse', but remaining as empty, abstract and unknowable as the law in Kant and Fichte; or, if it is knowable, *differance* must fall into some kind of presence – the only knowability acknowledged and spurned by Derrida. These alternatives could be avoided by the speculative exposition of *differance* as 'the unity and difference of identity and difference'.[45] But Derrida's eschatological reading of Hegel rules this out and produces instead a philosophy of history which oscillates between 'the enigma' and 'the fact' of self-consciousness as misappropriation. The history of reflection becomes merely the effect of a production, and a '*trick of writing* . . . through much unperceived mediation, must carry the entire burden of our question, a question that I shall provisionally call historical [*historiale*].'[46]

In the second chapter of the *Grammatology* Saussure's reflections on language seem to serve as the Kant to Derrida's Humboldt. Saussure, it is argued, places phonetic writing outside the concept of language, yet writing is implicit in his distinction between the signifier and the signified which establishes the idea of the sign:[47]

---

[43] Ibid., p.41, tr.p.26.
[44] Ibid.
[45] I take this formal statement from Hegel's *Encyclopaedia of the Philosophical Sciences*, Part I *Logic*, sec.21 (Addition).
[46] Derrida, *Of Grammatology*, p.38, tr.p.24.
[47] Ibid., p.96f., tr.p.30f.

'The very idea of institution – hence of the arbitrariness of the sign – is unthinkable before the possibility of writing and outside of its horizon.'[48] Saussure's attempt to maintain the distinction between the spoken language as primary and pure versus writing as derivative, secondary and external, obscures the way his thinking depends on the notion of institution or positing. However, the thesis of the arbitrariness of the sign hints at this 'deconstruction of the transcendental signified.'[49]

Transcendental justification is said to become the 'game of the world' once the absence of the transcendental signified is recognized.[50] 'Game', however, still implies rules and players, while the critical philosophy was originally founded on the absence of a transcendental signified – that was why it was called the *critical* philosophy. Derrida says that he calls the rules of the game 'writing' only because the word 'writing' 'essentially communicates with the vulgar concept of writing'.[51] He is using 'writing' metaphorically, but the metaphor is justified as *differance* itself: as the way of naming the law by which things are defined without implying any literalness at the source, as the occurrence of signification as such. But when we think of the law as written we are not just thinking metaphorically, transferring a literal meaning: a written law is one which is known because its definition specifies what falls under and what is excluded from its range of application. By using the word 'writing' Derrida reduces the meaning of law to differentiation as such and makes it enigmatic.

'Arche-writing' is not to be understood as the a priori condition of possibility but as 'movement of difference',[52] a '*pure* movement which produces difference'.[53] '*Differance* is therefore the formation of form. But it is *on the other hand* the being-imprinted of the imprint.'[54] This formulation corresponds, of course, to Humboldt's inner form, *typos*, the active principle which replaces Kant's a priori condition of possibility.[55] But Derrida disassociates

[48] Ibid., p.65, tr.p.44.
[49] Ibid., p.71, tr.p.49.
[50] Ibid., p.73, tr.p.50.
[51] Ibid., p.83, tr.p.56.
[52] Ibid., p.88, tr.p.60.
[53] Ibid., p.92, tr.p.62, emphasis in original.
[54] Ibid., p.92, tr.p.63.
[55] See chapter 7 above, p.112 and note 7.

himself from any metaphysics of virtuality or *dynamis*, and from Humboldt's distinction between *ergon* and *energeia*.[56] For this is his way of playing the 'game of the world': to put forward and then to retract the classic transcendental and metacritical moves. If 'Differance is articulation', then the *articulans* cannot itself be articulated, nor can it be articulate.[57] This 'unnameable movement of difference itself, that I have strategically nicknamed trace . . . Articulating the living upon the nonliving in general, origin of all repetition, origin of ideality . . . is not more real than ideal, not more intelligible than sensible, not more a transparent significa- tion than an opaque energy and *no concept of metaphysics* can describe it.[58] 'A form is imposed' but no 'classical model of causality' is thought. This game, this philosophical promiscuity, is apparently licenced by the admission that 'deconstruction always in a certain way falls prey to its own work'.[59]

In the *Grammatology* this licence is employed to undermine not metaphysics, but political and social theory. The work of Rous- seau and of Levi-Strauss is reconstructed so that the account of law is reduced to the discussion of writing. As a result, Rousseau is presented as a utopian, Levi-Strauss as an anarchist; both as mesmerized by the promise of an ideal speech-situation. Only Derrida knows

> There is no ethics without the presence *of the other* but also, and consequently, without absence, dissimulation, detour, differance, writing. The arche-writing is the origin of morality as of immorality. The non-ethical opening of ethics. A violent opening. As in the case of the vulgar concept of writing, the ethical instance of violence must be rigorously suspended in order to repeat the genealogy of morals.[60]

Derrida argues that 'writing' is the metacritical dimension of the 'social', which is defined instead by Levi-Strauss as the system of classification according to proper names: for a proper name implies 'the presence of a unique being' but functions 'within a

---

[56] Derrida, *Of Grammatology*, pp.265–6,439, tr.pp.187,311.
[57] Ibid., p.96, tr.p.66.
[58] Ibid., p.142,95, tr.pp.93,65, emphasis in original.
[59] Ibid., pp.39,410, tr.pp.24,290.
[60] Ibid., p.202, tr.pp.139–40.

classification and therefore within a system of differences.'[61] Proper names reveal the antinomy of law: 'proper' implies unique; 'name' implies a contrivance; 'when within *consciousness*, the name *is called* proper, it is already classified and is obliterated in *being named*. It is already no more that a *so-called* proper name.'[62] This exposition of naming is designed to show that Levi-Strauss's interest in the taboo on revealing proper names is misconceived, for, according to Derrida, Levi-Strauss's encounter with the young girls reported in *Tristes Tropiques* merely violates their classificatory system and provokes a revelation of the 'arche-violence' which opens and sustains it.[63]

Against Levi-Strauss Derrida argues that there can be no 'society without writing' because 'all societies capable of producing, that is to say of obliterating, their proper names, and of bringing classificatory differences into play, practice writing in general'.[64] All societies, that is, involve 'the death of absolutely proper naming, requiring in a language the other as pure other . . .'[65] All societies consist of three levels of 'violence': the first or originary naming; the second, reparative and protective, instituting moral and social consciousness and hiding the first; the third, the violence of reflection, the level of individual and empirical consciousness.[66]

If 'writing' is used in the sense of 'writing in general' then Levi-Strauss is more sensitive to it than Derrida: for in *Tristes Tropiques* the *graphein* is discerned by him in body-painting, in the lay-out of villages, in effect, wherever and however space is socially divided.[67] The real issue is revealed by Derrida's insistent use of 'violence' for the origin. 'Violence' stands for Derrida's middle voice; it is used to avoid the implication that politics and society are constituted by their members because that would imply the creativity of voices addressing each other in the first and second person when the first and second person only appear at the second,

[61] Ibid., p.159, tr.p.109.
[62] Ibid., p.161, tr.p.109.
[63] Ibid., pp.163–7, tr.pp.111–14.
[64] Ibid., p.161, tr.p.109.
[65] Ibid., p.162, tr.p.110.
[66] Ibid., pp.164–5, tr.p.112.
[67] Levi-Strauss, *Tristes Tropiques*, 1955, trans. John and Doreen Weightman, 1973, Harmondsworth, Penguin, 1976.

moral level. Hence 'violence' is used impersonally and non-relationally. In his equation of the 'social' and 'moral' Derrida reveals a further issue: 'From the moment that the proper name is erased in a system, there is writing, there is a subject . . . that is to say . . . from the first dawn of language.'[68] For Derrida the 'subject' is identical with the 'social' or 'moral'. This equation prevents him from distinguishing between different epochs: the social or ethical is said to be always moral, 'recognizing in a language the other as pure other'. Yet in some languages the 'other' is not recognized as 'pure other' but as *impure* other, as belonging to God, to His Holiness, to His name; this is the difference between communities where proper names are taboo and societies which are 'moral'. It is the deconstructionist not the anthropologist whose lament over law results in the universal imposition of an historically-specific distinction between the archetypical, the moral and the reflective levels of society.[69]

This spurious generalization is justified in principle when Derrida outlines the 'social': 'as soon as a society begins to live as a society, that is to say from the origin of life in general, when, at very heterogenous levels of organization and complexity, it is possible to *defer presence*, that is to say *expense* or consumption, and to organize production, that is to say *reserve* in general'.[70] This metaphorical use of economic terms to express *differance* as the defining of things as comparable, equal and unequal, so that resources may be organized and as that which gives rise to signification, captures the idea of contract. 'Writing' is Derrida's name for the social contract as set out in the *obiter dictum* cited here.

Levi-Strauss, on the other hand, is said to equate power and oppression, to see writing solely as constraint and enslavement, and not as liberation. His tone is said to be 'anarchic' for he implies that all political power is unjust, and forgets 'the other thesis, according to which the generality of the law is on the contrary the condition of liberty in the city'.[71] Levi-Strauss's 'Writing Lesson' in *Tristes Tropiques* is not the simple lament which Derrida reads it as being: it is an attempt to witness the transition from one form of

---

[68] Derrida, *Of Grammatology*, p.159, tr.p.108.
[69] Ibid., pp.167, tr.p.114.
[70] Ibid., p.190, tr.pp.130–31.
[71] Ibid., p.191, tr.p.131.

subjectivity to another, to witness an event when the law appears because it is changing.[72] Levi-Strauss's attention is strategic not innocent: he seeks to draw our attention to the precondition of a new form of subjective consciousness, that mix of freedom and bondage which Derrida claims Levi-Strauss does not know.

However, Derrida shifts his stricture on Levi-Strauss: 'I do not profess that writing may not and does not in fact play this role [of propaganda in the service of the state], but from that to attribute to writing the specificity of this role and to conclude that speech is exempt from it is an abyss one must not leap over so lightly.'[73] Levi-Strauss is now said merely to be wrong to consider writing more intrinsically corrupt than speech, more modifiable at will, and hence destabilizing: 'Which implies that oral formulae are not modifiable, not more modifiable at will than written formulae.'[74] The question, however, is not modifiability but the will: non-written law is known to be more modifiable than written law, but every modification does not necessarily raise the question of whose will is in operation, of sovereignty, as it does once the law is written.[75]

This examination of the 'deconstruction' of aspects of the work of Levi-Strauss proves how unjustifiable it is to take every empirical encounter with writing as evidence for the a priori; how opening 'the question of the γραφειν' occludes the question of law and of legal change.

Unlike Levi-Strauss Rousseau is said to have 'recognized this power which, inaugurating speech, dislocates the subject that it constructs', but, nevertheless, is 'more pressed to exorcise it than to assume its necessity'.[76] The 'economy of differance', on the other hand, 'does not resist appropriation, it does not impose an exterior limit upon it. *Differance* began by broaching [*par entamer*] alienation and it ends it by leaving reappropriation breached [*entamée*]'.[77] The litigious implication of the English word

---

[72] Ibid., p.192, tr.p.132.

[73] Ibid., p.194, tr.p.133.

[74] Ibid., p.193, tr.pp.132–3.

[75] See, for example, Peter Brown, 'Society and the Supernatural: A Medieval Change', in *Society and the Holy in Late Antiquity*, London, Faber and Faber, 1982, pp.302–32.

[76] Derrida, *Of Grammatology*, p.204, tr.p.141.

[77] Ibid., p.206, tr.p.143.

'breach', a broken state or gap in a fortification, hence breaking a contract or neglecting the privileges or rights of another, brings out how the 'economy' of *differance* depends on legal ideas, on concepts the literal meaning of which is metaphorical: which institute the range of relevance, that is, '*differance*'.

Rousseau, Derrida argues, can only see writing as evil, exterior to innocent and good nature;[78] he cannot see 'that this alteration does not simply happen to the self, that it is the self's very origin'.[79] Nature, said to be defined by Rousseau as 'absolute presence . . . [has] never existed; . . . what opens meaning and language is writing as the disappearance of natural presence'.[80] The opposition in Rousseau of pity, the law of the heart, to writing, which is 'without pity', amounts to an insinuation of a law of nature which repudiates the nature of law: 'The order of pity "takes the place of law", it supplements law, that is to say, instituted law.'[81] Rousseau's natural law, the 'natural condition of language', implies dispersion not presence, for language, like nature, implies order in space: 'Dispersion, as the law of spacing, is therefore at once pure nature, the principle of society's life and the principle of society's death.'[82] Rousseau's thought is said to be based on the 'juridical fiction' of 'pure nature'; within this concept of nature 'proximity is a distancing', 'the dispersion that is natural: space itself'.[83]

Reading Rousseau in this way as a guardian of natural law, Derrida obscures Rousseau's own strategy of transforming natural law into natural right which consisted in changing the meaning of 'God', 'law' and 'nature'. The 'God' who inscribes the law in our hearts rather than in the light of reason is humanity. The opposition of natural law to positive law is Rousseau's way of telling us that law is constituted: written and human. This opposition substitutes for the traditional opposition of law revealed in the Scriptures versus law evident to the light of reason: a contrast of two divine sources. Rousseau's interest lies in the

---

[78] Ibid., pp.208–9, tr.p.145.
[79] Ibid., p.221, tr.p.153.
[80] Ibid., p.228, tr.p.159.
[81] Ibid., p.257, tr.p.173.
[82] Ibid., p.388, tr.p.274.
[83] Ibid., p.331, tr.p.232.

antinomy which arises when law based on human authority perpetuates human inequality, for he knew the question of representation – in the political sense – to be the unresolvable problem of politics, the permanent condition of impermanence, the inevitable clash of particular and general will.[84]

Derrida justifies his 'exorbitant' choice of Rousseau's *Essay on the Origin of Languages*, for his discussion on the grounds that it offers a perspective on the age of logocentrism.[85] In fact this text becomes the pre-text for delineating a 'closed field of metaphysics' in which the rest of Rousseau's *oeuvre* and the history of subsequent attempts to rethink Rousseau's antinomies are to be inscribed. Rousseau's 'refusal of representation' – in politics, in the theatre, in writing – his desire for 'the order of pure law, which gives back to the people their liberty and to presence its sovereignty'[86] are seen as the *Urtext* of philosophical activity itself which supplements and compensates for primeval loss of presence by propagating the illusion of absence mastered.

The rhetorical question which Derrida addresses specifically to Condillac but intends to be taken generally begs for a metaphorical answer instead of the literal one: 'Why should writing be another name for the constitution of *subjects* and so to speak of constitution itself? of a subject, that is to say of an individual held responsible (for) himself in front of a law and by the same token subject to that law?'[87] The literal answer to this question is that constitutions are written. We know that what is formalized by being written excludes as well as includes; we know that individuals are inscribed in written law by the fiction of juridical personality, of the subject as active and passive, 'subject of' and 'subjected to'; and we know too that this fictional status may be complemented by a further fiction which presents the first fiction or function as a substance, a 'bearer of attributes'.

According to Derrida 'writing' creates these fictions, and, qua philosophy, writing as *episteme* seeks to restore the substance

---

[84] For a non-utopian reading of the problem of politics in Rousseau, see Émile Durkheim, 'Rousseau's *Social Contract*', in *Montesquieu and Rousseau*, 1892 and c.1901, trans. Michigan, Ann Arbor, 1965.

[85] Derrida, *Of Grammatology*, p.231, tr.p.161.

[86] Ibid., p.421, tr.p.298.

[87] Ibid., p.399, tr.p.281.

excluded by them: 'Philosophy is, within writing, nothing but this movement of writing as effacement of the signifier and the desire of presence restored, of being, signified in its brilliance and glory'.[88] This 'horizon of an infinite restitution of presence', wherever it occurs, 'within the practical order' or 'the graphic order' applies equally to Rousseau's providentialist 'finitism' as to Hegel's infinite teleology.[89] Derrida attributes a 'false reconciliation' to Hegel just as he does to Rousseau, deliberately overlooking the differences between them, and thereby also overlooking the way in which concepts change when they fail to reconcile irreconciliables. It is Derrida who makes history into the history – that is, the writing – of philosophy in a way alien to Hegel's thinking.

History for Derrida becomes the repetitive story of a 'closed field of metaphysics' which he himself has closed, and within which his 'indefinite [*sic*] exchange of "Rousseauist" and "Hegelian" positions (one might take other examples) obeys the laws inscribed within all the concepts that [he has] just recalled. It is possible to formalize these laws and indeed they are formalized.'[90] But for Hegel the philosophy of history is the history of the way law has been formalized, and he writes it in a way which eschews any philosophical ambition to formalize the law again: for the writing of law, that is, the history of the state, ancient and modern, can only be known by a writing that acknowledges its common origin with the state but does not continue to collude with the law.

Derrida makes a grave mistake when he says 'Hegel's formula must be taken literally: history is nothing but the history of philosophy, absolute knowledge is fulfilled'.[91] For a thinker who denies that meaning is literal this exception is particularly interesting since Hegel's meaning cannot be assimilated to the opposition of literal/metaphorical; the 'is' in Hegel is always speculative: it does not assert abstract identity but both identity and non-identity, which in the case of history and philosophy expresses the lack of connection between the two kinds of writing so that

---

[88] Ibid., p.405, tr.p.286.
[89] Ibid., pp.421–2, tr.p.298.
[90] Ibid., p.422, tr.p.299.
[91] Ibid., p.405, tr.p.286.

regional histories may be known too. It is Derrida who make all
history into the history of philosophy by attributing an abstract
identity to Hegel and reserving to himself that comprehension of
identity and non-identity, 'supplementarity', which he calls *differance* and says may be formalized.

Derrida indicts logocentrism in general by reference to Rousseau's longing for an 'order of pure law', presenting the latter's
critique of writing as resistance to the insinuation of 'usurpation
into the body of society'.[92] Yet it was Rousseau who changed
jurisprudence into social theory by founding a paradoxical concept
of the social in the *Second Discourse* on the simultaneous relieving
and reinforcing of inequality, on 'usurpation' in the literal sense.
This explains why Derrida writes the 'eschatology of the proper'
around Rousseau: for all that grammatology does is change the
signs, or as Derrida puts it, grammatology gives up the attempt to
'exorcise' the antinomy 'recognized' by Rousseau 'which, inaugurating speech, dislocates the subject that it constructs'.[93] Having
shown the 'interiority of exteriority which amounts to annulling
the ethical qualification and to thinking of writing beyond good
and evil' *differance* moves beyond good and evil.[94]

To argue that Derrida 'changes the signs' is not to argue that he
relapses into the classical metaphysical oppositions: it is to criticize
him for the way he tries to go beyond them. For to go beyond
good and evil in this grammatological way leaves good and evil,
or the antinomy of law, exactly where he finds it: in Rousseau's
mind. Derrida admits 'the impossibility of formulating the
movement of supplementarity within the classical logos', yet 'the
designation of that movement must borrow its resources from the
logic it deconstructs'.[95]

That Derrida has frozen history is confirmed by his proposal for
'a new transcendental aesthetic', for a rewriting of the forms of
intuition which would incorporate causality into the exposition of
space and time and which would no longer grant priority to time
as the 'inner sense'. 'When I say a form is imposed, I obviously do
not think of any classical model of causality . . . If the time–space

---

[92] Ibid., p.427, tr.p.302.
[93] Ibid., p.209, tr.p.141.
[94] Ibid., p.442, tr.p.314.
[95] Ibid., p.443, tr.p.314.

that we inhabit is a priori the time–space of the trace, there is neither pure activity nor pure passivity'. The new transcendental aesthetic 'must itself be guided not only by mathematical idealities but by the possibility of inscription in general, not befalling an already constituted space as a contingent accident but *producing* the spaciality of space' – emphasis added.[96] This need for causality in the transcendental aesthetic recalls the similar need in Schopenhauer and in Cohen who both rewrote the transcendental aesthetic around the idea of causality: the principle of sufficient reason in Schopenhauer, the typic of practical reason in Cohen.[97] But to incorporate causality into the aesthetic, as 'the unnameable trace', merely erects a metaphor at the source, and changes the mood, as it were, from lamentation to celebration of the unknowable. It takes the difference or non-identity implied by law as evidence of an unknowable and unnameable transfer, 'signification', instead of recognizing difference not as metaphor in general, but as evidence of a literal transfer effected by a specific written law that self-evidently declares that it excludes when it differentiates and legislates.

To replace concept and intuition by a blind but absolute causality at best replaces individual morality by an ethic of compassion and pity. Nietzsche, Derrida's vaunted mentor, showed how Schopenhauer's philosophy of the will regrounds a Rousseauian ethic of pity, how both Rousseau and Schopenhauer reinforce the decadence which they deplored.[98] Derrida's move beyond good and evil 'annuls the ethical' in the name of a 'transcendental aesthetic' in a spirit contrary to Nietzsche's genealogy of morals, contrary, that is, to what Nietzsche knew about law.

The 'trace', comparable with the 'cybernetic programme', recalls the neo-Kantian matheme: like Deleuze's *pur spatium*, it is no more inner than outer, no more temporal than spatial.[99] The

---

[96] Ibid., p.410, tr.p.290.

[97] See above, chapter 2, pp.42–3.

[98] See, for example, Nietzsche, on Schopenhauer, *The Gay Science, Werke*, II, trans. Walter Kaufmann, New York, Vintage, 1979, secs 99,127,346,357,370; on Rousseau, *Daybreak Thoughts on the Prejudices of Morality, Werke*, II trans. R.J. Hollingdale, Cambridge, Cambridge University Press, 1982, secs 163,459; on Rousseau and Schopenhauer, *Human all too Human*, Werke, I, sec.463.

[99] Derrida, *Of Grammatology*, p.19, tr.p.9.

connection in Derrida's thinking with this brand of neo-Kantianism emerges most clearly in his commentaries on Husserl which
are his least combative works.[100] In the essay '"Genesis and
Structure" and Phenomenology' the structural and genetic aspects
of Husserl's analysis of meaning are shown to share a common
concern with validity and with the 'original productivity' which
validity implies.[101] Husserl's geneticism is not psychological but
transcendental, constitutive, and intentional, 'simultaneously productive and revelatory, active and passive'.[102] Genesis in Husserl
means 'structural a priori'.[103]

Husserl's essay on the origin of geometry, to which Derrida has
written an introduction for the French edition, is a classic piece of
neo-Kantianism in the Marburg style: it seeks to justify an
exemplary or regional science not knowledge as such; it drops the
distinction between appearances and things in themselves; it turns
the question of transcendental possibility into a delineation of a
productive origin; and it defines the a priori metacritically as
'culture' or 'history'. 'Culture' or 'history' becomes the name for
the source of signification which repeatedly creates or posits its
idealities or validities: this historical beginning is defined as 'origin
in an accomplishment, first as a project and then as a successful
execution'.[104] The ideal-object which arises from this production
constitutes a 'tradition', a form of generality, of unconditioned
validity.[105] We understand this 'production' as grounding objective validity and not as merely psychological genesis by virtue of
the medium of this objectivity and ideality: writing. Writing

---

[100] Derrida, *Husserl: L'Origine de la geométrie, Traduction et introduction*, 1962,
Paris, Presses Universitaires de France, 1974, trans. *Edmund Husserl's Origin of
Geometry: An Introduction*, John P. Leavey, Stony Brook, New York,
Nicholas Hays, 1978; *La Voix et le phénomène: Introduction au problème du signe
dans la phénoménologie de Husserl*, 1967, Paris, Presses Universitaires de France,
1976 trans. *Speech and Phenomena and Other Essays on Husserl's Theory of Signs*,
David B. Allison, Evanston, Northwestern University Press, 1973.
[101] Derrida, *Writing and Difference*, p.231, tr.p.156.
[102] Ibid., p.235, tr.p.158.
[103] Ibid., p.231, tr.p.156.
[104] Husserl, 'The Origin of Geometry', 1936, Appendix III in *Husserliana*, VI,
Walter Biemel (ed.), The Hague, Nijhoff, 1962, p.367, trans. Appendix VI in
The Crisis of the European Sciences and Transcendental Phenomenology, David
Carr, Evanston, Northwestern University Press, 1970, p.356.
[105] Ibid., pp.365–6, tr.p.354–5.

permits that reactivation of self-evidence which characterizes a sphere of validity.[106]

This piece provides Husserl's sublation of the dichotomy which he had elaborated twenty years earlier in *Philosophy as a Rigorous Science* between natural and historical sciences.[107] For he now shows that validity is intrinsically historical: 'culture' is consciousness of historicality, that is, of validity, not because it observes a causality external to it, a succession of historical configurations, but because it 'involves the "coconsciousness" that it is something constructed through human activity'.[108] This self-evidence is the 'universal a priori of history', 'the initial movement of the existence and the interweaving of original formations and sedimentations of meaning'.[109] The origin of geometry is historical – where 'history' is writing or validity. Derrida comments that the eternal *apeiron*, promised in 1916, becomes the possibility of history itself.[110]

Derrida's strategy with Husserl is to change the signs: to take the idea of origin or unity as *differance*. The role of the origin in Marburg neo-Kantianism was always that of differentiation: it results from that revision of the transcendental turn which resolves the Kantian trinity – of appearances, things in themselves and the transcendental unity of apperception – into the productive *matheme*.

Derrida calls Husserl's *Origin of Geometry* a 'phenomenological history', and points out that Husserlian intuition of ideal objects of mathematics is 'absolutely constitutive and creative' in a way which is fundamentally different from Kantian constitution which concerns the 'history of an operation not of a founding'.[111] Derrida picks up the *quaestio quid juris* at the heart of Husserl's text: 'Writing, as the place of absolutely permanent ideal objectivities and therefore of absolute Objectivity', but he questions the implication that writing achieves the immediate and pure connection of

---

[106] Ibid., pp.370–72, tr.pp.359–61.
[107] See chapter 3 above, p.53.
[108] Husserl, 'The Origin of Geometry', p.379, tr.p.370: 'coconsciousness' '*sie . . . "mitbewuβt" ist*'.
[109] Ibid., p.380, tr.p.371.
[110] Derrida, *Edmund Husserl's Origin of Geometry*, p.169 n.1, tr.p.151 n.184.
[111] Ibid., p.23, tr.pp.40,41.

one Living Present to another, 'pure transcendental historicity'. Husserl's idea of writing reinforces the idea of history as what is conscious and known, as opposed to the idea of history as 'the entombment of lost intentions', and cannot understand intentionality as residual, as 'essential juridical failure'.[112]

In spite of this serious criticism of Husserl Derrida insists that we participate in the *'propaedeutic de jure'*.[113] The equation of ideal-meaning with history means that it is no longer necessary to perform a phenomenological reduction, for 'tradition' already means a reduction to ideal-sense. 'Traditionality is what circulates from one [*Logos*] to the other [*Telos*], illuminating one by the other in a movement wherein consciousness discovers its path in an indefinite reduction . . .'[114] Only phenomenology makes the *'de jure'*, that is, the *quaestio quid juris*, into the question of the possibility of the *'de facti'*, that is, the *quaestio quid facti*, by equating validity with the medium of writing in order to develop a notion of tradition which cuts across the conventional distinction between them.

On this new basis, phenomenology, first, 'exhausts . . . the question of historicity's sense and of historicity as sense' – the transcendental possibility of history, that is, of fact – and secondly, it opens up the questions '*Is there, and why is there any historical factuality?*' – the 'why' emerging from the possible non-being of historical factuality implied by the first question.[115] This is how Derrida wants to pose the question of Being: 'knowing what [ideal-]sense is as historicity I can clearly ask myself why there would be any history rather than nothing.'[116] In this way the 'question of the origin of Being as History', of 'factuality', may be apprehended on the one hand, without lapsing into metaphysics, and, on the other hand, without lapsing into empiricism.

In Kant, however, the *quaestio quid juris* is distinguished from the *quaestio quid facti* because a usurpation is suspected: 'the usurpatory concept' of freedom, and the critical deduction establishes the different procedures by which theoretical and practical

---

[112] Ibid., p.85, tr.p.88.
[113] Ibid., p.167, tr.p.150.
[114] Ibid., pp.165–6, tr.p.149.
[115] Ibid., p.167, tr.p.150, Derrida's emphasis.
[116] Ibid., p.168, tr.p.151.

claims may be justified. Heidegger understands the usurpation which leads to the crisis of critical self-justification as the Event of appropriation, *das Ereignis*. By making *das Ereignis* the way into the history of Being Heidegger makes it possible to pinpoint the historical specificity of authenticity, *Eigentlichkeit*, and its connection with modern subjectivity and morality. Derrida relegates all use of such ethical cognates to the 'eschatology of the proper' and prefers to draw the authority for his philosophical discourse from Husserl's phenomenology.[117]

> The impossibility of resting in the simple maintenance [nowness] of a Living Present, the sole and absolutely absolute origin of the De Facto *and* the De Jure, of Being *and* Sense, but always other in its self-identity; the inability to live in the innocent individedness [*indivision*] of the primordial Absolute because the Absolute is *present* only in being *deferrred-delayed* [*différant*] without respite, this impotence and this impossibility are given in a primordial and pure consciousness of Difference. Such a *consciousness*, with its strange style of unity, must be able to be restored to its own light. Without such a consciousness, without its proper dehiscence, nothing would appear.[118]

This pure consciousness is reclaimed here by changing the signs on Husserl's 'exemplary' statement of phenomenology in the *Origin of Geometry*.[119] Derrida grants a 'juridical priority' to phenomenology because it opens up history and being without encountering any usurpation, any appropriation, or any concept of freedom.[120] Husserl's Absolute is 'the Absolute *of* intentional historicity'[121] where the insistent 'of' is neither subjective nor objective, but 'the Absolute of *genetivity* itself as the pure possibility of a genetic relation . . .'[122] In this way Derrida returns the genealogy of morals to the genealogy of logic, but he has to reappropriate ethical and juridical terminology to restore this 'pure' philosophy to us.

[117] Ibid., p.167, tr.p.150.
[118] Ibid., p.171, tr.p.153.
[119] Ibid.
[120] Ibid., p.169, tr.p.151.
[121] Ibid., p.157, tr.p.142.
[122] Ibid., p.157, tr.pp.142–3.

How does Derrida restore this 'consciousness of Differance' to its own light? Its style of unity, as introduced in the passage cited, is indeed 'strange', for it involves both 'im-potence' and 'im-possibility'. Derrida is enjoying the philosophical promiscuity which *differance* permits him: alluding both to 'possibility' in the Kantian sense, and to 'potency', the recourse of those various attempts to change Kantian possibility into 'real possibility', 'virtuality', *dynamis*. Derrida wants to name his resolution of the antinomy of structuralism and phenomenology 'force', *Kraft*, and announce it as the new law to be engraved in the heart in the spirit of Nietzsche. But, unlike Nietzsche, Derrida knows that Hegel anticipated and criticized this move in the early section of the *Phenomenology of Spirit*, entitled 'Force and Understanding'. Furthermore, although this is not to my knowledge discussed by Derrida, Hegel also showed in the same book that the 'law of the heart' is no law at all.[123] Much of Derrida's shorter work can be read as a series of attempts on his part to defend grammatology as a Nietzschean jurisconsult against an Hegelian one.

In the first essay in *Writing and Difference* entitled 'Force and Signification' Derrida reminds us that Nietzsche's thinking developed from an opposition between Apollo and Dionysus in *The Birth of Tragedy*, between 'ardour' or '*élan*' and 'structure' in Derrida's terms, to 'all is but Dionysus'.[124] In *Thus Spoke Zarathustra*, the work which consummates the latter position, 'Nietzsche was certain, but Zarathustra was positive' in announcing a new law table and in appealing for help in engraving it in hearts of flesh. Derrida treats this as a recognition that knowledge is writing and writing is law: 'Writing is the outlet as the descent of meaning outside itself within itself . . .'[125]

This is said to be the only consistent position: one which does not stifle 'force under form' as in structuralism.[126] Derrida draws on Bergson to indict structuralism for turning 'meaning' into the simultaneity of space,[127] but, although Berson's *durée* explains

---

[123] Hegel, 'The law of the heart and the frenzy of self-conceit', *Phenomenology of Spirit, Theorie Werkausgabe*, 3, trans. A. V. Millar, Oxford, Clarendon Press, 1977, chapter V, B.b.
[124] Derrida, 'Force and Signification', *Writing and Difference*, p.47, tr.pp.28–9.
[125] Ibid., p.49, tr.p.29.
[126] Ibid., p.44, tr.p.26
[127] Ibid., p.42, tr.p.25.

differences of space as time-delayed, as intervals, Derrida extricates himself from the Bergsonian implications of his own position by the now familiar claim that he will transcend the oppositions on which Bergson relied to formulate the idea of *durée*: 'we maintain that it is necessary to seek new concepts and new models, an *economy*, escaping this system of metaphysical oppositions.'[128]

Hence, for Derrida, 'force' is not the force opposed to form, which would revive the old dichotomous schema, but nor is it, qua economy, 'an energetics of pure, shapeless force', which would be monocausal *dynamis*.[129] 'Economy' involves both 'differences of site *and* differences of force' – emphasis added.[130] By drawing on both the metaphysics of possibility (force versus form) and the metaphysics of potency (force as energetics) a 'third' force is produced: this strategy 'uses the strengths of the field to turn its own stratagems against it, producing a force of dislocation that spreads itself throughout the entire system, fissuring it in every direction and thoroughly delimiting it'.[131] The last phrase, written in the French '*dé-limitant de part en part*', emphasizes the new law which de-limits, which smokes out, as it were, the god of limits and boundaries.[132]

How can Derrida prevent this 'third' force from being taken as one of the other two, as a 'fact of consciousness', when it is being produced, inscribed, carried down into the valley? In two ways: he acknowledges it as a fact of his own writing by referring to his one comrade, Nietzsche, who is said to have done the same. And he faces and rebuts Hegel's convincing demonstration that to use 'force' as a principle of explication produces tautologies, by arguing that Hegel has merely demonstrated 'language's peculiar inability to emerge from itself in order to articulate its origin', but this does not rob us of 'the *thought* of force' (la *pensée* de la force) – Derrida's emphasis. 'Force is the other of language without which language would not be what it is'.[133] Force is to explain

---

[128] Ibid., p.34, tr.p.19.
[129] Ibid.
[130] Ibid., p.34, tr.pp.19–20.
[131] Ibid., p.34, tr.p.20.
[132] See Plato, *Laws*, Loeb Classical Library, trans. R.G. Bury, London, Heinemann, 1967, Book 8 843a, Book 9 879e,881.
[133] Derrida, 'Force and Signification', *Writing and Difference*, p.45, tr.p.27.

signification, but as the other of signification, force must be *thought*. 'Thought', however, is the illusory medium which 'signification' was intended to redescribe. In this way Derrida produces a definition: he stipulates what 'force' is to mean robbing us of its usual signification. Quite consistently, all he can do is carry on with the business of chiselling at the stone, that is, writing, and hope that his appeal to brethren who will carry the tablets, that is, read them, will be 'heard'.

In taking up his tools, however, Derrida has returned us to our thought – although we remember from the *Grammatology* that 'thought is here for me a perfectly neutral name, the blank part of the text, the necessarily indeterminate index of a future epoch of differance. *In a certain sense, "thought" means nothing*'.[134] The 'thought' of force waits for the production of *differance*; an example of the way our 'thought' may be directed once the question of thinking is transformed into the question of signification. 'Force' has an 'exemplary signification' – if I may borrow Husserl's portentous phrase with which Derrida concludes his Introduction to Husserl's *Origin of Geometry*, for it may now be seen as a ruse of *differance*.

In spite of his cavalier dismissal of Hegel's argument Derrida's thinking must be assessed in the light of the section 'Force and the Understanding' in the *Phenomenology*. The argument in that section is not simply that explanations which appeal to 'force' are invariably tautological; it consists of an exposition of the limitations of referring the conception of difference to 'force'. Hegel does not show that the origin cannot be articulated in language as Derrida claims he does; he shows that the thought of force is not the thought of the origin but the thought of law and difference: he shows, too, how on premises – which Derrida claims he is producing – that thought inevitably arises.

The oscillation between 'force' versus form, and 'force' as pure energy which leads Derrida to posit a third sense of force is shown by Hegel to arise out of a specific understanding of difference: 'The play of forces has merely this negative significance of being *in itself* nothing, and its only positive signification of that of being the *mediating agency*, but outside of the Understanding'.[135] The 'play of

---

[134] Derrida, *Of Grammatology*, p.142, tr.p.93.
[135] Hegel, *Phenomenology of Spirit*, p.119, tr.para. 148.

forces' implies an idea of law: an 'absolute flux' which in turn implies 'only difference as a universal difference, or as a difference into which many antitheses have been resolved'. This difference, as a universal difference, is consequently 'the *simple element in the play of force itself* and what is true in it. It is the *law of force*.'[136]

The idea of a 'play of forces' depends on the two meanings of 'force' as form and as pure energy: 'But these two relations are again one and the same; and the difference of form, of being the solicited and the soliciting Force, is the same as the difference of content, of being the solicited Force as such, viz, the passive medium on the one hand, and the soliciting Force, the active, negative unity or the one, on the other'.[137] The idea of Force which goes beyond 'force' versus form and 'force' as pure energy is simply the idea of 'universal difference' or the 'mere concept of law itself'.[138] If difference is understood as the play of forces 'the difference created since it is no difference cancels itself out . . . [for] it is the self-same which repels itself from itself',[139] or, to quote Derrida, '*differance*' names 'this sameness which is not identical'.[140]

The point is not that force is tautological when evoked as a principle of explanation, nor that language cannot articulate its origin, but that 'force' as the name for *differance*, as the thought of the other of signification, 'the negative signification of being *in itself* nothing', as Hegel put it, and, as Derrida, we have heard, wants to put it, '"*thought*" *means nothing*', can only be thought, that is, produced in Derrida's sense, as an absolute difference 'which repels itself from itself and posits an antithesis which is none'. It is, according to Hegel, these 'differences [which] are tautological; they are differences which are none'.[141]

Hegel brings out the ethical implications of thinking of 'force' as the Law of laws. 'Force' as the law of universal difference implies 'a tranquil kingdom of laws', a copy of the perceived world which retains the principle of change and alteration. On the other hand if 'force' is thought as self-repelling difference, then the perceived

---

[136] Ibid., p.120, tr.para. 148.
[137] Ibid.
[138] Ibid., pp.120,121, tr.paras 149,150.
[139] Ibid., p.127, tr.para. 156.
[140] Derrida, 'Difference', *Speech and Phenomena*, p.129.
[141] Hegel, *Phenomenology of Spirit*, pp.132,127, tr.paras 162,156.

world becomes internal to the overarching negative principle of change and alteration. Hence this second kind of supersensible world is different from itself, that is, different within itself: it is itself in being different from itself, or, the like is unlike itself, and, vice versa, its differences constitute its identity, or, its unlike is like itself. Hegel gives examples of the consequences: 'an action, which in the world of appearances is a crime would, in the inner world, be capable of being really good',[142] or 'The punishment which under the law of the *first* world disgraces and destroys a man, is transferred in its *inverted* world into the pardon which preserves his essential being and brings him to honour'.[143] These ethical paradoxes result from the thought of law as 'force': 'Thus the supersensible world, which is the inverted world, has at the same time overarched the other world and has it within it; it is *for itself* the inverted world, i.e. the inversion of itself; it is itself and its opposite in one unity. Only thus is it difference as *inner* difference, or difference *in its own* self, or difference as an infinity'.[144]

This implication of difference as an infinity Derrida sought to forestall in the *Grammatology*: 'It is precisely the property of the power of differance to modify life less and less as it spreads out more and more. If it should grow infinite – and its essence excludes this a priori – life itself would be made into an impassive, intangible, and eternal presence: infinite differance, God or death'.[145] This 'infinite differance' which Derrida would like to attribute to Hegel is implied by his own 'thought of force', for *differance* in Derrida is impervious to any knowledge of the mediations which would prevent it from 'growing infinite'. If such knowledge were permissible it would not be necessary to appeal to an 'unnameable', nor to try out the various names – 'force', 'trace', 'middle voice'.

In one sense Derrida could deny that *differance* is inner difference: it transcends the opposition of outer and inner as the criteria of space and time: 'by the silent writing of its a, it has the desired advantage of referring to differing *both* as spacing/temporalizing

[142] Ibid., pp.127–8, tr.para. 157.
[143] Ibid., p.129, tr.para. 158.
[144] Ibid., p.131, tr.para. 160.
[145] Derrida, *Of Grammatology*, p.191., tr.p.131.

and as the movement that structures each dissociation'.[146] The 'a' is to indicate the grammatical middle voice, but one which can no longer be heard:

> it rather indicates the middle voice, it precedes and sets up the opposition between passivity and activity . . . an operation which is not an operation, which cannot be thought of either as a passion or as an action of a subject upon an object, as starting from an agent or from a patient, or on the basis of, or in view of, any of these *terms*.[147]

Philosophy is said to have 'perhaps commenced by distributing the middle voice expressing a certain intransitiveness, into the active and passive and has itself been constituted in this repression'.[148] However, the difference of time and space not subject and object, action and passion, are presented as the defining features of *differance*: 'Constituting itself, dynamically dividing itself, this interval is what could be called spacing: time's becoming spatial or space's becoming temporal'.[149] The '*ance*' of *differance* captures this 'infinitive and active core of differing'.[150]

Yet this delineation of *differance* beyond the oppositions of metaphysics amounts to another version of that search for an inclusive difference which goes beyond the exclusive inner/outer; the search also conducted by Cohen, who found inclusive difference in Kant's concepts of reflection; by Bergson, who found the difference of intuited *durée* in opposition to the outer, homogenous difference of the Kantian forms of intuition; by Deleuze, who found inclusive difference in Kant's *Prolegomena* where the exposition of inner difference bursts the definition of time and space as outer relations; a search already subjected to criticism by Hegel. According to Derrida, as did Nietzsche, so could we

take up all the coupled oppositions on which philosophy is

---

[146] Derrida, 'Difference', *Speech and Phenomena*, pp.129–30, not all of this essay is included in the version in *Marges de la Philosophie*.

[147] Ibid., p.130; 'La Différence', *Marges de la Philosophie*, p.9, trans. in *Speech and Phenomena*, p.137.

[148] Ibid.

[149] Ibid., pp.13–14, tr.p.143.

[150] Ibid., p.9. tr.p.137.

constructed, and from which our language lives, not in order
to see the oppositions vanish but to see the emergence of a
necessity such that one of these terms appears as the
differance of the other, the other as 'differed' within the
systematic ordering of the same (e.g. the intelligible as
differing from the sensible, as sensible differed; the concept as
differed–differing intuition, life as differing–differed matter;
mind as differed–differing life; culture as differed–differing
nature; and all the terms designating what is other than *physis*
– *techne, nomos*, society, freedom, history, spirit, etc. – as
physis differed or *physis* differing: *physis in differance*).[151]

This emerging 'necessity' is the inclusive difference which Derrida
in effect acknowledges when he refers to 'the unfolding of the
same as differance'.[152]

Differance is comprehensive: 'Not only is differance irreducible to every ontological or theological – onto-theological-
reappropriation, but it opens up the very space in which onto-
theology-philosophy – produces its system and its history. It thus
encompasses and irrevocably surpasses onto-theology or philosophy'.[153] Derrida is here rehearsing Hegel's own argument against
Vorstellung, representation, and turning it against Hegel's idea of
philosophy: representational thinking, which Hegel distinguished
from philosophical thinking, is equated by Derrida with philosophy, while *differance* is introduced by him as the all-encompassing
and non-representational medium which Hegel called
'philosophy'.

Derrida acknowledges his debt to Hegel for the connotations of
differance as beyond active and passive, and as deferral, with
reference to a text from Hegel's Jena *Naturphilosophie* on time, but
not to the work of difference to be found throughout Hegel's
philosophy, the work of the middle voice, and the relationships
which the notion of the middle, *die Mitte*, imply. '*Diese Beziehung
ist Gegenwart, als differente Beziehung*' (this relation is (the) present,
as a different relation); in his discussion of this passage from
Hegel, Derrida overlooks how *differente Beziehung* is, for Hegel,

---

[151] Ibid., p.18, tr.pp.148–9.
[152] Ibid., pp.18–19, tr.p.149.
[153] Ibid., p.6, tr.pp.134–5.

above all a relationship since from the perspective of *differance* no relationship can be known.[154]

Derrida claims that his 'displacement' of Hegelian language is 'both infinitesimal and radical',[155] when it is, in effect, predictable and knowable within the Hegelian system. The 'middle voice' is best traced not by Derrida's 'playful' lapses into transcendental and phenomenological (in the Husserlian sense) terminology, but by the metaphor which he designs for his infinitesimal but radical 'shift' of Hegelianism: 'general economy' which competes with Hegel's purported 'restricted economy'.

A restricted economy such as Hegel's is 'one having nothing to do with an unreserved expenditure'; it 'accounts for' *differance*, while, contra Hegel, a general economy *'takes account of* what is unreserved', and 'fails to' account for *differance*.[156] Yet, contra Levinas, Derrida shows how from the position of general economy a classically Hegelian defence may be mounted: he defends the negative as the condition of the totality when Levinas distinguishes between the totality as history and the infinite as radically other and beyond history. Derrida argues that the radically other is the condition of the totality itself; the infinite is in the finite not beyond it: 'Infinity cannot be understood as Other except in the form of the in-finite'.[157] The infinite is not beyond history: it opens it up; *'Within history* . . . not history in the sense given to it by Levinas (totality), but . . . the history of departures from totality, history as the very movement of transcendency of the excess over the totality without which no totality would appear as such'.[158]

However, Hegel's 'economy' is said to be restricted because it implies that 'deferred presence can always be recovered, that it simply amounts to an investment that, only temporarily and without loss, delays the presentation of presence, that is, the perception of gain or gain of perception'.[159] Hegel is said not to

[154] Ibid., p.15, tr.p.144.
[155] Ibid., p.15, tr.p.145.
[156] Ibid., pp.20–21, tr.p.151.
[157] Derrida, 'Violence and Metaphysics', *Writing and Difference*, p.188, tr.p.114.
[158] Ibid., p.173, tr.p.117.
[159] Derrida, 'La Différence', *Marges de la Philosophie*, p.21, trans. in *Speech and Phenomena*, p.151.

'take account' of *differance* except by equating pure presence with absolute loss. Borrowing from Bataille, Derrida argues that this amounts to a preoccupation with circulation of objects whose value is already established: 'The circularity of absolute knowledge could dominate, could comprehend only this circulation, only the circuit of reproductive consumption. The absolute production and destruction of value, the exceeding energy as such, the energy which "can only be lost without the slightest aim, consequently without any meaning" – all this escapes phenomenology as restricted economy'.[160] In Hegel's economy difference and negativity are only moments: 'the negative side' is the 'reassuring *other* surface of the positive'.[161]

It sounds as if Derrida is developing another kind of 'conservative' reading of Hegel's thinking and reserving its radicality for his own thinking. 'Absolute knowledge' is said to represent the governance or sovereignty of Hegel's pen – albeit one that knows the close relation of sovereignty and servitude. But Derrida himself points out that the oscillation of reactionary and revolutionary readings of Hegel provides evidence of the limitation of Hegelian *Aufhebung*, according to which writing can only be sovereign or servile. Absolute knowledge of the 'we' is opposed to the restricted knowledge of 'natural consciousness', so that the passage of experience is conceived 'as the circulation of meaning and value' from slave to master and from natural to philosophical consciousness.[162]

It is Derrida's writing which produces a restricted economy within the more 'general economy' of Hegelianism. The very metaphor of economy is the point of restriction. Hegel called his discourse 'speculative', which – to continue for the moment in Derrida's terms – means that it defers itself, or, it is never finished. It recognizes an inclusive absolute whereas Derrida proposes a 'productive' one which postpones its other indefinitely, and thereby reinforces the very law it claims to question by making it indefinite and unknowable. This writing becomes the precipitate of a law which it merely reproduces: precisely what a speculative discourse avoids.

---

[160] Ibid., p.381, tr.p.259.
[161] Derrida, 'From Restricted to General Economy: an Hegelianism without Reserve', *Writing and Difference*, p.399, tr.p.271.
[162] Ibid., pp.406–7, tr.pp.275–6.

The idea of a 'general economy', taken from Bataille, is designed to circumvent the sovereignty of writing by making 'apparent that excesses of energy . . . cannot be utilized'.[163] Bataille wants to argue that his 'transgression of discourse . . . like every transgression conserve[s] or confirm[s] that which it exceeds' but to justify this ineluctable confirmation as dispelling 'the prohibition without suppressing it', a truly Hegelian scruple of making the law knowable without legislating it again. Bataille does not erect a new unknowable principle as the authority of his transgression but speaks of the 'effects' of 'unknowledge'.[164]

Derrida, however, is worried that Bataille has stifled his Dionysian laughter and lapsed into an Hegelian seriousness. Reading 'Bataille against Bataille' Derrida wants to affirm that transgression of discourse may succeed in dispacing 'discourse (and consequently law in general, for discourse establishes itself only by establishing normativity or the value of meaning, that is to say the element of legality in general)', since writing, 'the speculative concept par excellence' may interrupt the serene Hegelian 'circulation of meaning and value'.[165] Derrida overlooks the speculative relation to writing which characterizes Hegel's texts themselves. He produces not a reactionary or a revolutionary reading of Hegel but a naive one.

To discuss Hegel in terms of economy already restricts philosophy to the *oikos nomos*, the law of the household: it insinuates a specific kind of law into the ostensibly neutral move to 'general economy'. The idea of speculative discourse is to allow the law, the universal form of the particular, to show itself in this contrariness within philosophy – and not to pre-empt its appearance by legislating it again. This is what 'phenomenology' in the Hegelian sense means: presentation of the drama between 'discourses', such as the 'philosophemes' of Kant and Fichte, and their 'excess'.[166] Derrida restricts Hegel's enterprise by forcing Hegel's concept to designate that excess. By calling his own enterprise a 'general economy' Derrida makes the law of his philosophical household into an unknowable absolute. A restricted economy which recognizes the limited place of its law, its 'discourse',

[163] Ibid., pp.396–7, tr.p.270.
[164] Ibid., pp.403–4, tr.p.274.
[165] Ibid., pp.403–4,406, tr.pp.274,275.
[166] Ibid., p.406, tr.p.275.

would tell us more about the law which gives rise to the illusion that it is 'general', and which only knows the other as death: 'Thus there is the vulgar tissue of absolute knowledge and the mortal opening of an *eye*. A text and a vision. The servility of meaning and the awakening to death.'[167]

Derrida recommends that 'the imperalism of the *Logos*' be counteracted by the liberation of 'the mathematization of language', for mathematical notation would break the illusion of perfect mediation produced by phonetic writing.[168] This new imperialism of the *matheme* is also to serve as a rebuttal of the Hegelian concept, the medium of media, and of the Hegelian debasement of mathematical notation as the abstract thought of exteriority. 'What Hegel, the *relevant* interpretor of the entire history of philosophy, *could never think* is a machine that would work. That would work without, to this extent being governed by an order of reappropriation'.[169] This remark of Derrida's is evidence that his thinking remains dependent on the metaphysical oppositions which he would disown, on the bad infinite, a charge which he brings himself against Levinas's infinite. Yet, in another place, Derrida accepts the designation of his position as 'materialist', as 'irreducible heterogeneity' or 'radical alterity' in opposition to Hegel's resolving of alterity.[170] This apparent inconsistency is Derrida's philosophical 'play': to affirm, contra Levinas, that the Other opens up history, but contra Hegel, that the Other is not captured by history. The other is other and same, heterogenous and homogenous. This is the strategy of economy which is based on 'the point of greatest obscurity, on the very enigma of differance, on how the concept we have of it is divided by a strange separation'. *Differance* keeps changing its position because 'system and nonsystem, the same and the absolutely other, etc. cannot be conceived *together*'.[171]

What this strategy reveals, to read Derrida against Derrida, is that 'the question of the γϱαφειν' remains closer to the Kantian *quaestio quid juris*, 'that dry, necessary and somewhat facile

[167] Ibid., p.407, tr.p.276.
[166] Derrida, *Positions*, p.47, tr.p.34.
[169] Derrida, 'The Pit and the Pyramid', *Margins of Philosophy*, p.126, tr.p.107.
[170] Derrida, *Positions*, pp.82,87, tr.pp.60,64.
[171] Derrida, 'Difference', *Speech and Phenomena*, p.20, tr.p.151.

question', than to the Hegelian question 'With what must the science begin?' which he seems to be asking for grammatology, albeit as a positive science: '*Where and how does it begin . . .?*' a question which itself raises and postpones the question of the origin.[172] The idea of 'general economy' is Derrida's 'radical shift' of Hegel's absolute method: it permits the unauthorized intervention of *differance* to break up everyone else's economy, but, if challenged, to justify these displacements either as transgression of legality in general, or, as a shift and re-commencing 'of the very project of philosophy under the privileged heading of Hegelianism'.[173] Under the new empty heading of general economy or system – general versus the restricted economy both of Hegel and of political economy, which is apparently 'restricted to commercial values' – Derrida draws our attention away from the metaphors he employs.[174] Political economy does not deal with 'commercial values': the economic is political because it is the realm of transferred and fetishized meaning and we can see it as such without positing any literal or natural meaning. The economic is the realm of law: the realm in which activity, product and personality acquire juridical form. The economy, like writing, can stand for *differance* because the illusion of literalness does not attach to it even in its paradigmatic meaning.

With his use of the economic metaphor Derrida returns us to the logic of illusion: 'This economic aspect of differance . . . confirms that the subject, and first of all the conscious and speaking subject, depends upon the system of differances and the movement of differance, that the subject is constituted only in being divided from itself, in becoming space, in temporizing, in deferral . . .' but he prevents us from knowing illusion as such.[175] For Derrida philosophy is 'metaphorical': it is *differance* dissembled as writing and revealed as economy or 'unknowledge'; for Hegel, metaphor, whether writing or economy, is semblance – *Schein* – a realm of transferred meaning whose law may be known. For Derrida the 'exergue' which stands at the beginning of the *Grammatology* and

---

[172] Derrida, *Of Grammatology*, p.104, tr.p.74.
[173] Derrida, 'Difference', *Speech and Phenomena*, p.21, tr.p.151.
[174] Quoted from Bataille, Derrida, 'From Restricted to General Economy', *Writing and Difference*, p.396, tr.p.270.
[175] Derrida, *Positions*, pp.40–41, tr.p.29.

at the beginning of the essay on metaphor and philosophy, 'White Mythology', stands for the writing on the coin, for value in general, while for Hegel and for Marx it stands for the writing of a contract, for specific but formalized exchange relations.[176]

'Exergue' means the inscription on the reverse of a coin in the space below the principle device. For Derrida it captures the metaphor of writing as an economy, a circulated law, which divides subjects from themselves, in becoming space, in temporizing. He admits that 'Inscription on coinage is most often the intersection, the scene of the exchange between the linguistic and the economic,' but takes this connection as evidence for two supplementary types of signifying discussed in the problematic of fetishism in Nietzsche as well as in Marx.[177] However, fetishism in Nietzsche is referred solely to the passage quoted above from the early essay on truth but not to Nietzsche's mature work on the *Genealogy of Morals* where the 'moralization of concepts' is traced to specific legal forms of contract and exchange.[178] Similarly Marx's discussion of fetishism is relegated in Derrida's notes to a brief quotation from *Capital* and a longer one from Marx's exposure of Max Stirner's false etymologies in the *German Ideology*.[179] 'Fetishism' is made by Derrida into the unaddressable absolute in Marx and Nietzsche when it is the point of address in their work: the point where legal forms indicate the historically specific economy which they serve.

Derrida should be taken literally when he argues that the metaphors of philosophy – value, gold, the sun – are drawn along in the movement of tropes because philosophy is rhetorical.[180] Calling philosophy 'rhetorical' does not mean that it is self-referential, or that it is a game for the initiated. It means that it serves a law, or, that it is written: 'I am not sure that the imperative of taking a position in philosophy has so regularly been considered "scandalous" in the history of metaphysics, whether one considers this position taking to be implicit or declared'.[181]

---

[176] Derrida, 'White Mythology', *Margins of Philosophy*, p.249, tr.p.209.
[177] Ibid., p.257, tr.p.216.
[178] For Nietzsche's early essay on truth, see the opening of chapter 7 above.
[179] Derrida, 'White Mythology', *Margins of Philosophy*, pp.257–8 notes 8,9, tr.pp.216–17 notes 12,13.
[180] Ibid., p.260, tr.p.218.
[181] Derrida, *Positions*, p.129., tr.p.93.

Philosophy is the exergue, the writing on the coin, which means, as Nietzsche insinuated in the early essay on truth and made explicit later, that the philosopher stamps an inscription or legislates: '*Genuine philosophers, however, are commanders and legislators*: they say "*thus* it *shall* be . . ."'[182]

However, the exergue could also remind us that the philosopher's writing is precipitated, de-posited, but caught in the illusion that it posits or commands. Derrida defies us to classify metaphors or collect them from any literal meaning, from the presence they promise. But we do not want to do that: we want to draw attention to Derrida's rhetoric, to what it includes and excludes. For the minted coin, the 'being imprinted of the imprint' or *typos* which is opposed to any idea of philosophy as *telos*, makes a metaphor literal. Meaning or signification is typed not collected – only flowers are gathered, we are told[183] – for Derrida can only conceive re-collection, *Erinnerung*, as '*interring* difference in a self-presence'.[184] He ignores the inseparability in Hegel of productive memory, signs and contract by stopping his commentary on imagination in the *Encyclopaedia* at the paragraph before the introduction of productive memory and the reference to deed of contract, and refers instead in a note to the discussion of productive memory in the much earlier *Nürnberger Schriften*.[185] The exergue in Derrida becomes the cypher of an eternal circulation of signification for its law as contract remains unknowable.

Derrida argues that rhetorical elaboration of philosophical metaphor reinforces the idea of a unitary tradition: 'Each time that a rhetoric defines metaphor , not only is *a* philosophy implied, but also a conceptual network in which philosophy *itself* has been constituted'.[186] The rhetoric of the exergue is not immune from this implication either, while the exergue as rhetoric, the stamp on the coin, arises from the opposition between particular and

---

[182] Nietzsche, *Beyond Good and Evil, Werke*, III, trans. Walter Kaufmann, New York, Vintage, 1979, sec.211; it is in this light that the passage on truth as coin cited at the opening of chapter 7 above should be read.
[183] Derrida, 'White Mythology', *Margins of Philosophy*, p.262 n.12, tr.p.220 n.21.
[184] Derrida, *Positions*, p.59, tr.p.43.
[185] 'The Pit and the Pyramid', *Margins of Philosophy*, p.101 and n.6, tr.p.87 and n.15.
[186] Derrida, 'White Mythology', *Margins of Philosophy*, p.274, tr.p.230.

universal which establishes the value inscribed and validates the law. For Derrida the rhetoric of metaphor is either mistakenly taken as literal or must remain enigmatic. So Aristotle is said incidentally to invoke 'the case of a *lexis* that would be metaphorical in all its aspects' but, even so, a 'secret narrative' would lead us to a proper name.[187] Derrida reduces the meaning of *physis* in Aristotle to 'natural presence', projecting onto Aristotle – who is said to confuse words with things – the oppositions which later ages bring to their reading of him.[188] Derrida generalizes the historically specific problem of reflection under the legal title of 'general economy', instead of asking whether the reflection he evinces everywhere does not belong to a restricted economy – for 'economies' can only be restricted.

Instead we are circumscribed by 'tropes' qua inscribed figures, and 'tropic' qua movement, just the kind of etymology by resemblance which Derrida deplores. We are re-positioned by Derrida's *Positions*. If we accept his account of 'the question in which we are posed', we will find ourselves reclining guests at Belshazzar's feast: the hand is writing on the wall – '*Mene mene tekel u-pharsim*' – but we cannot read the words and there is no Daniel to read the names of the three weights and tell us what they foretell.[189] For, according to Derrida, the writing on the coins becomes the coin as writing, as the stamping not the calibrating. Daniel's interpretation did not alter the course of events – Belshazzar would have perished anyway. But in the Biblical story he perished knowing the judgement. Derrida would have us perish without knowing why, for he leaves the law as unknowable as it was before he raised the question of the *graphein*.

---

[187] Ibid., p.290, tr.p.243.

[188] Compare Heidegger, 'On the Being and Conception of *Physis* in Aristotle's *Physics*, B,1' in *Wegmarken*, Frankfurt am Main, Klostermann, 1978, pp.237–99, trans. Thomas J. Sheeham in *Man and World* 9/3 (1976), 219–70.

[189] Daniel 5 1–31; the three weights: the mine, shekel and the half-shekel, are read by Daniel and interpreted to mean 'numbered', 'weighed', 'divided': 'Here is the interpretation: *mene*: God has numbered the days of your kingdom and brought it to an end; *tekel*: you have been weighed in the balance and found wanting; *u-pharsim*: and your kingdom has been divided and given to the Medes and Persians,' (verses 26–9). See Raymond Hammer, *The Book of Daniel*, 1976, in the *Cambridge Bible Commentary*, Cambridge, Cambridge University Press, 1976, pp.60,64–5.

Writing cannot be picked out as definitive of metaphor by stipulating that it is to be understood as 'what gives rise to an inscription in general', since this is its literal meaning. Law is recognized as such when it is inscribed – on a stone, with a reed, and so on. Prior to any inscription law is customary – in that state of permanent change which the fiction or metaphor of 'custom' connotes. Derrida reads the tradition too literally when he read only the denigration of writing as the confirmation of presence and does not read the celebration of writing as the battle for sovereignty and initiative. Why else do foundation myths attach to the giving of law on Mount Sinai when we know it was written by priests in exile and frequently rejected by the people, or to the decemvirs who formulated and published the Twelve Tables of Roman Law to outmanoeuvre the demands of the plebians for a share in the law and managed to leave them dependent on tribunate power in spite of the codification? Why would Derrida take the memory of events which we know initiated new forms of contest as nostalgia for an ideal speech-situation which we know to imply the absurdity of an ideal law-situation?

Derrida reminds us of the uneasy opposition of *phone* (voice) and writing, but he might have reminded us of *ius-dicere*, declaring the law, the different forms which the battle over jurisdiction have taken.[190] For once law is inscribed its 'declaration' changes. Even if the writing claims merely to 'discover' the law, the possibility of legislation and the question of sovereignty can no longer be disguised by the fiction of custom. Derrida's 'history of writing' understands law only as dissemblance, not as celebration nor as contestation and hence not as semblance. His history of writing takes the metaphor of writing far more literally than those it indicts. It cannot think the history of writing for it makes its own writing the servant of signification as such: formal, static and ahistorical.

Before the exergue, the inscribed or minted coin, came the scales and copper. Does Derrida's *differance*, the middle voice, distributed by society into active and passive, serve as a reminder that

---

[190] See, for example, Georges Dumézil, *Archaic Roman Religion: With an Appendix on the Religion of the Etruscans*, 1966, trans. Philip Krapp, Chicago, The University of Chicago Press, 1970, p.122.

the figure of justice is not only blind but gagged and voiceless: that the scales and copper balance themselves – the one symbol that Saussure concedes is not arbitrary?[191] Why should Derrida tell us that non-truth, metaphor, is a minted coin when we have already been told that truth is not a minted coin to be scooped into the pocket?[192] Because Derrida legislates while Hegel seeks to recognize and cease philosophical legislation.

Derrida replaces the old imperialism of the *Logos*, the old law table, by the imperialism of the *grapheme*, prepared as a new law table, but displaying the old Marburgian dream – as naturalized and as utopian as any which Derrida indicts – to be carried down into the valley and engraved in hearts of flesh. He might be reminded of those who entomb effaced Holy Script, for, contrary to such celebration of the law, his reference to writing does not raise the question of law – it buries it.[193]

[191] Saussure, *Cours de linguistique générale*, 1915, Tullio de Mauro (ed.), Paris, Payot, 1979, p.101, trans. *Course in General Linguistics*, Wade Baskin, Glasgow, Fontanta/Collins, 1974, p.68.

[192] Hegel, Preface, *Phenomenology of Spirit*: 'truth is not a minted coin that can be given and pocketed ready-made,' (p.40, tr.para. 39).

[193] See, for example, the story of the Cairo *Genizah* summarized in the Introduction, *The Penguin Book of Hebrew Verse*, T. Carmi, Harmondsworth, Penguin, 1981, pp.22–3.

9

Legalism and Power: Foucault

Derrida offers us Zarathustra's new law table; Foucault offers us Zarathustra's 'powers'. Derrida turns law and knowledge into writing; Faucault turns law and knowledge into speech: 'discourse'. Derrida tells us that writing is pre-legal, prior to the law; Foucault tells us that discourse is post-legal, after the stage of law, a norm. Derrida posits the origin of law as *differance* (validity); Foucault posits the origin of law as 'power' (value). Derrida's new law table is inscribed with the end of law, the *telos*; Foucault is opposed to merely turning the table which opens up the space of the court-room – on the judge. He recommends that we smash it, and he is sanguine that the end of law, the *finis*, can be executed.[1]

Foucault's 'bio-history' affirms and denies a typology of legal history which reproduces a Saint-Simonian triarchy of the theological or feudal, the metaphysical or juridical, and the positive stages; in Foucault's terms: the monarchical, the reforming jurist, and the disciplinal stages.[2] This history is affirmed within an even larger sweep which contrasts archaic Greek justice

---

[1] For the idea of the table in Foucault compare Preface, *Les Mots et les choses: Une archéologie des sciences humaines*, Paris, Éditions Gallimard, 1966, p.9, trans. *The Order of Things: An Archeology of the Human Sciences*, New York, Vintage, 1973, p.xvii; and 'On Popular Justice: A Discussion with Maoists' in *Power/Knowledge: Selected Interviews and Other Writings 1972–1977*, Colin Gordon (ed.), New York, Pantheon, 1980, p.8.

[2] For Saint-Simon, see Durkheim, *Socialism*, c.1895, trans. and Alvin W. Gouldner (ed.), New York, Collier, 1962, p.165; Foucault, *Histoire de la sexualité 1. La Volonté de savoir*, Paris, Éditions Gallimard, pp.183–91, trans. *The History of Sexuality*, Volume One, *An Introduction*, Robert Hurley, Harmondsworth, Penguin, 1981, p.139–45; and *Surveiller et punir: Naissance de la prison*, Paris, Éditions Gallimard, 1975, pp.133–4, trans. *Discipline and Punish: Birth of the Prison*, Alan Sheridan, Harmondsworth, Penguin, 1979, pp.130–31.

and early medieval legal process, when the distribution of justice was directly and immediately connected with political struggle, with the evolution, since the beginning of Roman law, of juridical forms which are separate from the rest of social and political life, and which depend on distinct forms of knowledge and on a 'series of subjected sovereignties'.[3]   This typology of legal change is denied by a theory which abolishes itself as theory, an ultimate self-perficient nihilism. For, according to Foucault, theory posits itself as the neutral voice of 'the whole of society', but acts a bogus third or judge of the juridical stage, and colludes in its judgements which are no longer of innocence and guilt, but of normal and abnormal, in the administrative technology of the post-legal stage.[4] Nihilism is to complete two revolutions in one: to cut off the king's head and the head of the specious administrator.[5] To the objection that this practice is blind and runs the risk of reinforcing what it seeks to abolish, Foucault reiterates his celebration of the 'dark moment', for all eyes are implicated in the old order; he affirms an absolutely different future, and reminds us of the powers that are waiting to be taken.[6]

As a result of his concern to disassociate his work from structuralism Foucault's notion of history changes from one which aspires to the condition of archeology to 'bio-history' or genealogical history.[7] This change from delineation of *episteme* to delineation of 'powers' marks a move from an interest in the idea of law as the justification of scientific regularities to an interest in 'real' law, the juridical stage, and its presupposition, power, as the unjustifiable source which conforms to no regularity. For 'the archive' as 'the law of what can be said, the system that governs the appearance of statement as unique events', was taken by Foucault's critics as a recasting of the idea of law, as an emphasis

---

[3] Foucault, 'History of Systems of Thought', and 'Revolutionary Action: "Until Now"', in *Language, Counter-Memory, Practice: Selected Essays and Interviews*, Donald F. Bouchard (ed.), Ithaca, New York, Cornell University Press, and Oxford, Basil Blackwell, 1977, pp.203–4,221–2.

[4] Ibid., p.233.

[5] Foucault, 'Truth and Power', *Power/Knowledge*, p.121.

[6] This is what Foucault seems to be proposing at the end of the discussion 'Revolutionary Action: "Until Now"', *Language, Counter-Memory, Practice*, p.233, although in *The History of Sexuality* 'power' is said to be something that cannot be 'acquired, seized, or shared', (p.123, tr.p.94).

[7] For 'bio-history', see *The History of Sexuality*, vol. 1. p.188, tr.p.143.

on regularity, albeit *sans* origin or goal, subject or continuity, when Foucault had sought to tilt the scales further towards the regional, the particular, the imperative, and the event.[8] Hence the move from *episteme* to power, from archeology to genealogy, is a move from a new justification or validity to a force before justification or value, from regularity without *telos* (*episteme*) to powers without regularity (bio-history), from excavation of the structure of dead remains to the affirmation of life.

From this perspective the litigious nature of Kant's *Critique of Pure Reason* corresponds to the juridical stage of law and politics. The critical court of knowledge has now become an administrative tribunal, and the original attempt to investigate a case of suspected usurpation has become the classification of normality and abnormality. Critique has turned into discourse as the court of theoretical reason has turned into the court of practical reason. The attempt to justify a suspected usurpation is unveiled as the hypocrisy of a power which cannot be justified, which is always usurpatory, and which increasingly abuses its authority in its present classificatory role. In Foucault's work the intrinsic but unacknowledged connection in the critique of theoretical reason between technical terms of law and the conditions of legitimate knowledge is exposed from the perspective of the era of the post-critical tribunal. The internal construction of knowledge changes to conform to the successive epochs of law which it serves.

Foucault claims that his genealogy of power is like Nietzsche's because it is presented without any reference to political theory.[9] It aims to replace legal terminology in both its political and theoretical uses by the delineation of the practice of power.[10] It refuses the three conventional elements of neutrality: the role of the third; the reference to the universal rule of justice; and decision with power of enforcement, for these are 'three characteristics of the courts which are represented in anecdotal fashion by the table in our society'.[11] Yet, like all nihilist programmes, this one insinuates a new law disguised as beyond politics. For Foucault's

---

[8] Foucault, *L'Archéologie du savoir,* Paris, Éditions Gallimard, 1969, p.170, trans. *The Archeology of Knowledge,* A. M. Sheridan-Smith, London, Tavistock, 1974, p.129.

[9] Foucault, 'Prison Talk', *Power/Knowledge,* p.53.

[10] Ibid., p.51.

[11] 'On Popular Justice', ibid., p.11.

case relies on the theological and military terminology of the feudal stage: body and soul; war and deployment; strategy and tactics. It also falls back on the civil law concepts supposedly left behind in the juridical stage. True to the rejection of Nietzsche's politics it reverts from Nietzschean 'will to power' to a pre-Nietzschean metaphysic of 'will to life'.

Once power is made prior to justification, whether legal or philosophical and scientific, the history of law and the history of knowledge are treated as 'a single, process of "epistemologico-juridical" formation'.[12] In *Discipline and Punish* history becomes the genealogy of the present 'scientifico-legal complex'.[13] The sanction of punishment, the standard indicator of criminal justice and of law, is seen instead as a 'tactic' or 'technology' of power in general and the changing modalitites of punishment are thereby detached from any general theory of social change. This produces a one-dimensional account of legal change which does less justice than either Durkheim or Weber to the paradoxes and antinomies of law in capitalist societies.

This perspective is introduced both as a set of methodological prescriptions, 'make the technology of power the very principle of the humanization of the penal system and of the knowledge of man', and as a historical thesis, a law of three stages, over the course of which punishment has become 'technical', corrective and disciplinal.[14] These elisions of method and thesis, technology and technique, strategy and tactic, are the sleights-of-hand by which Foucault dissolves politics into 'powers'.

The three stages consist of: monarchical law, when punishment was a ceremonial of sovereignty, both public and ritual; the law of the reforming jurists, when punishment was a procedure for requalifying individuals as juridical subjects; and disciplinal law, when punishment has become the normalization of individuals by reforming their 'habits', understood as a training and mastery of the body.[15] The four rules employed to produce this typology consist in taking punitive mechanisms, first, in terms of their

---

[12] Foucault, *Discipline and Punish*, p.28, tr.p.23.

[13] Ibid., 'Une généalogie de l'actuel complexe scientifico-judicaire', p.27, tr.p.23.

[14] Ibid., pp.28,133–4, tr.pp.23,130–31.

[15] Ibid., pp.133–4, tr.pp.130–31; and chapter 1, 'The Body of the Condemmed', pp.9–35, tr.pp.3–31.

positive not their negative effects; secondly, as political tactics *sui generis*, and not as 'indicators' of law or social structure; thirdly, as indicators of a technology of power shared by the single matrix of law and science; and fourthly, as the valorization of the body in the name of the soul.[16] Following these stages and rules reveals the apparent humanization of punishment to be the effect of an extension of control, and not, as one would have expected, the benevolent vehicle of its diminution. This extension of control, traced by conceiving of individuals not as 'persons' but as 'bodies', culminates in the disciplinal, a 'form of justice which tends to be applied to what one is, this is what is so outrageous when one thinks of the penal law of which the eighteenth century reformers had dreamed, and which was intended to sanction, in a completely egalitarian way, offences explicitly defined by the law'.[17]

This tone of indictment indicates Foucault's infidelity to his rules: for the ground of his outrage remains the ideal of legal–formal equality which rests in effect on a formal and inequitable egalitarianism of the deed. What Foucault's study of disciplinal punishment demonstrates is that the change to the egalitarianism of the intention is equally formal and inequitable. Yet his rules bid him present the 'mask' of this new power, its 'exorbitant singularity', as 'panopticism', and as 'medico-judical treatment', and to leave unexamined the bearer of the mask, the new 'economy of illegalities', developed to administer absolute bourgeois property, since the civil law concepts on which this thesis and his sense of outrage manifestly depend have been surpassed by the approach of the 'plurality of powers'.[18]

By way of *obiter dictum* Durkheim's famous essay, '*Deux Lois de l'évolution pénale*', is dismissed on the grounds that it posits increasing individuation as the cause rather than the effect of the 'new tactics of power'.[19] However, the position attributed to Durkheim is the Spencerian thesis which Durkheim sought to

---

[16] Ibid., p.28, tr.pp.23–4.
[17] Foucault, 'About the Concept of the "Dangerous Individual" in 19th-Century Psychiatry', trans. Alain Baudot and Jane Couchman, *International Journal of Law and Psychiatry* 1 (1978), 17.
[18] Foucault, *Discipline and Punish*, pp.27,89, tr.pp.22–3,87.
[19] Ibid., pp.27–8, tr.p.23; Durkheim, 'Deux lois de l'évolution pénale', in *L'Année Sociologique* IV (1900), 65–95, trans. "The Evolution of Punishment", in *Durkheim and the Law*, Steven Lukes and Andrew Scull (eds.), Oxford, Martin Robertson, 1983, pp.102–32.

refute in *The Division of Labour in Society*.[20] By referring solely to Durkheim's essay on penal law Foucault avoids any confrontation with Durkheim's more complex discussion of the connection between punishment and social change in *The Division of Labour in Society*. Nevertheless his own account of penal transition is deeply indebted to Durkhiem's more schematic statement in the essay on penal evolution. Foucault merely adds a third stage to Durkheim's two laws of penal evolution: the law of quantitative variation – that the intensity of pain inflicted increases in less developed societies and in societies whose central power is more absolute; and the law of qualitative variation – that the pain of privation of liberty and of libery limited to a period proportional to the gravity of the crime tends gradually to become the normal type of repression.[21]

In *Discipline and Punish* Durkheim's two laws correspond to the transition from punishment as the public ceremonial of pain to punishment as the requalification of juridical subjects. The third additional stage is that of the reform of the body defined as a knowable soul that is not subjected to physical pain, or simply deprived of rights, but doctored out of its propensity to commit crimes against itself. It is argued that these three mechanisms overlap with, but cannot be reduced to, three theories of law; but the interesting point is not the overlap or reduction of three mechanisms of punishment to three theories of law but what those three theories of law are and how they are related.[22] Like Foucault other theorists make general analytical and historical distinctions between social orders based on status, on contract and on socio-technical norm.[23] It has been argued too that capitalist and state socialist societies are at present undergoing a transition from domination by associative or contract law to domination by bureaucratic or administrative law; in other terms, from law to regulation, from courts to tribunals, from justice to administra-

---

[20] Durkheim, *The Division of Labour in Society*, 1893, 2nd edn 1902, trans. George Simpson, London, Free Press, 1964, p.200f.
[21] Durkheim, 'Deux lois de l'évolution penale', 64,78, tr.pp.102,114.
[22] Foucault, *Discipline and Punish*, p.134, tr.p.131.
[23] See R. H. Neale, 'Property, Law and the Transition from Feudalism to Capitalism', in Eugene Kamenka and R. H. Neale (eds), *Feudalism, Capitalism and Beyond*, London, Edward Arnold, 1975, pp.7–8.

tion, from private to public law, and from individual property rights to rights of communal property.[24]

However, like Foucault's, these arguments simplify the paradox into separate categories or stages which provided the pivotal tension of the classic sociological tradition. In *The Division of Labour in Society* Durkheim's thesis of the transition from repressive to restitutive penal law serves to open up the larger question of social cohesion in a society which is based at the same time on contractual and on cooperative law, on negative and on normative law, and to delineate the antomic division of labour which results from this antinomy of freedom and control.[25] Similarly Weber focuses on the legitimacy of that combination of the value-rationality of the free individual together with the formal rationality of the technical organization of command as the paradox of legal-rationality which leads from the this-worldly asceticism of the autonomous individual to the encompassing bars of the iron cage. By making knowledge a precipitate of power as such Foucault presents as a simple success story, as 'the power of normalization', those paradoxes and antinomies of law and social control which have been identified as definitive of industrial or capitalist society by non-Marxist and by Marxist sociology alike.[26]

Furthermore Foucault's 'rules' have belonged to the sociological curriculum ever since Durkheim criticized Spencer for conceiving of law solely as negative and progressive, and formulated *The Rules of Sociological Method*, which define crime, one of his major examples, as a normal, creative and positive effect of social control.[27] Similarly Weber's concept of power is designed to provide a criterion for the creation of power when it is apparently being limited in capitalist society by the developments of rights: 'Even a formal legal order which offers and guarantees many "rights of freedom" and "empowerments" and few positive and negative norms can, nonetheless, serve a quantitative and qualitative

---

[24] See Eugene Kamenka and Alice Erh-Soon Tay, 'Beyond Bourgeois Individualism: The Contemporary Crisis in Law and Legal Ideology', ibid., p.128.

[25] Durkheim, *The Division of Labour in Society*, Book Three.

[26] Foucault, *Discipline and Punish*, p.314, tr.p.308; and the last sentence of the English edition which does not appear in the French.

[27] Durkheim, *The Rules of Sociological Method*, 1895, in *The Rules of Sociological Method and Selected Texts on Sociology and its Method*, trans. W.D. Halls, London, Macmillan, 1982, pp.77–83.

increase not only in general coercion but an increase in the authoritarian character of coercive command'.[28]

By treating 'knowledge' solely as a resource of power Foucault can make no distinction between forms of apprehension for which critical self-reflection is intrinsic – which are preoccupied, as were Durkheim and Weber, with the connection with the place from which they speak and their form of speaking – and formalized or clinical practices such as medicine or penal law; that is, he cannot distinguish between the 'technical' notion of power or command, which he recommends and employs, and the object or actuality to be apprehended. As a result his own thesis of a change and increase in social control is presented in military–theological terms which conjure up the politics and society of a bygone age. Yet even though the vocabulary of 'strategy', 'tactics', and 'techniques' is derived from warfare, its use avoids the risks of war, for, although resources are 'deployed', no battle is ever fought, lost or won.

Similarly the 'fiction of a juridical subject' is replaced by the apparently material reality of control over bodies.[29] But this materialism is spurious; it deliberately revives the theological opposition of body and soul, distracting us from Foucault's abandonment not of the fiction of the juridical subject but of the complex reality of legal personality, especially the relation between personality as a legal and as a social and psychological category. Foucault's translating of the juridical subject back into religious terminology is his way of discrediting modern psychology which, as he sees it, assimilates the logos of the *psyche* to the traditional idea of the soul, while sciences which seek to comprehend the mix of dependence and independence, the correlate of a law based on persons, are the unblushing servants of social control. Yet to transcribe individual experience into terms of the body reaffirms the soul/body dichotomy once again and replaces a fiction by a chimera.[30]

Quite inconsistently Foucault develops a sociological theory, and one, moreover, which depends on civil law concepts. For the

---

[28] Max Weber, *Economy and Society, Studienausgabe*, Tübingen, J.C.B. Mohr, 1976, p.440, trans. Guenther Roth and Claus Widdich (eds), Berkeley, University of California Press, vol. 2, p.731, amended.

[29] Foucault, *Discipline and Punish*, p.310, tr.p.303.

[30] Consider 'the soul, prison of the body', ibid., p.34, tr.p.30, amended.

change from punishment as ceremonial to punishment as juridical is associated with the development of specifically capitalist private property and the new 'administration of illegalities' which this required.[31] This rhetoric of supervision of illegality is also applied to the 'new economy of power', consisting of mechanisms of discipline and surveillance which are said to play 'a specific' but unspecified 'role in profit'.[32] However, apart from stressing their creativity as forms of control and their multiplicity as part of the decentralized apparatuses of production, these mechanisms are presented independently of any theory or history of the successes and failures of the bourgeois state. The refusal to develop any theory which explicitly involves juridical concepts results in an insinuated set of unexamined juridical concepts.

The idea of an 'economy of power' uses the idea of economy and the idea of power in two conflicting senses: 'economy' is used as the neutral description of the management of finite resources, which Foucault calls, 'political anatomy',[33] and as a system which 'masks its exorbitant singularity', where the universal laws of circulation mask the particularity of underlying relations, which he calls in places 'political economy';[34] while, correspondingly, 'power' is used in both the Parsonian sense of a circulating resource like credit or purchasing power which can be increased overall, 'the technology of power', and in the zero-sum sense according to which one person's power is another's lack of power, implied by his redress to the civil law concepts of civil society and the bourgeoisie. Drawing on the former sets of connotations legal terminology is transcribed into the discipline of the body.[35] The concept of labour-power is understood as the dissociation of an increased aptitude from the body, and its transformation into a relation of strict subjection – a disciplinary coercion of the body. But 'labour-power' distinguishes the acts, not the force, of production from rights over the product and not simply from the physical or corporeal object produced; it distinguishes between the individual as a thing and as a person in relation to others who are

[31] See ibid., p.91, tr.p.89.
[32] Ibid., p.310,314, tr.pp.304,308.
[33] Ibid., p.33,16, tr.pp.28,11.
[34] Ibid., p.27, tr.p.23 and *The History of Sexuality*, vol. 1, p.98, tr.p.73.
[35] Foucault, *Discipline and Punish*, pp.138–40, tr.pp.136–8.

also things and persons. To derive 'subjected', 'practised' and 'docile bodies' by analogy with legal terminology is to reduce the complex relations of persons and things, of politicization and depoliticization, to a deliberately anarchronistic dichotomy of body and soul. To transcribe experience into terms of the body as Foucault does is to rob persons of experience altogether.

The peculiar features of Foucault's conception of power and law in *Discipline and Punish* become more intelligible when his reasons for discarding his earlier idea of an archeology of knowledge are appreciated. 'We are doomed historically to history, to the patient construction of discourses about discourses and to the task of hearing what has already been said.'[36] This doom, announced in the Preface to *The Birth of the Clinic* provides an important clue for how to read *Les Mots et les Choses* (*The Order of Things*). For the deliberate conflating of *res gestae, Geschichte*, events and deeds, with *historia rerum gestarum, Histoire*, historical knowledge, reveals the circularity of Foucault's archeology of the human sciences, which reconstructs the changing relation between words and things in a way which justifies its own position. The misunderstanding of this work as structuralist, which led Foucault to produce the companion volume, *The Archeology of Knowledge*, is immensely instructive both in relation to structuralism itself and in relation to Foucault's subsequent move from archeology to genealogy of power.[37]

Foucault reconstructs the history of knowledge as a transition from the classical *episteme*, where representation corresponds to things in themselves, to the modern *episteme*, where 'Representation is in the process of losing its power to define the mode of being common to things and to knowledge. The very being of that which is represented is now going to fall outside representation itself'.[38] This point of contrast is designed to pinpoint the centrality of *anthropos*, of 'finite man', in the modern *episteme*.

---

[36] Foucault, *Naissance de la clinique: Une archéologie du regard médical*, 1963, Paris, Presses Universitaires de France, 1972, p.xiii, trans. *Birth of the Clinic: An Archeology of Medical Perception*, A. M. Sheridan-Smith, London, Tavistock, 1973, p.xvi.

[37] Foucault, Introduction, *The Archeology of Knowledge*, pp.25–7, tr.pp.14–17; and Foreword to the English Edition, *The Order of Things*, tr.p.xiv.

[38] Foucault, *The Order of Things*, pp.252–3, tr.p.240.

Although the main comparison of classical and modern *episteme* is concentrated on economics, natural history/biology, and linguistics, the transition from classical to modern is established by reference to Kant's three critiques. The argument around which the work is organized that the idea of sovereign but finite 'man' is definitive of the modern *episteme* is sustained by relating all subsequent developments to the Kantian dichotomy between the transcendental and the empirical aspects of 'man'.[39] Foucault himself speaks from a post-*anthropos* position, acknowledging Nietzsche as his only predecessor, and modern linguistics as the only aspirant to this new office.

On a closer examination, however, Foucault's own position and his monotone account of post-Kantian developments yield to a different reading. For the story he tells describes a circle from the 'retreat' of the classical 'mathesis' to the return of a post-modern mathesis.[40] The mathesis is the 'gravitational centre' of classical thought, understood, not as the dominance of mathematics, but as a universal science of measurement and order.[41] Signs and things have become divorced but their relationship is transparent and neutral. Kant's critical philosophy is said to separate representation from things in themselves, the transcendental from the empirical, and the formal from the transcendental. It is Foucault's attention to the last of these separations, that of the formal and transcendental, that makes it possible for him to assimilate all post-Kantian thinking to the same parameters:

> From Kant onward the problem is quite different; knowledge can no longer be deployed against the background of a unified and unifying mathesis. On the one hand, there arises the problem of the relation between the formal field and the transcendental field (and at this level all the empirical contents of knowledge are placed between parentheses, and remain suspended from all validity); and, on the other hand there arises the problem of the relation between the domain of empiricity and the transcendental foundation of knowledge (in which case the pure order of the formal is set apart

[39] Ibid., pp.256–61, tr.pp.243–9.
[40] Ibid., pp.71,361,393–5, tr.pp.57,349,381–4.
[41] Ibid., pp.70,71, tr.pp.56,57.

as non-pertinent to any account of that region in which all experience, even that of the pure forms of thought, has its foundation).[42]

Foucault concedes that 'the human sciences, unlike the empirical sciences since the nineteenth century, and unlike modern thought [*sic*], have been unable to find a way around the primacy of representation'.[43] Like 'the whole of Classical knowledge', they tend to 'reside within' representation, but their inherent activity of critical self-reflection disqualifies them from settling in to a new mathesis. This qualification is to be found in the 'pure', non-reflective, sciences of economics and linguistics, especially the latter, which does not speak of 'man', and which offers a 'principle of primary decipherment', not a reworking of knowledge acquired elsewhere:[44]

> Linguistic analysis is more a perception than an explanation: that is, it is constitutive of its very object. Moreover, we find that by means of the emergence of structure (as an invariable relation within a totality of elements) the relation of the human sciences to mathematics has been opened up again . . . a question which is central if one wishes to know the possibilities and rights, the conditions and limitations, of a justified formalization.[45]

It is in the context of this aspiration to a new mathesis, the return of 'man' to that 'serene non-existence in which he was formerly maintained by the imperious unity of Discourse' that Foucault's appeal to a bowdlerized, proudly depoliticized reading of Nietzsche must be set.[46] For the new mathesis is to abolish the question of law as well as critical reflection. It is revealing that a book which has traced from Velázquez's painting, *Las Meninas*, the replacement of the king as sovereign centre of signification by sovereign 'man', concludes with the question of the death of God and the end of his murderer. This indifference in relation to the

---

[42] Ibid., p.260, tr.p.247.
[43] Ibid., p.375, tr.p.363.
[44] Ibid., p.393, tr.p.381.
[45] Ibid., p.393, tr.p.382.
[46] Ibid., p.397, tr.p.386.

question of 'man' between the killing of God and the beheading, as it were, of the king, testifies to Foucault's indiscriminate separation of politics and knowledge. For when Nietzsche wrote, the king's head had long since grown back on; Nietzsche's madman was crazed with his self-imposed but, as he saw it, impossible task of alerting people to their *ressentiment*, to their turning of their 'will to power' against themselves, a tendency which persists whether the law is seen as divine or natural, or as human and positive.[47] Far from setting us, as Foucault would have it, the methodological task of contemplating 'the enigma of divided origin', or 'the absolute dispersion of man', a new integrity of Discourse, which will allow us to retreat behind masks and dissolve into laughter,[48] Nietzsche's thought aims at a new integrity: independence beyond *ressentiment* – a new politics.[49]

The Order of Things should be read not as the first attempt since Nietzsche to interrupt our anthropological slumber but as a renewed attempt to drug us into the far deeper sleep of the mathesis. This perspective illuminates Foucault's objections to the label 'structuralist' which he elaborates in the Foreword to the English edition, drawing attention to the stress on discontinuities, the refusal of the concept of mind, and the historical approach which inform the work.[50] Quite consistently, he rejects any account of the work which assimilates it to either side of the Kantian dichotomy: *quaestio quid juris* versus *quaestio quid facti*, or, in the terms of this debate, structure versus genesis; for his fundamental argument identifies this very distinction as the anthropological distinction of transcendental versus empirical which characterizes the 'modern' as such and from which he wishes to dissociate his own position. This explains his manifest annoyance with the careless description of his work as 'structuralist', for it assimilates it to the anthropology which he is attacking in

---

[47] For the 'madman' in Nietzsche, see *The Gay Science, Werke*, II, Schlechta, Frankfurt am Main, Ullstein, 1979, trans. Walter Kaufmann, New York, Vintage, 1979, sec.125.

[48] Foucault, *The Order of Things*, pp.397,395, tr.pp.385,383.

[49] As an example see the description of Mirabeau in Nietzsche, *The Genealogy of Morals, Werke III*, trans. Walter Kaufmann and R.J. Hollingdale, New York, Vintage, 1969, First Essay, sec.10.

[50] Foucault, *The Order of Things*, p.xiv.

general as well as to Levi-Strauss's anthropology in particular. 'Archeology' is Foucault's term for the new mathesis which goes behind, as it were, the Kantian and post-Kantian dichotomies. It also explains why, when he later turned to 'genealogy' he needed to take greater pains, under the guise of discussing Nietzsche, to distinguish genealogy from the other side of the Kantian opposition, the question of genesis, and from the implication of a new logos.[51]

Yet Foucault's 'archeology' is deeply allied to a different school of structuralism which was founded to transcend the finite and anthropological Kantian dichotomy of transcendental versus empirical by dropping both the thing in itself and the transcendental subject. Marburg neo-Kantianism, like Foucault's, is based on the mathesis of the origin, inscribed by means of the Kantian concepts of reflection, identity and difference; 'it is the identity of the Return of the Same with the absolute dispersion of man'.[52] It is the rules of this Marburgian method which Foucault rehearses in the Foreword of *The Order of Things* and which he projects back into the eighteenth century before the discovery of 'man', and which he claims to rediscover in recent linguistics and in Nietzsche.

This attempt to replace the Kantian oppositions by a neo-Kantian mathesis receives its most formal defence, however, in *The Archeology of Knowledge*, after which Foucault took an apparently radical turn but, in effect, a predictable one, from archeology to genealogy, from *episteme* to power. The idea of the mathesis is retained, but all association with the question of justification or validity and even with regularity is abandoned and replaced by 'power', the dynamic and forceful-sounding equivalent of Heidelbergian 'value'. For we are assured that 'power' has nothing to do with politics, with justification, with law – even construed as regularity, as *Gesetzmässigkeit*, but precedes all political and epistemological validity. True to this switch in the positing of the matheme the style of Foucault's texts change from the legal and juridical terminology of the *episteme* and the

---

[51] Foucault, 'Nietzsche, Genealogy, History', *Language, Counter-Memory, Practice*, pp.139–64.
[52] Foucault, *The Order of Things*, p.397, tr.p.385.

magisterial Marburgian tone of *The Archeology of Knowledge*, to
the anarchic terminology designed for the Heidelbergian warfare
without politics of the later works. References to Nietzsche are
made to serve both of these positions.

The four 'Directions for Use' outlined in the Foreword to the
English edition of *The Order of Things* are classically Marburgian:
concern with 'well-defined' empirical regularities; with regional
areas of knowledge; with the origin, which is unknown but
positive, for although 'the rules of formulation are never formulated' they constitute a spatial order or *episteme* which may be
intuited; with a productivity which is not of the epistemological
subject, but of 'a spontaneous movement of an anonymous body
of knowledge', a pure *Gesetzmässigkeit* without subject, origin or
end, which merely needs to be described.[53] In the Preface to the
first edition Foucault dilates on this fundamentally spatial frame
of validity where 'language has intersected space' which he calls 'a
pure experience or order'. This third domain of order is
apparently distilled from the difference between the primary codes
of a culture, or first domain, and the reflexive theories of those
codes, the second domain. Yet it is clearly posited by Foucault
since he fails to clarify how the primary codes may be identified
separately from the secondary theories.[54] In effect Foucault's 'pure
experience' consists of the order which divides systems of
positivities 'before presenting them to the understanding', the
episteme or mathesis, and delineates a classic *Geltungslogik*, a logic
of validity.[55]

From within the circle of this mathesis where the origin is the
end Foucault indicts modern empirical and human science for
operating within a methodological space opened up by the
metaphysics of the natural beginning and utopian end of history:
'The great dream of an end to History is the utopia of causal
systems of thought, just as the dream of the world's beginning
was the utopia of the classifying systems of thought.'[56] Within

---

[53] Ibid., pp.ix–xii; for the Marburg School of neo-Kantianism, see Rose, *Hegel
Contra Sociology*, chapter 1.
[54] Foucault, *The Order of Things*, pp.9,11–3, tr.pp.xvii,xx–xxi.
[55] Ibid., p.14, tr.p.xxii; for *Geltungslogik*, see Rose, *Hegel Contra Sociology*,
chapter 1.
[56] Ibid., p.275, tr.p.263.

these historical parameters he provides a methodological account of post-Kantian developments in which the analytic of life, labour and language appears in three stages: as new transcendental/empiricities, as reflexive, human sciences, and as aspirants to pure science.[57]

However, the transcendental/empirical approach (Ricardo – Marx, Cuvier, Bopp), is said to fall back into 'pre-critical naïveté' – even though we have been told that the pre-critical is not naive; the reflexive, human sciences, by extending knowledge of 'man' beyond the limits of representation, 'imitate' the classical 'philosophical posture of the eighteenth century'; while the third category, the aspiring 'pure' sciences, brings us to the threshold of the new mathesis.[58] In short, in spite of the apparent complexity of the discussion, Foucault's reduction of post-Kantian thought to an anthropological mean tends to undermine the distinctions he wishes to establish between the classical and the modern, along with those he wishes to establish within the modern itself.

This categorization is determined by Foucault's extremely general interest in the 'retreat of the mathesis' which makes him equate the 'finite' with 'man'.[59] Since 'finite' is a relational term Foucault judges all approaches according to how they dispose of the non-finite residue. In this way, for example, a positivist and eschatological reading of Marx's theory of labour is produced as a commitment to History and anthropological finitude that assimilates Marx's thought to the kind of historical jurisprudence which both he and Hegel attacked.[60] Marx was not concerned with 'man' or with 'labour' but with labour-power, with a juridical category, and with the civil and political society which it presupposes. In his discussion of all three stages of modern knowledge Foucault resolutely ignores the recasting of the question of law: how, since the Kantian critiques, the question of law destroyed the idea of 'man'. Or, when in relation to the human sciences he does admit

[57] Foucault, *The Order of Things*, pp.257–8,375,364–5, tr.pp.244,364,353–4.
[58] Ibid., pp.331,375,364–5, tr.pp.320,363–4,353.
[59] Ibid., p.361, tr.p.349.
[60] Hegel, Introduction, *Philosophy of Right, Theorie, Werkausgabe*, Frankfurt am Main, Suhrkamp, 1977, 7, para. 3 (Remark); Marx, 'The Philosophical Manifesto of the Historical School of Law', 1842, in Marx and Engels, *Collected Works*, vol. 1, London, Laurence and Wishart, 1975, pp.203–10.

this – 'three pairs of *function* and *norm, conflict* and *rule, signification* and *system* completely cover the entire domain of what can be known about man' – he has to admit, too, their affinity with the classical paradigm which knew 'man' not.[61] Foucault's book does not disperse 'man'; it dissolves the politics of everyone else's work by construing their questions as easy solutions to an anthropology which is irrelevant to their work. True to the nihilist project Foucault's mathesis aims to complete and perfect the scientific experience of the determination of 'man' by affirming it not as 'the never-completed formation of Difference', but as 'the ever-to-be accomplished unveiling of the Same'.[62]

In *The Archeology of Knowledge*, intended to clarify *The Order of Things*, the idea of the mathesis is presented directly, and without the circular history, as an alternative to the old idea of validity which depended on the distinction between transcendental and empirical: 'The archive is first the law of what can be said, the system that governs the appearance of statements as unique events.'[63] A new balance is proposed between law and event, between universal and particular: the idea of a regularity as opposed to a teleological origin or end. However, to set out the rules of a method (even those of an anti-method) risks reinscribing the universality which is to be redefined. The inscription of re-gional validities of discourse is opposed to a spurious universality of general validity but still reinstates and depends on the idea of validity: 'How General Grammar defines a domain of *validity* for itself . . . how it constitutes a domain of normativity for itself . . .'[64] Given this dilemma Foucault opts for a compromise: 'The statement then must not be treated as an event . . . but neither is it an ideal form . . . Too repeatable to be entirely identifiable with the spatio-temporal correlates of its birth . . . too bound up with what surrounds it and supports it to be free as pure form . . . the statement may be *repeated* but always in strict conditions.'[65]

The resultant vagueness of the idea of the 'archive' accounts for the subsequent development in Foucault's work from the delineation

---

[61] Foucault, *The Order of Things*, p.359, tr.p.357.
[62] Ibid., p.351, tr.p.340.
[63] Foucault, *The Archeology of Knowledge*, p.170, tr.p.129.
[64] Ibid., p.81, tr.p.61, emphasis in original.
[65] Ibid., pp.137–8, tr.pp.104–5.

of regional validities to the emphasis on power, from validity to value. For 'power', like 'value', sounds singular rather than universal, imperative and forceful rather than regular and lawlike. This explains also why Foucault works so hard to divorce 'power' from politics, from another realm of justification, for, like neo-Kantian 'value', 'power' is prior to all law whether the universality of the regular or the justification of the right, judidical or litigious. *The Archeology of Knowledge* depended on the oppositions which 'power' transcends: between 'positivities' and their 'precondition', even though the relation was conceived as regulative not as constitutive. It depended too on mere inversions; for to valorize instead of denying or resolving 'contradictions' and 'discontinuities' involves a simple dialectic of contraries: continuity/discontinuity; negative/positive; repression/release; negation/limitation. As a result the perspective of archeology appeared as arbitrary as the one indicted, and, thus far, the nihilist project of changing the signs was indistinguishable from the dialectic of contraries from which it sought to distance itself.

Foucault's attribution of a preoccupation with 'man' to all post-classical thought in *The Order of Things* is the correlate of his own preoccupation with the concept of life. 'Life' is the overarching, absolute concept which unifies his *oeuvre*, whether the individual works are organized as studies of *episteme*, or, later, of 'power'. Since 'life' may be conceived as infinite – the life of God(s) – or finite – the life of 'man' – it may provide a perspective from which the relational aspect of the finite becomes discernible. For 'finite' implies something limited and hence also either the law of its limitation or the other of its finitude.

In *The Birth of the Clinic* Foucault traces the way the history of the development of the idea of finite life presupposes the historical development of the idea of finite death, understood as a change in *episteme*, in the relation of universal and particular. Clinical medicine succeeds deductive medicine: the suzerainty of the gaze achieves priority over the a priori classification of cases from which the particular case is simply inferred.[66] Examination at the bedside mediates the body of available knowledge: intuition, albeit controlled, determines the choice of concept. This clinical notion of life presupposes a clinical notion of death, one whose

[66] Foucault, *The Birth of the Clinic*, p.2, tr.p.4.

universality no longer partakes of the divine or ceremonial, but may be found in the space of every body: 'it is when death becomes the concrete a priori of medical experience that death could detach itself from the counter-nature and become *embodied* in the *living bodies* of individuals'.[67] This medical definition of death is another correlate of the transition of life into the human, finite life of 'man': 'The individual is not the initial most acute form in which life is presented. It was given at last to knowledge only at the end of a long movement of spatialization whose decisive instruments were a certain use of language and a difficult conceptualization of death.'[68] Foucault argues, contra Bergson, that immortality, that is, 'living individuality', may be found not in 'inner time' but in space, for it is in the clinical space of the body that the relation to its other is recognized and the modern concept of life is located.[69] It is in clinical space that the new regularity without law – neither of God nor of the polis – is to be found.

In *The Birth of the Clinic* Foucault delineates a regularity without law, a change in the relation between the universal and the particular, where law is still understood as the 'pure experience of order' in a general a priori sense. History is understood in relation to conceptions of life, but as 'bio-episteme', as it were. In *The History of Sexuality* history is understood as 'bio-power', contra law in the political and legal sense and in any a priori sense of regularity as such: 'If one can apply the term *bio-history* to the pressures through which the movement of life and the processes of history interfere with one another, one would speak of *bio-power* to designate what brought life and its mechanisms into the realm of explicit calculations and made knowledge-power an agent of transformation of human life.[70] This introduction of the idea of 'bio-power' where 'bio' means 'life' and 'power' means 'force' – for it may not mean, as we shall see, anything juridical, whether regular or justified – indicates how far Foucault's thinking is from Nietzschean 'will to power' and how close it is to the pre-Nietzschean ancestry of 'will to life'.[71]

[67] Ibid., p.200, tr.p.196.
[68] Ibid., pp.174–5, tr.p.170.
[69] Ibid., p.175, tr.p.170.
[70] Foucault, *The History of Sexuality*, vol. 1, p.188, tr.p.143.
[71] For the comparison of 'will to life' and 'will to power', see, for example, Nietzsche, 'On Self-Overcoming', *Thus Spoke Zarathustra*, Second Part, sec.12.

'. . . you would have us believe, that you have rid yourself of the problem of law . . .'[72] In *The History of Sexuality* the opposition between repressive law and creative norm is both tool and object of 'genealogy', just as in *The Archeology of Knowledge* 'discontinuity' is said to be both tool and object of investigation.[73] In the first four parts of *The History of Sexuality* the social control of sexuality is reconceptualized as a positive effect of an increasing power, while in the fifth part the historical transition from the juridical to the adminstrative stage of society and law presupposed in the first four parts is itself outlined.

In *The History of Sexuality* Foucault challenges the progressive and liberating claims of psychoanalytic theory and practice in the name of their social meaning by reference to a sociological typology of legal change. He argues that psychoanalysis adheres to an antiquated notion of law and hence misrecognizes its past and its future, its continuity with the Catholic confessional and its service in the present and projected administration of secularized life. Foucault poses three questions which his work seeks to address: an historical one – has there been repression? an historical-theoretical one – is power best conceived negatively as prohibition, censorship, denial? and, an historic-political one – does psychoanalysis fulfil its promise of liberation or reinforce a power while it claims to surpass a law?[74]

However, in the course of the study Foucault's concentration on an answer to the second of these questions prevents him from tackling the third: for he replaces the 'repressive' concept of power by a 'technical' account of the creation of power, so that all mechanisms of social control are seen solely as positive effects of power in a way which rules out in principle the judgement that any particular mechanism perpetuates the impotence that it challenges. A dialectic of power and impotence is inconceivable in an exclusive universe where 'laws' are said to define negative objects and 'norms' to define positive objects. Foucault does not falsely rid himself of 'the problem of law'; he sets himself up for three topoi of inconsistency: he betrays his promiscuity of powers

---

[72] Foucault, *The History of Sexuality*, vol. 1, p.108, tr.p.82.
[73] Foucault, *The Archeology of Knowledge*, p.17, tr.p.9.
[74] Foucault, *The History of Sexuality*, vol. 1, p.18, tr.p.10.

by relying on juridical concepts of the civil and of feudal law; he mistakes effects for causes and falls into vicious circularity; he cannot dissociate his own position from the 'administrative nihilism' which he claims, in effect, to identify.[75]

Once again Foucault does not transcend the dichotomy repression/creation, but merely affirms it by taking the sociological perspective that life is organized by imperatives which perform a classificatory and creative function in relation to sexuality as in relation to all other aspects of behaviour. In classic sociological style he compares the Western development of a science of sex with the Eastern erotic art, as the difference between inquisition and initiation, two kinds of legal process: inquisition in a society where authority is divorced from the individual and knowledge is detached from ritual; initiation where the ritualized process of accusation and ordeal reconcile the whole community.[76] Western sexuality is assimilated to this change in litigious practice whereby sex becomes a form of knowledge and the transition from ignorance to knowledge indicates the operation of organized power.[77]

Foucault then radicalizes this thesis of the constitutive nature of normative power to attack the idea of constitution as such for implying juridico-discursive order. He identifies the theoretical notion which he wishes to abandon by reference to political history. Western monarchies are said to have replaced the multiplicity of feudal powers by developing unitary regimes based on law.[78] This history is said to provide the origin of our idea of law as the negative basis of order and hence of intelligibility, as prohibition, as censorship and as uniformity.[79] Not only does this simplify legal development by conflating sovereignty with monarchy and government with sovereignty, but all theoretical thinking is to be identified by reference to this egregious

---

[75] 'Administrative nihilism' is how Huxley reproached Spencer's work, cited and considered in the context of 'will to power' by Nietzsche in *The Genealogy of Morals, Werke III*, Second Essay, sec. 12.

[76] *The History of Sexuality*, vol. 1, pp. 76–80, tr. pp. 57–9.

[77] Ibid., pp. 74–5, tr. pp. 69–70.

[78] Ibid., p. 114, tr. p. 87.

[79] Ibid., pp. 110–12, tr. pp. 83–5.

representation of political change.[80] The 'constitution' of the social
in the sociological sense is not to be understood by analogy with
the political congress of founding fathers but 'technically' by
conceiving right as technique, law as normalization, punishment
as control, and the state in terms of civil society.[81] Thus Foucault
rehearses the birth of sociological thinking by translating what he
takes to be political concepts, whether they occur in the social
world or in theoretical work, into neutral, scientific concepts.[82]

However, since Foucault has destroyed the question of the
specific relation between civil society and the state by equating all
questions of law and sovereignty with monarchical government,
the concept of law with which he works is equally monolithic and
uniform. By making sovereignty and monarchical government
synonymous he insinuates that all exercise of power is arbitrary
and despotic and prevents any discrimination of universal claims
and particular relations. In classic sociological style Foucault offers
rules for this method to ensure that the 'objective viewpoint' is not
conceived as a form of regularity. 'Power' is to be seen as mobile,
'a moving substrata [*socle*] of force relations';[83] and plural, 'a
multiplicity of force relations'; it is not acquired, seized or shared,
but exercised from and on innumerable points, 'furrowed across
individuals, cutting them up and remoulding them, marking off
irreducible regions in them, in their bodies and minds'.[84] These
rules are intended to avoid using any idea of law whether litigious
right and justice or juridical regularity: instead, 'power' is
'intentional and nonsubjective'.[85]

This stipulation captures the inversion of *The Archeology of
Knowledge*: regularity without a purpose has become purpose
without regularity. But this position cannot be maintained
because it is inconceivable: the proposition that 'power is distributed in irregular fashion' uses and denies the idea of regularity in

---

[80] Foucault appears to obliterate Rousseau's famous distinction between the
Sovereign and the State, see the chapter 'Government in General' in 'The
Social Contract', *The Social Contract and Other Discourses*, trans. G. D. H. Cole,
London, Dent, 1973, Book III, chapter 1, p.208.

[81] Foucault, *The History of Sexuality*, vol. 1, p.135, tr.p.102.

[82] Ibid., 'Method', pp.121–35, tr.pp.92–102.

[83] Ibid., pp.122–3, tr.p.93.

[84] Ibid., p.127, tr.p.96.

[85] Ibid., p.124, tr.p.94.

the same phrase: distribution/irregularity.[86] In fact the main theses are couched in the terminology of strategy and tactics: the Roman army in the place of Roman law, as it were. Power is not divided between the dominators and the dominated, but consists of 'a multiplicity of discursive elements that can come into play in various strategies', and we hear of 'tactical productivity' and 'strategic integration'.[87] This clarifies the earlier call for a 'political economy of the will to knowledge', by which is meant not the gain of one party amounting to the loss of another but the circulation of pre-political resources, a natural law of power.[88]

'Strategy' and 'tactics', purposive but irregular, are the technical mode of exposition, a counterpart of the thesis presented elsewhere that the peace installed in civil society, like all power, is 'war continued by other means', an inversion of Clauswitz's dictum that 'war is politics continued by other means'.[89] However, even if 'warfare' were the appropriate conception of power this would not make knowledge of the connections between civil society and the state redundant, for 'war' remains a political concept even when apparently perpetual. Indeed Weber's sociology might be considered an exposition of the organization of defence and warfare as the indicator of the connection between private and public law, of the area of social life where power otherwise dispersed into distinct social and political channels can be apprehended as a whole. Similarly, a technical notion of power does not destroy the question of the legitimacy or illegitimacy of command, but, as Weber showed, returns us to it as the question of the form rather than the substance of authority. Foucault's rules do not change the concept of law into the idea of the norm, they demolish the relational nature of all concepts.

This becomes evident in the parts of *The History of Sexuality* where Foucault moves from outlining the tool of research and the rules for its use to the socio-historical thesis that a transition has occurred from 'deployment of alliance' to 'deployment of sexuality', and from 'right of death' to 'power over life'.[90] The

---

[86] Ibid., p.127, tr.p.96.
[87] Ibid., pp.133,135, tr.pp.101,102.
[88] Ibid., p.98, tr.p.73.
[89] Foucault, 'Two Lectures', *Power/Knowledge*, p.90.
[90] Foucault, *The History of Sexuality*, vol. 1, Parts Four and Five.

superimposition of deployment of sexuality on the earlier deployment of alliance is defined in terms of a transition from control by juridical means to control by non-juridical administrative means. Deployment of alliance is defined as 'a system of marriage, of fixation and development of kinship ties, of transmission of names and possessions . . . built around a system of rules defining the permitted and the forbidden, the licit and illicit, whereas the deployment of sexuality operates according to mobile, polymorphous, and continuous techniques of power'. The first of these is concerned with 'links between partners and definite statuses; the second is concerned with the sensations of the body, the quality of pleasure, the nature of impressions however tenuous or imperceptible these may be'.[91] These contrasts, drawn by use of 'deployment', another military term, confuse a concept of law, marriage, with a concept of force, sexuality; a legal relationship which presupposes all sorts of contrary particular experiences with a notion of plural and physical powers which does not draw on law in any regular or litigious, justified or justifiable sense: 'For this is the paradox of a society which, from the eighteenth century to the present, has created so many technologies of power that are foreign to the concept of law . . .'[92]

In effect Foucault demonstrates that this is the paradox of a tradition which has not been restricted to monarchical sovereignty. This juridical complexity is further indicated by the four domains which are listed for future research: hysterization of women's bodies; pedagogization of children's sex; socialization of procreative behaviour; psychiatrization of perverse pleasure.[93] Had he adhered to his own four rules or 'cautionary prescriptions' of immanence, continual variations, double conditioning, technical polyvalence of discourse, Foucault would never have been able to identify and describe these domains since they employ the juridico-discursive concepts which have been abandoned on principle.[94]

It is in the course of the concluding general discussion of the socio-historical transition from right over death to power over life

[91] Ibid., pp.140–41, tr.p.106.
[92] Ibid., p.144, tr.p.109.
[93] Ibid., pp.137–9, tr.pp.104–5.
[94] Ibid., pp.129–35, tr.pp.98–101.

that the positing of effects as causes, which results from Foucault's attempt to conceive of social forms as the effects of power mechanisms, emerges most clearly. Foucault argues that power has changed from 'the ancient right to *take* life or *let* live' which was contested by the struggle for political rights, to the function of administering life, 'to *foster* life or *disallow* it to the point of death', indicated by the demand for the 'right' to rediscover what one is and all that one can be.[95] Crucial for the identification of this transition from the juridical to the administrative stage is the shift in the boundary between life and death. In the juridical stage death was the public, ceremonial, political point at which a limited, terrestrial sovereignty gave way to a more powerful divine sovereignty, whereas in the present stage, power is 'situated and exercised at the level of life' and death is a merely private and secret event.[96] Like Hannah Arendt, Foucault takes the rhetorical shift from negative to positive freedom, from the contest for formal to apparently substantial equality, as evidence for the end of politics and the inception of technical control, for he cannot distinguish between appeals and institutions nor discern the continuity of control that results in prima facie changing appeals.[97]

The sociology of suicide is taken as testimony of the rediscovery of the 'strange and persistent' desire to die in a society dedicated to fostering life.[98] But Durkheim's sociology of suicide was based on the realization that suicide is not a personal, private and wholly individual event. It demonstrated that Protestant confession is connected with the burden of Protestant individuality, that even suicide is mediated, as are all forms of death, by relation to the community. Durkheim's investigation of suicide showed that 'ceremonial' or the law of the community is implicated in individual death in general and that the suicide rate varies directly with the degree of individual right in a community. He did not rediscover the perverse desire to die, but the conflicting pressures

[95] Ibid., pp.181,191, tr.pp.138,145; with allusion to Rousseau's chapter 'The Right of Life and Death' in 'The Social Contract' in *The Social Contract and Other Discourses*, p.189.

[96] Ibid., p.180, tr.p.137.

[97] Hannah Ardent, *On Revolution*, Harmondsworth, Penguin, 1979, and 'The Concept of History: Ancient and Modern', in *Between Past and Future: Eight Essays in Political Thought*, Harmondsworth, Penguin, 1980, pp.41–90.

[98] Foucault, *The History of Sexuality*, vol. 1, p.182, tr.pp.138–9.

of individual rights, whether positive or negative: that Weber's worldy-ascetics, those apparently strong Protestants, paradoxically turn out to have the highest suicide rate. By taking ostensible changes in ceremony as an indicator of fundamental change in the nature of power, Foucault links visible effects directly with causes, conflates the ideas of life and death with the sociological category of the individual and the legal category of suicide.

'Power would no longer be dealing simply with legal subjects over whom the ultimate dominion was death but with living beings and the mastery it would be able to exercise over them would have to be applied at the level of life.'[99] By translating legal concepts into concepts of life and death in order to characterize an historical transition, Foucault perpetuates the legal illusion which he is trying to undermine. For power was always situated and exercised at the level of life, whatever juridical concept covers that life and however much of life any set of legal concepts admits and excludes. If we have moved from the idea of a legal person to the ideal of the integral personality that is not a move from law to administration but from one law to another, from one kind of administration to another – if indeed either a new law or a new administration is implied. 'For millenia man remained what he was for Aristotle: a living animal with the additional capacity for a political existence; modern man is an animal whose politics places his existence as a living being in question.'[100] But Aristotle did not say that man had an additional capacity for politics: he said that politics defined human life; now as then it puts life in question, for politics like life implies death. To make his rehetorical point Foucault has to attribute to Aristotle a distinction of nature and culture that is entirely his own and on which he depends in his 'post-legal' discourse of life and death.

Foucault's turning of the effects of power into principles of power is crowned by his paradoxical contrast between Fascism and Freud. Fascism is said to be an example of administrative mechanism of power coupled with the old symbolism of blood associated with the order of sovereignty. The Freudian analysis of sex is said to characterize the administrative stage, but, in Freud's

[99] Ibid., pp.187–8, tr.pp.142–3.
[100] Ibid., p.188, tr.p.143.

case, to be linked to the former system of law and the symbolic order of sovereignty.[101] This stubborn adherence of Freud to the legal model of power is said to be to his 'practical credit', yet *The History of Sexuality* began by discrediting precisely that model.[102] In fact Foucault's argument is that psychoanalysis or the analytics of sex serves the adminstration of bodies, and he is now trying to wriggle out of the scandalous consequence that his typology of power fails to distinguish between Fascist *ressentiment* and the Freudian analysis of *ressentiment*. This results from simplifying 'will to power' so that 'power' comes to describe effects and techniques at the level of life.

'Clearly nothing was more on the side of the law, death, transgression, the symbolic and sovereignty than blood; just as sexuality was on the side of the norm, knowledge, life, meaning, the disciplines and regulation'.[103] Since Foucault associates any non-descriptive or explanatory account of an effect with 'symbolics' all he can do is assign things to one side or another of this egregious contrary: 'And yet to conceive the category of the sexual in terms of the law, death, sovereignty . . . in the last analysis is a historical retro-version.'[104] This is to discredit a mode of explanation by listing its working concept in an indifferent, inoperative order, contrasting it with the proposed innovation and projecting the drawbacks into a dissenting mouth which complains that it amounts to 'groundless effects, ramifications without roots, a sexuality without sex'.[105] Yet the proposed innovation is more extreme than this complaint which represents its principle as intelligibility (sexuality) but not constitution (sex), as *Zweckmässigkeit ohne Zweck*, purposiveness without purpose, when this has been deliberately inverted into *Zweck ohne Zweckmässigkeit*, insistently engineered purpose with no regularity. The notion of sexuality has been destroyed along with the notion of sex.

The innovation is to define 'power' as 'an *effect with a meaning value*'.[106] In spite of the rules which forbid any constitutive

---

[101] Ibid., pp.193–5,197–8, tr.pp.147–8,150.
[102] Ibid., pp.197–8, tr.p.150.
[103] Ibid., p.195, tr.p.148.
[104] Ibid., p.198, tr.p.150.
[105] Ibid., p.200, tr.p.151.
[106] Ibid., p.195, tr.p.148.

deduction Foucault concludes that 'sex is the most speculative, most ideal, and most internal element in a deployment of sexuality organized by power in its grip on bodies and their materiality, their forces, energies, sensations and pleasures'.[107] This account implies that the 'body' is a neutral term and Foucault insists that he has not inverted the approach of the history of mentalities to produce a rival corporeal focus for the history of 'meaning bestowal', but an account of 'the manner in which what is most material and vital in them [that is, bodies] has been invested'. 'Investment' versus 'bestowal' is a distinction without a difference; while the discourse of 'forces' and 'energies' is no more material than spiritual. Its introduction amounts to an attempt, not indeed to turn mentalities into bodies, but to avoid all juridical and litigious terminology, and above all, to eschew the concept of a person with its mix of legal and psychological connotations.

It is this self-defeating ambition that results in Foucault's own historical 'retro-version': his theological and military terminology and his replacing of 'will to power' by 'will to life': 'The Faustian pact, whose temptation has been instilled in us by the deployment of sexuality, is now as follows: to exchange life in its entirety for sex itself, for the truth and sovereignty of sex. Sex is worth dying for. It is in this (strictly historical) sense that sex is indeed imbued with the death instinct.'[108] Foucault has defined not 'power' but 'life' as an 'effect with a meaning value', and made 'life' into the criterion of all his interpretations and judgements.

He considers, however, that he has changed the conception of power from negative to positive; from universal to particular: 'power is not built up out of wills (individual or collective)'; from monolithic and singular to plural and myriad; from cause to effect; from law to norm.[109] In this way the procedures of power are no longer linked to the law of prohibition, the homogenous, negative, pure enunciation: 'Thou shalt not.'[110] Power 'never ceases its interrogation, its inquisition, its registration of truth'. But this does not change the idea of power or law at all: it retains the form of the *Sollen*, the ought: 'Thou shalt not' becomes 'Thou

107 Ibid., p.205, tr.p.155.
108 Ibid., p.206, tr.p.156.
109 Foucault, 'The History of Sexuality', *Power/Knowledge*, p.188.
110 'Power and Strategies', ibid., pp.139–40.

shall' and is renamed 'norm' in order to underline its imperative force and to emphasize that 'force' precedes justification. However, the idea of law and the idea of norm are inseparable in the tradition although their order of priority has always been disputed: *non ex regula jus sumatur, sed ex jure quod est regulae fiat*: law is not taken from rule – rules come into being from existent law. This maxim from Paulus has been interpreted in contrary senses to mean that norms derive from law and that law derives from norms.[111] Kant's criterion of universalizability involved trying out the legality of a maxim by considering it as a norm: 'Ought one to do x?' becomes 'What if everyone did x?' Unlike Hegel and Nietzsche Foucault does not move from questioning the pure form of the moral law to exposing the custom of morality or the morality of custom, *die Sittlichkeit der Sitte*, which it presupposes. He retains the form of the abstract imperative, affirms its force, and examines instead *the relation to life* which it indicates since he cannot discern the 'will to power' or its correlate, *ressentiment*, on which it rests.

This position rests furthermore on an eclectic sociology of civil society: the bourgeois class 'provided themselves with a certain number of methods for distancing the proletarianised from the non-proletarianised people . . . the army, colonisation and prisons'.[112] These means fail to distinguish the bourgeoisie from any other ruling class for all world empires have engaged in warfare, colonization and imprisonment. 'The penal system has had the function of introducing a certain number of contradictions among the masses, and one major contradiction, namely the following: to create mutual antagonisms between the proletarianised common people and the non-proletarianised common people . . . The third role of the penal system: is to make the proletariat see the non-proletarianised people as marginal, dangerous . . .'[113] Foucault makes use of a mixed sociology of contradiction and function, class relations and marginalization. Yet 'All the literary, journalistic, medical, sociological and anthropological rhetoric about criminals . . . plays this role [of separating the

---

[111] See Hans Kelsen, *The Communist Theory of Law*, London, Stevens and Sons, 1955, p.64f.

[112] Foucault, 'On Popular Justice', *Power/Knowledge*, pp.16–17.

[113] Ibid., pp.14–15.

poletariat from non-proletarianized people]'.[114] 'Countless people have sought the origins of sociology in Montesquieu and Comte. That is a very ignorant enterprise. Sociological knowledge (*savoir*) is formed rather in practices like those of the doctors.'[115] In this blatant way Foucault discredits sociology but uses its central concepts and theses, smuggling in the main sociological recasting of the question of law: the use of 'function', 'role', 'resource' and 'system' are, on Foucault's premises, unacceptably universal, structural and institutional; while the theory of the organized perception of others as 'marginal' depends on assumptions concerning legitimacy and illegitimacy which smack of justification, right and subjectivity.

Foucault's arguments in *The Order of Things* that the illusion of theoretical apprehension is no longer sustainable, and that archeology offers a neutral description of the theoretical practices of others turn out to be unsound. For his own position is manifestly embedded in a theory of civil society which he dissociates from Hobbes's *Leviathan* on the grounds that Hobbes develops a theory of sovereignty, but which bears much resemblance to Hobbes's state of nature, the war of all against all, since 'warfare' is the only category which Foucault justifies.[116] He overstates the distinction between descriptive and theoretical apprehension: for theory claims to redescribe or represent its object just as all description involves theoretical assumptions; his own stipulations that 'discontinuity' or 'power' are both tool and object of research argue as much.[117] By drawing on a theory of civil society without a theory of the state Foucault does not open up the perspective of myriad powers in place of the conventional sovereign and singular power, he introduces or posits a spurious universal: warfare.

> . . . the basis of the relationship of power lies in the hostile engagement of forces . . . for convenience, I shall call this Nietzsche's hypothesis . . . on this view, repression is none other than the realisation, within the continual warfare of this

[114] Ibid., p.15.
[115] 'The Eye of Power', ibid., p.151.
[116] 'Two Lectures', ibid., pp.97–8.
[117] Foucault, *The Archeology of Knowledge*, p.17, tr.p.9.

pseudo-peace, of a perpetual relationship of force (. . . not abuse, but . . . on the contrary, the mere effect and continuation of a relation of domination).[118]

Elizabeth Forster-Nietzsche believed that the spectacle of regiments of German cavalry rushing by to almost certain death on the fields of battle in 1870 impressed on the recumbent Nietzsche the idea of 'will to power' – the highest 'will to life' as a 'will to conflict', as opposed to Schopenhaurian 'will to sympathy'.[119] This misunderstanding of 'will to power' makes it a simple inversion of Schopenhauer's will to life. Foucault produces a similar travesty of the idea when he makes will to power mean 'the hostile engagement of forces', for he makes it a matter of blindness versus sight, and of force versus politics.

Zarathustra was not created and represented by Nietzsche as a blind force: he is full of law and his dramatized story is political – a story of impotence and power. This drama offers a practical complement to the theoretical knowledge developed in *The Genealogy of Morals*:

> The tremendous labour of that which I have called 'custom of morality [*Sittlichkeit der Sitte*]' . . . the labour performed by man upon himself during the greater part of the existence of the human race, his entire *prehistoric* labour finds in this its meaning . . . man was actually *made* calculable . . . If we place ourselves at the end of this tremendous process where the tree at last brings forth fruit, where society and the custom of morality at last reveal *what* they have simply been the means to: then we discover that the ripest fruit is the *sovereign* individual, like only to himself, liberated again from the custom of morality (for 'autonomous' and 'moral [*sittlich*] are mutually exclusive), in short the man who has his own independent, protracted will, who may promise – and in him a proud consciousness, quivering in every muscle of *what* has at length been achieved and become flesh in him, a

---

[118] Foucault, 'Two Lectures', *Power/Knowledge*, pp.91,92.
[119] See Elizabeth Forster-Nietzsche (ed.), *The Nietzsche-Wagner Correspondance*, trans. Caroline V. Kerr, New York, Liveright, 1949, pp.66–7.

consciousness of his own freedom and power, a sensation of humankind come to completion.[120]

Nietzsche argues that the distinction cherished by Kant as the criterion of the good will between the disinterested self-imposition of the moral law and the interested conformity to an external law produces instead either the supra-moral individual who, by overcoming of heteronomous motives, achieves independence of the self-denying moral law itself; or the sub-moral or resentful individual whose repeated attempts to achieve moral autonomy and suppress natural desire and inclination perpetuates in the name of the moral law a syndrome of self-hatred and self-destruction. The first, supra-moral individual is full of power in the political sense of sovereignty over his own warring factions: self-overcoming; while the second, sub-moral individual is full of force, impotent in the political sense of doing violence to his warring factions: self-defeating but able to justify himself by his conformity to the moral law as an ideal – and hence full of vainglory and *ressentiment*.

'Will to power' is a compound idea: 'will' 'to' 'power' not a simple notion of the plurality of hostile forces nor a pre-political *mathesis* which precedes law in the senses of juridical regularity and litigious justification. According to Nietzsche 'power' certainly cannot be justified: it is always usurped; but it can be used or abused. Myth is the form of its active use, and *ressentiment* the form of its reactive, displaced abuse. Nietzsche did not develop a natural law, as so many would ascribe to him, nor its converse, a natural history of positive law, for which some criticize him. But that was not because he was unconcerned with politics and law, but because his lesson applied to all historically specific positive law. He distinguishes politically between the strong warfare of the Roman Republic and the inverted warfare of the Babylonian exile as a way of illuminating that mix of strength and weakness which characterizes the modern individual, and above all, to pinpoint the cruelty of the impotent to themselves and to others.[121]

---

[120] Nietzsche, *The Genealogy of Morals, Werke*, III Second Essay, sec.2, p.801, trans. Walter Kaufmann and R.J. Hollingdale, New York, Vintage, 1969, p.59, amended.

[121] Ibid.; the second essay provides the context for the first essay which concerns *ressentiment* and for the third which concerns asceticism.

The utterly different spirit of Foucault's thinking robs 'war' and 'power' of their connection with law. and politics. Life as such and not the dynamic of self-reference and relation to other becomes the guiding criterion and gives rise to the methodologism evinced by the *oeuvre*. Foucault's discussion of Nietzschean 'genealogy' is structured by the four Deleuzian principles of eschewing identity, analogy, resemblance and opposition.[122] In *L'Ordre du discours* the concept of history is likewise reduced to four methodological principles – reversal (archeology), discontinuity, specificity and exteriority (genealogy), which gives us history as 'event' plus series, as effect 'on the level of materality', or as 'incorporeal materalism', but which exactly reproduces Kant's definition of history as the appearance of the noumenal in the phenomenal world.[123]

Like Heidegger's Event of appropriation, *das Ereignis*, this notion of the event captures Foucault's 'interrogation of the limit' and search for a language to express the act of transgressing the limit which would be what dialectics was 'in earlier times' for totality and contradiction.[124] Like Jünger and Heidegger, Foucault's questioning of law draws him to the image of the 'narrow zone of a line', as the place where the limit of finitude has been set by Kant, and where we discover 'that our path is circular and that, with each day, we are becoming more Greek'.[125] However, the difference between Heidegger's perfecting of this nihilist circle and Foucault's 'totally different form of time' is the difference between Heidegger's *telos*, the Lighting, before *Moira* divides time or space, and Foucault's 'tauromachy', the bull-fight, taken from Bataille's *The History of the Eye*.[126] The tauromachy is

---

[122] Foucault, 'Nietzsche, Genealogy, History', *Language, Counter-Memory, Practice*, pp.139–64; and compare the list in *L'Ordre du discours*, 1970, Paris, Éditions Gallimard, 1971, pp.53–4, trans. 'The Discourse on Language', Rupert Swyer, Appendix to the US edition of *The Archeology of Knowledge*, New York, Pantheon, 1972, tr.p.229.

[123] Ibid., p.60, tr.p.231; and compare Kant, 'Idea for a Universal History from a Cosmopolitan Point of View', *Werkausgabe*, XI, p.33, trans. in *On History*, Lewis White Beck *et al.*, New York, Bobbs-Merrill, 1963, p.11.

[124] Foucault, 'Preface to Transgression', originally in an edition of *Critique* devoted to Georges Bataille: *Critique* XIX (1963), 759,767, trans. in *Language, Counter-Memory, Practice*, pp.40,50.

[125] Ibid., 757, tr.p.37.

[126] Foucault, 'Nietzsche, Genealogy, History' in *Language, Counter-Memory,*

not the Dionysian sacrifice of a bull, but the night of an enucleated eye engorged during the bull-fight and the absolute darkness of the body which precedes and succeeds all sight.[127] 'We do not experience the end of philosophy, but a philosophy which regains its speech and finds itself again only in the marginal region which borders its limits: that is, which finds itself either in a purified metalanguage or in the thickness of words enclosed by their darkness, by their blind truth'.[128]

For Foucault the question of the limit or border of the finite, which Kant raised but relegated to anthropology, finally becomes the experience of the death of God who is still the unknowable guarantor of the border in Kant.[129] This 'death' occurs when sexuality is discovered to be the 'perpetual movement that nothing can ever limit (because it is, from its birth and in its totality, constantly involved with the limit) . . . On the day that sexuality began to speak and to be spoken language no longer served as a veil for the infinite; and in the thickness it acquired on that day, we now encounter the absence of God, our death, limits and their transgression.'[130] This 'death of God is not merely an "event" that gave shape to contemporary experience as we know it; it continues tracing indefinitely its great skeletal outline.'[131] It is not *an* event, it is *the* Event, *das Ereignis*, and Foucault conceptualizes it so as to deny that his self-reference of the limit is the source of new life or new light, new work or new power. It is seen solely as a self-sacrifice in the time of the 'ungraspable instant'.[132]

'Transgression contains nothing negative, but affirms limited being – affirms the limitlessness into which it leaps as it opens this zone to existence for the first time. But correspondingly, this affirmation contains nothing positive: no content can bind it, since by definition no limit can possibly restrict it.'[133] Foucault tries to

---

Practice, p.160; and Georges Bataille, *The Story of the Eye*, 1928, trans. Joachim Neugroschel, Harmondsworth, Penguin, 1982.

[127] Foucault, 'Preface to Transgression' in *Language, Counter-Memory, Practice*, pp.768–9, tr.pp.51–2.

[128] Ibid., p.760, tr.p.41.

[129] Ibid., pp.757–8, tr.p.38.

[130] Ibid., pp.754,767–8, tr.pp.33,51.

[131] Ibid., p.752, tr.p.32.

[132] Ibid., p.769, tr.pp.52, and 'Nietzsche, Genealogy, History', pp.163–4.

[133] Preface to Transgression', ibid., p.756, tr.pp.35–6.

maintain this idea of transgression as a plenitude of repetition, but betrays the empty self-reference which it implies: 'Transgression opens on to a scintillating and constantly affirmed world, a world without shadow or twilight, without that serpentine "no" that bites into fruits and lodges their contradictions at their core.'[134] Yet there would be no scintillation in a world without shadow: in absolute light as in absolute darkness nothing can be seen – there would be no 'world'. The language speaks against its author's ambition: 'Contestation does not imply a generalized negation but an affirmation that affirms nothing, a radical break of transitivity.'[135] Transitivity is not broken if nothing is affirmed: for if nothing is affirmed, then something has been affirmed. Foucault's language shows him firmly within that dialectic which he claims to have transgressed: 'Transgression then is not related to the limit as black to white, the prohibited to the lawful . . . rather, their relationship takes the form of a spiral which no simple infraction can exhaust.'[136] The serpent instead of swallowing its tail, that old symbol of dialectic, has twisted itself into a spiral, and this is announced as the detaching of existence, 'so pure and so complicated . . . from its questionable association to Ethics'.[137]

Foucault plunders Bataille's *The History of the Eye* to capture the darkness of his Event contra the lighting of Heidegger's Event:

> the flash of lightning in the night which, from the beginning of time, gives a dense and black intensity to the light it denies, which lights up the night from the inside, from top to bottom, and yet owes to the dark the stark clarity of its manifestation, its harrowing and poised singularity; the flash loses itself in this space it marks with its sovereignty and becomes silent now that it has given a name to obscurity.[138]

The eye, similarly, 'a small white globe that encloses its darkness, traces a limiting circle only sight can cross . . . it is the figure of being in the act of transgressing its own limit.'[139] This imagery

---

[134] Ibid., p.757, tr.p.37.
[135] Ibid., p.756, tr.p.36.
[136] Ibid., p.755, tr.p.35.
[137] Ibid., p.756, tr.p.35.
[138] Ibid., pp.755–6, tr.p.35.
[139] Ibid., p.763, tr.pp.44–5.

brings out the reversal which occurs when the limit becomes a circle or spiral, for the limitless or infinite, no longer a notion of time, becomes the space which encompasses the zone of the line. The distinction between inner sight and outer object of sight collapses as the sovereignty of the inner space is questioned. The white of the eye is blind and 'the circular night of the iris is made to address the central absence which it illuminates with a flash, revealing it as night'.[140]

This image of the 'enucleated or upturned eye' serves as a rival to any experience of transgression which might mark it as a celebration of Dionysus – Foucault replaces Nietzsche's vision by reference to 'the cries of the madman in the streets of Turin', the moment of Nietzsche's final breakdown;[141] or as a new work – Foucault refers to 'laughter, tears, the overturned eyes of ecstasy' in place of 'man as a worker and producer'; but above all, as new power or new life.[142] Foucault takes us from the law court to the bull-ring the 'tauromachy', so that we may try to grasp the momentary vision which comes out of the night carried in the threat of the bull's horn. He wants us to witness the speaking of absence by sex which in the 'flash of the act' only serves to return 'the white of the pale and skinless seed' to the original night of the body. This is to signify not the beginning of new life but the murder of the toreador who is blinded and killed by the horn of the bull at the very same instant when the woman is penetrated and the young man's eye emerges from his head. And for us voyeurs this is the promised 'ungraspable instant' in which he 'seems' to touch her.[143]

It is this refusal to transcend the exclusive opposition between the 'death' of God and the life of 'man' that brings Foucault to this point. For it was by eating the sacrificed god each year that the life of the new god and of the community was renewed: Dionysus was the sacrificial bull before he was anthropomorphized.[144] But Foucault remains within the exclusive opposition of the death of

[140] Ibid., p.769, tr.p.46.
[141] Ibid., p.761, tr.p.42.
[142] Ibid., pp.765,766, tr.pp.48,49.
[143] Ibid., pp.768–9, tr.pp.51–2.
[144] See Jane Harrison, *Prolegomena to the Study of Greek Religion*, 1903, London, Merlin, 1980, chapter VIII 'Dionysus', pp.363–453.

the infinite/life of the finite, and hence the only sacrifice he can propose is that of the bull-ring or of knowledge: 'Where religion once demanded the sacrifice of bodies, knowledge now calls for experimentation on ourselves, calls us to the sacrifice of the subjects of knowledge.'[145] This sacrifice, however, is in vain, for it produces no work, no renewed life and no power. Neither positive nor negative such affirmation is without determination or characteristic; it does not represent an encounter with the power of another but an ecstasy of blind laughter or blinding tears, which, unlike Heidegger's ecstatic time, is simply that old familiar despair.[146]

From magical nihilism to this administrative nihilism which completes itself as despair, that political voluntarism erupts to affirm the equally characterless 'beyond', which Foucault calls the 'until now' and which will most surely repeat just that.[147] The nihilism which most explicitly engages with law would most dangerously blind us to it.

---

[145] Foucault, 'Nietzsche, Genealogy, History', *Language, Counter-Memory, Practice*, p.163.

[146] Compare the idea of 'ecstatic time' in Heidegger, *Sein und Zeit*, 1927, Tübingen, Niemeyer, 1972, trans. *Being and Time*, John Macquarrie and Edward Robinson, Oxford, Basil Blackwell, 1967, H.329, with 'the giving of time' as a four-dimensional realm, in "Time and Being", in *Zur Sache des Denkens*, Tübingen, Niemeyer, 1969, p.17, trans. *On Time and Being*, Joan Starbaugh, New York, Harper & Row, 1972, p.17.

[147] Foucault, 'Revolutionary Action: "Until Now", *Language, Counter-Memory, Practice*, p.233.

Conclusion:
Dialectic of Nihilism

The various claims, some of which have been considered in this essay, that metaphysics has been surpassed, have turned out to be rhetorical – whether advanced against the knowledge of God (Kant), against the positing of abstract entities (Comte), against the traditional Aristotelian categories (Heidegger to Derrida) – in the strong, original meaning of rhetoric as guard and guide to the law. Metaphysics, pre-critical and post-critical, pre-Nietzschean and post-Nietzschean, has not been overturned by its transmogrification into positive science, nor by the return to its archaic beginning, nor by the timeless and tireless reception of our disowned and projected powers. For these glimpses into the metajuridical vault are still purchased with those Aristotelian categories we were just using: science (*episteme*); principle or beginning (*arche*); timeless (*apeiron*); power (*dynamis*). The invariable reversal of such attempts to cashier metaphysics reveals in each case a speculative jurisprudence: a story of the identity and non-identity of law and metaphysics retold by the rhetor in the mask of the *histor*.

The choice urged upon us whether of genealogy versus dialectics, of Husserlian versus Hegelian phenomenology, or of post-structuralism versus structuralism, is not a choice at all. Not that these oppositions are insignificant but that they now partake in a tradition and this places their signification beyond any question of choice. The fundamental categorial contraries which are said to capture the differences at stake, such as, repetition/contradiction, description/constitution, and, lately, structure/event, do not only imply and depend upon each other, but, on examination of their jurisprudential claims and connotations, display a deeper mutual involvement, an identity and non-identity, which is historically discernible. Just as 'subject is substance' is not a simple inversion of Aristotle's 'substance is not in a subject' but opens and holds open in that frail yet uninnocent 'is' the question of the political and historical experience that makes the assertion of the original proposition and of its inversion equally apposite, so, too, the Heideggerian lesson that essential being is accidental being, that *ousia* is *symbebekos*, the Event of appropriation, is not a simple inversion of the preliminary Aristotelian distinction between essential and accidental being, but opens up the history contained in the Being which shows in that 'is' and which seems to serve such contrary positions.

Similarly, the cases we have witnessed for grammatological *differance* and for genealogical Event have yielded the history which their founding contraries would hold at a great distance, and which they yet, ever so partially, relate. It has not been a question here of construing *differance* as a new transcendental argument, or 'power' as a new metacritique, but of comprehending why the moment when Zarathustra comes down from the mountain has had to be invoked, why it has become the new image for the unity of theory and practice. To witness this event is to witness the moment at which the rationality of the critical philosophy based on the drama of the fictions of Roman law – persons, things, and obligations – is phantasized into an Orientalism which borrows the identity of wandering Dionysus or Persian Zoroaster, but which, in its celebration of writing, returns the concept of tradition to an Hebraic setting. The opposition between *phonos* and *logos* on which the Derridean reconstruction of the tradition is based has been belied by the visit to the critical court-room where the proceedings ('discourse') were dominated by the voices of the manifold persons of the law. Grammatology takes Husserl's idea of writing as the realm which transcends the critical distinction of validity and genesis, changes the cerebral plenitude of Husserl's notion into eternal and invisible absence, and calls on Nietzsche's personified *voice* to initiate us into this monolithic but unknowable fate. What did Nietzsche call for? Qua scholar, he asked that the law tables be subjected to philological and historical investigation since he would have us know more not less about the law.

Genealogy calls on Nietzsche, qua scholar, to change traditional history into sacrificial history, to reinvent *wirkliche Historie*, the sublime instant of the unconditioned act, to relieve us of the burden of seeking to know. Concentrating on Nietzschean perspectivism, on truth as rhetorical value, Foucault would blind us to the truth both of Nietzsche's and of his own rhetoric. 'Will to power' is not thought by Nietzsche to fill the blind spot of the critical philosophy with the gratuitous act, but to develop a new kind of reflection on the seemingly unbudgeable habit of moral rigorism; this perspective beyond good and evil involves the most strenuous immersion in historical labour and imbues our acts with a greater not a sparer density. The genealogical reconstruction of the tradition with its would-be exclusion of 'law' from 'power' cripples our reason as it does Nietzsche's – for we cannot think the one without the other. Foucault sacrifices his own rule enough to apprehend us of the advent of administrative power and the demise of the civil law, but not enough to give us any space in which to relate to the ubiqitous and infinite points of power.

The cost of proceeding without Nietzsche's 'conscience of method' has become clear. His reminder that truth is a value has been taken as a turn to language. Yet the claim that representation is a matter of linguistic convention, not a synthesis of concept and intuition, presupposes both the concept of language and the concept of convention. To try to finish off metaphysics by exposing the 'promise of presence' which still lingers at the heart of the linguistic theory of value reaffirms the starting point yet again: for to say either that representation may be traced to linguistic 'contract' or that it contains a 'promise' reintroduces the question of the third or mediate term implied by these quintessential legal concepts. To leave us with the broken promise of presence attributed merely to the ruse of language, and with the 'force' of *differance* or with 'power' as the origin of representation, is to leave us at the bottom rung of the phenomenological ladder, at, respectively, *das Meinen*, and *Kraft und Verstand*; it reaffirms representation as an obscuring and obdurate medium and will not confront the paradox of the concept: of contracts and promises and language as the *Mitte*, the third. This foolhardy innovation prevents us from understanding why Hegel and why Nietzsche, equally anti-method but respectful of the limits of innovation, of the ineluctable cross of metaphysics and law, carefully reinstate an 'absolute method' and a 'conscience of method'.

It was sociology which inherited this conscience; and the trajectory followed here – from the *quaestio quid iuris* to 'writing' and 'power' as names designed to take our thinking beyond the opposition of genesis and validity, and their latter-day equivalents, action and structure, without reinscribing a metacritical circle but reproducing the antinomy of culture in the different and repeated Event – rededuces the development of sociological thinking. Socio-logic relieved transcendental logic of that unending trial of reason by taking the persons of the law out of the critical court-room and recasting them as social actors, by taking rights and obligations and treating them as status and role, by turning juridical things into social interaction. Weber's first major work on Roman agrarian history captures *die Zulassung der Usukapion*, the moment when the concept of property changed from *modus* (area) to *locus* (boundary), and which we saw initiating the critical crisis of reason in the Kantian and neo-Kantian justifications. Adapting Emil Lask, Weber proceeded relentlessly to translate the contraries of rationality and irrationality into the historical fate of actors and legal-rational authority, domination legitimized as authority – *dominium* justified as *usucapio*. The Parsons–Schutz correspondance can be read as the exchange of imperial rescripts: their struggles over the delineation of actors, things and obligations, the working out of a new edition of Justinian's *Institutes*, where the difficulty is to return the titles to their original setting of things and obligations without the discursive accretions of modern rights. Sociological repetition of structure and action arises from its status as the jurisprudence of actor and obligation; it may be that we have become so accustomed to thinking that law blinds us to the social that we overlook how socio-logic blinds us to law.

If this work has addressed itself to the 'question' of law it has been neither an unabashed revision of Heidegger's 'question of Being', nor an attempt to avoid the theory of justice or the concept of law, nor a refusal of Hegel's *Begriff*. It has been an attempt to return to the beginning, to the *locus classicus* which we share: Kant's strange way of not answering his own question, the *quaestio quid iuris*. Yet this unanswered question founds the idea of method we still revere and grounds the oppositions which still condition us – metaphysics and science; theory and practice; freedom and necessity; history and form. The discovery that the form of reason and the form of law imply each other did not become the occasion to devise a reformed *Kriticismus*, but to acknowledge the complexity of our continuing witness which went on to divulge further strata of litigious experience disciplined even by the forms of intuition, space and time, themselves. This involvement served as the touchstone from which to reassess that recent philosophical labour which would split again its interest in reason from the sociological interest in rationality and yet claim the most radical innovatory credentials. From the midst of the tradition, embroiled as it is in the antinomy of law, these interlocutors are heard to speak – not, as they would have it, against the naturalized beginning or utopian end of the Rousseauian, dialectical or structuralist heritage, but against their middle: against the exposition of civil society and civil law which they explicitly or implicitly present.

The exposition begun here of some of those confrontations with that middle has been partisan neither to a renewed indictment of the ever-encroaching irrationality of reason, nor to sketching an erstwhile civilizing process now uncivil: for these developmental theses would presuppose a safe place in the 'life-world' or in 'configuring science'. The procedure in this work has been both more implicated and more preliminary; by drawing out the legal arguments and the legal history at the heart of post-metaphysical reason, an attempt has been made to draw us back into the antinomy of culture, into the tradition which holds us, and, so, to open it again – in this aporetic way – under the title, if there must be one, of jurisprudential wisdom.

Bibliography

The bibliography is limited to works cited in the text.

Aarsleff, Hans, *From Locke to Saussure: Essays on the Study of Language and Intellectual History*, London, Athlone, 1982.

Adorno, T. W., *Negative Dialektik*, 1966, *Gesammelte Schriften*, 6, Franfurt am Main, Suhrkamp, 1973, trans. *Negative Dialectics*, E. B. Ashton, London, Routledge and Kegan Paul, 1973.

Altmann, Alexander, *Moses Mendelssohn: A Biographical Study*, London, Routledge and Kegan Paul, 1973.

Aquinas, *Selected Political Writings*, A. P. d'Entrèves (ed.), Oxford, Basil Blackwell, 1979.

Arendt, Hannah, 'The Concept of History: Ancient and Modern', in *Between Past and Future: Eight Essays in Political Thought*, Harmondsworth, Penguin, 1980.

—— *On Revolution*, Harmondsworth, Penguin, 1979.

—— 'On Violence', in *Crises of the Republic*, Harmondsworth, Penguin, 1973.

Aristotle, *The Categories*, The Loeb Classical Library, trans. Harold P. Cooke, London, Heinemann, 1973.

—— *The Physics* I, Books I–IV, The Loeb Classical Library, trans. Philip H. Wickstead and Francis M. Cornford, London, Heinemann, 1970.

—— *Metaphysics*, I–IX, and X–XIV, The Loeb Classical Library, trans. Hugh Tredennick, London, Heinemann, 1980 and 1977.

Augustine, *The City of God*, trans. John Healey, London, Dent, 1973, vol. 1.

Barthes, Roland, *Elements of Semiology*, 1964, trans. Annette Lavers and Colin Smith, London, Cape, 1972.

Bataille, Georges, *The Story of the Eye*, 1928, trans. Joachim Neugroschel, Harmondsworth, Penguin, 1982.

Benveniste, Émile, *le vocabulaire des institutions indo-européenes*, 1 and 2, Paris, Les Éditions de Minuit, 1969.

—— *Problèmes de linguistique générale*, 1, Paris, Éditions Gallimard, 1966.

Bergson, Henri, *Essai sur les données immédiates de la conscience*, 1889, Paris, Presses Universitaires de France, 1976, authorized trans. *Time and Free Will*, F. L. Pogson, London, George Allen and Company, 1912.

—— *Matter and Memory*, 1896, authorized trans. Nancy Margaret Paul and W. Scott Palmer, London, George Allen and Company, 1911.

—— *Creative Evolution*, 1907, authorized trans. Arthur Mitchell, London, Macmillan and Co., Ltd. 1911.

—— *Two Sources of Morality and Religion*, 1932, trans. R. Ashley Audra and Cloudesley Brereton, New York, Doubleday Anchor, 1954.

—— *The Creative Mind*, n.d., c.1903–23, trans. Mabelle L. Andison, New Jersey, Littlefield, Adams and Co., 1975.

Bernstein, Jay, 'Kant and The Problem of Transcendental Realism', unpublished Ph.d. thesis, University of Edinburgh, 1975.

Brentano, Franz, *Von der mannigfachen Bedeutung des Seienden nach Aristoteles*, 1862, trans. *On the Several Senses of Being in Aristotle*, 1862, trans. Rolf George, Berkeley, University of California Press, 1975.

Brown, Peter, *Society and the Holy in Late Antiquity*, London, Faber and Faber, 1982.

Buckland, W. W., *A Manual of Roman Private Law*, 1st edn, Cambridge, Cambridge University Press, 1928.

Bultmann, Rudolf, *Theology of the New Testament*, 1948, trans. Kendrick Gabel, vols I and II, London, SCM, 1978.

Carmi, T., *The Penguin Book of Hebrew Verse*, Harmondsworth, Penguin, 1981.

Cassirer, Ernst, *Substance and Function and Einstein's Theory of Relativity*, 1910, trans. William Curtis and Marie Collins Swabey, New York, Dover, 1923.

—— *The Philosophy of Symbolic Forms*, vol. 1 *Language*, 1923, trans. Ralph Mannheim, New Haven, Yale University Press, 1970.

Caygill, Howard, '*Aesthetics and Civil Society: Theories of Art and Society 1640–1790*', unpublished D. Phil thesis, University of Sussex, 1982.

Clements, Ronald E., *Exodus*, 1972, in *The Cambridge Bible Commentary* on the *New English Bible*, Cambridge, Cambridge University Press.

Cohen, Hermann, *Kants Theorie der Erfahrung*, Berlin, Ferd. Dummler, 1871.

—— *System der Philosophie*, 3 parts, Berlin, Bruno Cassirer:
  1. *Logik der reinen Erkenntnis*, 1902;

2. *Ethik des reinen Willens*, 1904;

3. *Ästhetik des reinen Gefühls*, 1, 2, 1912.

—— *Religion der Vernunft aus den Quellen des Judentums*, 2nd edn, Wiesbaden, Fourier, 1978.

Comte, Auguste, *Introduction to Positive Philosophy*, 1830, trans. Frederick Ferre, Indianapolis, Bobbs–Merrill, 1976.

—— *The Foundation of Sociology*, Kenneth Thompson (ed.), London, Nelson, 1976.

—— *Catéchisme Positiviste*, 1852, Paris, Garnier–Flammerion, 1966.

Copleston, Frederick, S.J., *Medieval Philosophy*, Part II *Albert the Great to Duns Scotus*, New York, Image Books, 1962.

Cornford, F. M., *From Religion to Philosophy: A Study in the Origins of Western Speculation*, 1912, Brighton, Harvester, 1980.

Daube, David, *Forms of Roman Legislation*, Oxford, Clarendon Press, 1956.

—— *The Exodus Pattern in the Bible*, 1963, Westport, Connecticut, Greenwood, 1979.

—— *Roman Law, Linguistic, Social, and Philosophical Aspects*, Edinburgh, Edinburgh University Press, 1969.

David, René and Brierley, John E. C., *Major Legal Systems in the World Today*, London, Stevens and Sons, 1978.

Deleuze, Gilles, *Le Bergsonisme*, Paris, Presses Universitaires de France, 1966.

—— *Nietzsche et la philosophie*, Paris, Presses Universitaires de France, 1962, trans. *Nietzsche and Philosophy*, 1962, Hugh Tomlinson, London, Athlone, 1983.

—— *Différence et répétition*, Paris, Presses Universitaires de France, 1972.

Derrida, Jacques, *Husserl: L'Origine de la géométrie, traduction et introduction*, 1962, Paris, Presses Universitaires de France, 1974, trans. *Edmund Husserl's Origin of Geometry: An Introduction*, John P. Leavey, Stony Brook, New York, Nicolas Hays, 1978.

—— *La Voix et le phénomène: Introduction au problème du signe dans la phénoménologie de Husserl*, 1967, Paris, Presses Universitaires de France, 1976, trans. *Speech and Phenomena and Other Essays on Husserl's Theory of Signs*, David B. Allison, Evanston, Northwestern University Press, 1973.

—— *De la grammatologie*, Paris, Les Éditions de Minuit, 1967, trans. *Of Grammatology*, Gayatri Chakravorty Spivak, Baltimore, The Johns Hopkins University Press, 1976.

—— *L'Écriture et la différence*, Paris, Éditions du Seuil, 1967, trans. *Writing and Difference*, Alan Bass, London, Routledge and Kegan Paul, 1981.

—— *Marges de la philosophie*, Paris, Les Éditions de Minuit, 1972, trans. *Margins of Philosophy*, Alan Bass, Brighton, Harvester, 1982.

—— *Positions*, Paris, Les Éditions de Minuit, 1972, trans. *Positions*, Alan Bass, London, Athlone, 1981.

Dodd, C.H., *The Bible and the Greeks*, 1935, London, Hodder and Stoughton, 1954.

Dumézil, Georges, *Archaic Roman Religion: With an Appendix on the Religion of the Etruscans*, 1966, vols 1 and 2, trans. Philip Krapp, Chicago, University of Chicago Press, 1970.

Duns Scotus, *Philosophical Writings*, trans. Allan Wolter, Indianapolis, Bobbs-Merrill, 1978.

Durkheim, Émile, *Montesquieu and Rousseau: Forerunners of Sociology*, 1892 and c.1901, trans. Michigan, Ann Arbor, 1965.

—— *Socialism*, c.1895, trans. Alvin W. Gouldner (ed.), New York, Collier, 1962.

—— and Marcel Mauss, *Primitive Classification*, 1901–02, trans. Rodney Needham, London, Cohen and West, 1970.

—— 'Deux lois de l'évolution pénale' in *L'Année Sociologique* IV (1900), 65–95, trans. in *Durkheim and the Law*, Steven Lukes and Andrew Scull (eds.), Oxford, Martin Robertson, 1983, pp.102–32.

—— *The Division of Labour in Society*, 1893, 2nd edn 1902, trans. George Simpson, London, Free Press, 1964.

—— *The Rules of Sociological Method and Selected Texts on Sociology and its Method*, trans. W.D. Halls, London, Macmillan, 1982.

—— *The Elementary Forms of the Religious Life*, 1912, trans. Joseph Ward Swain, London, George Allen and Unwin, 1968.

—— *Leçons de sociologie*, Paris, Presses Universitaires de France, 1969.

Ehrlich, Eugen, *Fundamental Principles of the Sociology of Law*, 1936, trans. Walter L. Moll, New York, Russell and Russell Inc., 1962.

Eissfeldt, Otto, *The Old Testament An Introduction*, trans. Peter Ackroyd, Oxford, Basil Blackwell, 1974.

Eliade, Mircea, *The Myth of the Eternal Return or, Cosmos and History*, 1949, trans. Willard R. Trask, Princeton, Bollingen, 1974.

d'Entrèves, A.P., *Natural Law: An Introduction to Legal Philosophy*, London, Hutchinson's University Library, 1951.

Forster-Nietzsche, Elizabeth (ed.), *The Nietzsche–Wagner Correspondence*, trans. Caroline V. Kerr, New York, Liveright, 1949.

Foucault, Michel, *Naissance de la clinique: Une archéologie du regard médical*, 1963, Paris, Presses Universitaires de France, 1972, trans. *The Birth of the Clinic: An Archeology of Medical Perception*, A.M. Sheridan Smith, London, Tavistock, 1973.

—— *Les Mots et les choses: Une archéologie des sciences humaines*, Paris, Éditions Gallimard, 1966, trans. *The Order of Things: An Archeology of the Human Sciences*, New York, Vintage, 1973.

—— *L'Archéologie du savoir*, Paris, Éditions Gallimard, 1969, trans. *The Archeology of Knowledge*, A. M. Sheridan Smith, London, Tavistock, 1974.

—— *L'ordre du discours*, 1970, Paris, Éditions Gallimard, 1971, trans. 'The Discourse on Language', Rupert Swyer, Appendix to US edn. of *The Archeology of Knowledge*, New York, Pantheon, 1972.

—— *Surveiller et punir: Naissance de la prison*, Paris, Éditions Gallimard, 1975, trans. *Discipline and Punish: The Birth of the Prison*, Alan Sheridan, Harmondsworth, Penguin, 1979.

—— *Histoire de la sexualité 1. La Volonté de savoir*, Paris, Gallimard, 1976, trans. *The History of Sexuality*, Volume One *An Introduction*, Robert Hurley, Harmondsworth, Penguin, 1981.

—— *Language, Counter-Memory, Practice: Selected Essays and Interviews*, Donald F. Bouchard (ed.), Ithaca, New York, Cornell University Press, and Oxford, Basil Blackwell, 1977.

—— *Power/Knowledge: Selected Interviews and Other Writings 1972–1977*, Colin Gordon (ed.), New York, Pantheon, 1980.

—— 'About the Concept of the "Dangerous Individual" in 19th-Century Psychiatry', trans. Alain Baudot and Jane Couchman, *International Journal of Law and Psychiatry* 1 (1978), 1–18.

Friedrich, Carl Joachim, *The Philosophy of Law in Historical Perspective*, 1958, Chicago, University of Chicago Press, 1963.

Gierke, Otto von, *Natural Law and the Theory of Society, 1500–1800*, vols I and II, trans. Ernest Barker, Cambridge, Cambridge University Press, 1934.

Goldman, Lucien, *Immanuel Kant*, 1945, trans. Robert Black, London, New Left Books, 1971.

—— *Lukács and Heidegger: Towards a New Philosophy*, 1973, trans. William Q. Boelhower, Routledge and Kegan Paul, 1977.

Gurvitch, Georges, *L'Idée du droit social: Notion et système du droit social, histoire doctrinale depuis le XVIIe siècle jusqu'à la fin du XIXe siècle*, 1932, Aalen, Scientia, 1972.

—— *Sociology of Law*, London, Routledge and Kegan Paul, 1947.

Hamann, J. G., *Schriften zur Sprache*, Josef Simon (ed.), Frankfurt am Main, Suhrkamp, 1967.

Hammer, Raymond, *The Book of Daniel*, 1976, in *The Cambridge Bible Commentary* on the *New English Bible*, Cambridge, Cambridge University Press.

Harrison, Jane, *Prolegomena to the Study of Greek Religion*, 1903, London, Merlin, 1980.

—— *Themis: A Study of the Social Origins of Greek Religion*, 1911, London, Merlin, 1977.

Hart, H. L. A., *The Concept of Law*, 1961, Oxford, Oxford University Press, 1981.

Hartmann, Eduard von, *Kategorienlehre*, Leipzig, Hermann Haacke, 1896.

Hartmann, Klaus, 'On Taking the Transcendental Turn' in *Review of Metaphysics* XX (1960), 223–49.

Hegel, G. W. F., *Theorie Werkausgabe*, 2, 3, 7, 8, 10, 12, Frankfurt am Main, Suhrkamp, 1977.

—— 'Natural Law', 1802–03, *Theorie Werkausgabe*, 2, trans. T. M. Knox, Pennsylvania, University of Pennsylvania Press, 1975.

—— 'The Difference between Fichte's and Schelling's System of Philosophy', 1801, *Theorie Werkausgabe*, 2,9–138, trans. H. S. Harris and Walter Cerf, Albany, State University of New York Press, 1977.

—— *Phenomenology of Spirit, Theorie Werkausgabe*, 3, trans. A. V. Millar, Oxford, Clarendon Press, 1977.

—— *Philosophy of Right, Theorie Werkausgabe*, 7, trans. T. M. Knox, Oxford, Oxford University Press, 1967.

—— *Encyclopaedia of the Philosophical Sciences*, 1830, Part I *Logic*, Part III *Philosophy of Mind, Theorie Werkausgabe*, 8 and 10, trans. William Wallace, Oxford, Clarendon Press, 1975 and 1971.

—— *The Philosophy of History, Theorie Werkausgabe*, 12, trans. J. Sibree, New York, Dover, 1956.

—— *Science of Logic*, vols I and II, 1813, Hamburg, Felix Meiner, 1969, trans. A. V. Millar, London, Allen and Unwin, 1969.

Heidegger, Martin, 'Der Zeitbegriff in der Geschichtswissenschaft', in *Zeitschrift für Philosophie und philosophische Kritik* 161 (1916), 173–88, trans. 'The Concept of Time in the Science of History', Harry S. Taylor and Hans W. Uffelmann, in *Journal of the British Society for Phenomenology* 9/1 (1978), 3–10.

—— *Die Kategorien- und Bedeutungslehre des Duns Scotus*, Tübingen, J. C. B. Mohr, 1916.

—— *Sein und Zeit*, 1927, Tübingen, Niemeyer, 1972, trans. *Being and Time*, John Macquarrie and Edward Robinson, Oxford, Basil Blackwell, 1967.

—— *Kant und das Problem der Metaphysik*, 1929, 4th edn, Frankfurt am Main, Klostermann, 1973, trans. *Kant and the Problem of Metaphysics*, James S. Churchill, Bloomington, Indiana University Press, 1965.

—— *Die Frage nach dem Ding: Zu Kants Lehre von den transcendentalen Grundsätzen*, 1935–36, Tübingen, Niemeyer, 1975, trans. *What is a Thing?* W. B. Barton Jr and Vera Deutsch, Indiana, Regnery, 1967.

—— *Nietzsche*, I and II, Pfullingen, Neske, 1961.

—— *Holzwege*, 1950, Frankfurt am Main, Klostermann, 1980, trans.: 'The Word of Nietzsche: "God is Dead"', 1943, in *The Question concerning Technology and Other Essays*, William Lovitt, New York, Harper, 1977; 'The Origin of the Work of Art', 1935/36, abridged and based on 1960 edn by H.-G. Gadamer, in *Basic Writings*, David Farrell Krell (ed.), London, Routledge and Kegan Paul, 1978 (complete trans. in Albert Hofstadter (ed.), *Poetry, Language, Thought*, New York, Harper, 1977); *Hegel's Concept of Experience*, 1942–43, translation prepared by Harper and Row with a section from Hegel's *Phenomenology of Spirit* in the Kenley Royce Dove translation, New York, Harper and Row, 1970.

—— *Einführung in die Metaphysik*, 1953, Tübingen, Niemeyer, 1958, trans. *Introduction to Metaphysics*, Ralph Mannheim, New York, Doubleday, 1961.

—— *Vorträge und Aufsätze*, 1954, Pfullingen, Neske, 1978; trans.: 'The Thing', in Albert Hofstadter (ed.), *Poetry, Language, Thought*, New York, Harper, 1977; 'The Question concerning Technology' and 'The Turning' in *Basic Writings*, David Farrell Krell (ed.), London, Routledge and Kegan Paul, 1978, and *The Question concerning Technology and Other Essays*, William Lovitt, New York, Harper, 1977; 'Moira' in *Early Greek Thinking*, David Farrell Krell and Frank A. Capuzzi, New York, Harper and Row, 1975.

—— *Was Heißt Denken?* Tübingen, Niemeyer, 1954, trans. *What is called Thinking?* Fred D. Wieck and J. Glenn Gray, New York, Harper and Row, 1972.

—— *The Question of Being*, 1955, German text and translation, London, Vision Press, 1959.

—— *Identity and Difference*, 1957, German text and translation, Joan Stanbaugh, New York, Harper and Row, 1969.

—— *Wegmarken*, 1967, Frankfurt am Main, Klostermann, 1978, trans.: 'Letter on Humanism', 1946–47, in *Basic Writings*, David Farrell Krell (ed.), London, Routledge and Kegan Paul, 1978, 'On the Being and Conception of *Physis* in Aristotle's *Physics*, B,1', 1939, Thomas J. Sheeham in *Man and World* 9/3 (1976), 219–70.

—— *Zur Sache des Denkens*, Tübingen, Niemeyer, 1969, trans. *On Time and Being*, Joan Stanbaugh, New York, Harper and Row, 1972.

Herder, J.G., 'Verstand und Erfahrung, Vernunft und Sprache, eine Metakritik der reinen Vernunft', 1799, *Werke*, Hildesheim, Georg Olms, 1967.

Homer, *Iliad*, trans. Richard Lattimore, Chicago, Chicago University Press, 1961.

Hughes, H. Stuart, *consciousness and society: the reorientation of European social thought 1890–1920*, London, Macgibbon and Kee, 1967.

Humboldt, Wilhelm von, *Schriften zur Sprache*, Miachael Böhler (ed.), Stuttgart, Reclam, 1973.

Husserl, Edmund, *Philosophie als strenge Wissenschaft*, 1910–11, Frankfurt am Main, Klostermann, 1981, trans. 'Philosophy as a Rigorous Science' in *Phenomenology and the Crisis of Philosophy*, Quentin Lauer, New York, Harper and Row, 1965.

—— *Vorlesungen zur Phänomenologie des inneren Zeitbewußtseins*, 1905, M. Heidegger (ed.), 1928, Tübingen, Niemeyer, 1980, trans. *The Phenomenology of Internal Time Consciousness*, James S. Churchill, The Hague, Martin Nijhoff, 1964.

—— 'The Origin of Geometry', 1936, Appendix III in *Husserliana*, VI, Walter Biemel (ed.), The Hague, Nijhoff, 1962, trans. Appendix VI in *The Crisis of the European Sciences and Transcendental Phenomenology*, David Carr, Evanston, Northwestern University Press, 1970.

Ihering, Rudolf von, *Geist des römischen Rechts*, 1852–58, 3 parts, Aalen, Scientia, 1968.

—— *Der Zweck im Recht*, 1877–81, Leipzig, Breitkopf und Härtel, vol. I 3rd edn, 1893, vol. II, 2nd edn, 1886, vol. I trans. *Law as a Means to an End*, Isaac Husik, New York, Augustus Kelley, 1913.

Jolowicz, H. F., *Historical Introduction to the Study of Roman Law*, Cambridge, Cambridge University Press, 1932.

—— *Roman Foundations of Modern Law*, Oxford, Oxford University Press, 1957.

Jones, J. Walter, *The Law and Legal Theory of the Greeks*, Oxford, Clarendon Press, 1956.

Jünger, Ernst, 'Über die Linie', Martin Heidegger zum 60. Gerburtstag, 1950, *Werke*, 5, Stuttgart, Ernst Klett, 1960, 247–89.

Justinian, *The Institutes of Justinian*, trans. and ed. Thomas Collett Sanders, London, Longmans, Green and Co., 1917.

Kafka, Franz, *Der Prozess*, 1925, Frankfurt am Main, Fischer, 1980, trans. *The Trial*, Willa and Edwin Muir, Harmondsworth, Penguin, 1975.

—— 'The Problem of Our Laws', German and English trans. in *Parables and Paradoxes*, New York, Schocken, 1975.

Kamenka, Eugene, and Tay, Alice Ehr-Soon, 'Beyond Bourgeois Individualism: the Contemporary Crisis in Law and Legal Ideology', in Eugene Kamenka and R. H. Neale (eds), *Feudalism, Capitalism and Beyond*, London, Edward Arnold, 1975.

Kant, Immanuel, *Werkausgabe*, III, IV, V, VII, VIII, X, XI, Wilhelm Weischedel (ed.), Frankfurt am Main, Suhrkamp, 1980.

—— *Critique of Pure Reason, 1781/87, Werkausgabe*, III and IV, trans. Norman Kemp Smith, New York, St Martin's, 1965; and *Concise Text*, trans. Wolfgang Schwarz, Aalen, Scientia, 1982.

—— *Groundwork of the Metaphysics of Morals, Werkausgabe*, VII, trans. H.J. Paton, New York, Harper and Row, 1964.

—— *Critique of Practical Reason, Werkausgabe*, VII, trans. Lewis White Beck, Indianapolis, Bobbs-Merrill, 1956.

—— *Prolegomena to any Future Metaphysics that will be able to present itself as a Science, Werkausgabe*, V, trans. Peter G. Lucas, Manchester, Manchester Press, 1971.

—— *The Metaphysical Elements of Justice*, abridged trans. of the first part of *Die Metaphysik der Sitten, Werkausgabe*, VIII, John Ladd, Indianapolis, Bobbs-Merrill, 1965.

—— *Metaphysical Foundations of Natural Science, Werkausgabe*, IX, trans. James Ellington, Indianapolis, Bobbs-Merill, 1970.

—— *Critique of Judgement, Werkausgabe*, X, trans. J.H. Bernard, New York, Hafner, 1972.

—— 'Idea for a Universal History from a Cosmopolitan Point of View', *Werkausgabe*, XI, trans. in *On History*, Lewis White Back *et al.*, New York, Bobbs-Mcrrill, 1963.

Kelsen, Hans, *Society and Nature: A Sociological Inquiry*, Chicago, University of Chicago Press, 1943.

—— *The Communist Theory of Law*, London, Stevens and Sons Ltd. 1955.

Lask, Emil, *Gesammelte Schriften*, Eugen Herrigel (ed.), Tübingen, J.C.B. Mohr, 1923–24:

    Band 1 'Fichtes Idealismus und die Geschichte', 1902; 'Rechtsphilosophie', 1905, trans. in *The Legal Philosophy of Lask, Radbruch and Dabin*, Kurt Wiek, Cambridge, Mass., Harvard University Press, 1950;

    Band 2 'Die Logik der Philosophie und die Kategorienlehre', 1910; 'Die Lehre vom Urteil', 1911;

    Band 3 Nachlass.

Lefebvre, Henri, *Le langage et la société*, Paris, Éditions Gallimard, 1966.

Levi-Strauss, Claude, *The Elementary Structures of Kingship*, 1944, trans. James Harle Bell *et al.*, London, Eyre and Spottiswoode, 1969.

—— *Tristes Tropiques*, 1955, trans. John and Doreen Weightman, 1973, Harmondsworth, Penguin, 1976.

—— *Totemism*, 1962, trans. Rodney Needham, Harmondsworth, Penguin, 1969.

—— *Structural Anthropology*, trans. Claire Jacobson and Brooke Grundfest Schoepf, Harmondsworth, Penguin, 1979.

—— *The Savage Mind*, 1962, London, Weidenfeld and Nicolson, 1974.

Liebmann, Otto, *Kant und die Epigonen*, 1865, Berlin, Reuther und Reichard, 1912.

Lukács, Georg, 'Emil Lask', in *Kantstudien* XXII (1913), 349–70.

—— *Frühe Schriften zur Ästhetik, 1912–16, Gesammelte Werke*, vols 16–17, Darmstadt, Luchterhand, 1979.

MacDowell, Douglas M., *The Law in Classical Athens*, London, Thames and Hudson, 1978.

Macquarrie, John, *An Existentialist Theology: A Comparison of Heidegger and Bultmann*, 1955, Harmondsworth, Penguin, 1973.

Maine, Henry Sumner, *Ancient Law*, 1861, London, George Routledge & Sons, nd.

Marx, *Early Writings*, trans. Rodney Livingstone and Gregory Benton, Harmondsworth, Penguin, 1977.

—— *Capital*, vol. 1, trans. Ben Fowkes, Harmondsworth, Penguin, 1976.

—— and Engels, *Collected Works*, vol. 1 (1835–43), London, Laurence and Wishart, 1975.

Mill, John Stuart, *Auguste Comte and Positivism*, 1865, Michigan, Ann Arbor, 1973.

Mommsen, Theodor, *The History of Rome*, 1854–56, trans. W. P. Dickson, vols I–IV, 1868, London, Dent, n.d.

Murray, Gilbert, *The Rise of the Greek Epic*, 1907, Oxford, Oxford University Press, 1934.

—— *Five Stages of Greek Religion*, 1912, London, Watts and Co., 1943.

Neale, R. H., 'Property, Law and the Transition from Feudalism to Capitalism', in Eugene Kamenka and R. H. Neale (eds), *Feudalism, Capitalism and Beyond*, London, Edward Arnold, 1975.

Nietzsche, Friedrich, *Werke*, I, II, III, Schlechta, Frankfurt am Main, Ullstein, 1979.

—— Über Wahrheit und Lüge in aussermoralischen Sinn', *Werke*, III, trans. 'On Truth and Lies in a Nonmoral Sense' in *Philosophy and Truth: Selections from Nietzsche's Notebooks of the early 1870s*, Daniel Breazeale, Brighton, Harvester, 1979; extracts in *The Portable Nietzsche*, Walter Kaufmann, Harmondsworth, Penguin, 1981; and in Oskar Levy (ed.) vol. II, *Early Greek Philosophers and Other Essays*, London and Edinburg, T. N. Foulis, 1911.

—— *Human all too Human, Werke*, I.

—— *Daybreak Thoughts on the Prejudices of Morality, Werke*, II, trans. R. J. Hollingdale, Cambridge, Cambridge University Press, 1982.

—— *Thus Spoke Zarathustra: A Book for All and None, Werke*, II, trans. in *The Portable Nietzsche*, Walter Kaufmann, Harmondsworth, Penguin, 1981, and by R. J. Hollingdale, Harmondsworth, Penguin, 1961.

—— *The Gay Science: With a Prelude in Rhymes and an Appendix of Songs, Werke*, II, trans. Walter Kaufmann, New York, Vintage, 1979.

—— *Beyond Good and Evil: Prelude to a Philosophy of the Future, Werke*, III, trans. Walter Kaufmann, New York, Vintage, 1966.

—— *Genealogy of Morals, Werke*, III, trans. Walter Kaufmann and R.J. Hollingdale, New York, Vintage, 1969.

—— *Ecce Homo, Werke*, III, trans. Walter Kaufmann, New York, Vintage, 1969.

—— *The Will to Power*, Stuttgart, Kroner, 1964, trans. Walter Kaufmann and R.J. Hollingdale, New York, Vintage, 1968.

—— *The Nietzsche-Wagner Correspondence*, Elizabeth Forster-Nietzsche (ed.), trans. Caroline V. Kerr, New York, Liveright, 1949.

Nisbet, R. A., *The Sociological Tradition*, London, Heinemann, 1967.

Plato, *Laws*, I and II, Loeb Classical Library, trans. R. G. Bury, London, Heinemann, 1967.

Poncelet, Roland, *Cicero traducteur de Platon: L'Expression de la pensée complexe en latin classique*, Paris, E. de Boccard, 1957.

Puelma, Mario, 'Cicero als Platon-Übersetzer', in *Museum Helveticum* 37 (Juli 1980), 137–78.

Radcliffe and Cross, *The English Legal System*, 6th edn, London, Butterworths, 1977.

Robinson, H. Wheeler, *Inspiration and Revelation in the Old Testament*, Oxford, Clarendon Press, 1946.

Rommen, Heinrich A., *Die Ewige Wiederkehr des Naturrechts*, 1936, trans. *The Natural Law: A Study in Legal and Social History and Philosophy*, Thomas R. Hanley, St Louis, B. Herder Book Co., 1947.

Rose, Gillian, *The Melancholy Science: An Introduction to the Thought of Theodor W. Adorno*, London, Macmillan, 1978.

—— *Hegel contra Sociology*, London, Athlone, 1981.

Rousseau, J.-J., *The Social Contract and Discourses*, trans. G. D. H. Cole, London, Dent, 1973.

Ste Croix, G. E. M. de, Class Struggle in the Ancient Greek World from the Archaic Age to the Arab Conquests, London, Duckworth, 1981.

Saussure, Ferdinand de, *Cours de linguistique générale*, 1915, Tullio de Mauro (ed.), Paris, Payot, 1979, trans. *Course in General Linguistics*, Wade Baskin, Glasgow, Fontana/Collins, 1974.

Schelling, F. W. J., *System des transcendentalen Idealismus*, 1800, Hamburg, Felix Miener, 1957.

Schleiermacher, F. D. E., *Hermeneutik und Kritik*, Manfred Frank (ed.), Frankfurt am Main, Suhrkamp, 1977.

Schopenhauer, Arthur, *On the Basis of Morality*, 1841, *Zürcher Ausgabe* VI, Zürich, Diogenes, 1977, trans. E. F. J. Payne, Indianapolis, Bobbs-Merrill, 1965.

—— *The World as Will and Representation*, vol. 1, 1819, *Zürcher Ausgabe II* Zürich, Diogenes, 1977, trans. E. F. J. Payne, New York, Dover, 1966.

Scotus, *see* Duns Scotus.

Seung, T. K., *Structuralism and Hermeneutics*, New York, Columbia University Press, 1982.

Sherwin-White, A. N., *Roman Society and Roman Law in the New Testament*, Oxford, 1963, reprinted Grand Rapids, Baker Book House, 1981.

Simmel, Georg, *Schopenhauer und Nietzsche*, 1907, München und Leipzig, Duncker und Humblot, 1920.

—— *Philosophie des Geldes*, 1900, trans. Tom Bottomore and David Frisby, London, Routledge and Kegan Paul, 1978.

Spencer, Herbert, *On Social Evolution*, J. D. Y., Peel (ed.), London, University of Chicago Press, 1972.

Spinoza, Baruch, *Ethics* in *Works of Spinoza*, trans. R. H. M. Elwes, (ed.), New York, Dover, 1955.

Stammler, Rudolf, *Wirtschaft und Recht nach der materialistischen Geschichtsauffassung*, Leipzig, Veit und Comp, 1896.

—— *Die Lehre von dem richtigen Rechte*, Berlin, J. Guttentag, 1902, trans. *The Theory of Justice*, Isaac Husik, New York, Augustus M. Kelley, 1925.

Stein, Peter, *Regulae Iuris: From Juristic Rules to Legal Maxims*, Edinburgh, Edinburgh University Press, 1966.

—— *Legal Evolution: The Story of an Idea*, Cambridge, Cambridge University Press, 1980.

Stirner, Max, *Der Einzige und sein Eigentum*, 1845, trans. *The Ego and his Own*, New York, Dover, 1973.

Strauss, Leo, *Natural Right and History*, 1953, Chicago, the University of Chicago Press, 1971.

Tacitus, *Germania*, Lateinisch/Deutsch trans. Arno Mauersberger, VMA-Verlag, Wiesbaden, n.d., English trans. H. Mattingly, revised S. A. Handford, Harmondsworth, Penguin, 1970.

Trendelenberg, Adolf, *Geschichte der Kategorienlehre*, 1846, Hildesheim, Georg Olms, 1963.

Vaihinger, H., *The Philosophy of 'As If': A System of the Theoretical, Practical and Religious Fictions of Mankind*, 1911, trans. C. K. Ogden, New York, Harcourt, Brace and Co., 1925.

Vinogradoff, Paul, *Outlines of Historical Jurisprudence*, vol. 1 *Tribal Law*, vol. 2 *The Jurisprudence of the Greek City*, Oxford, Oxford University Press, 1920–22.

Watson, Alan, *Society and Legal Change*, Edinburgh, Scottish Academic Press, 1977.

—— *The Making of the Civil Law*, Cambridge, Mass., Harvard University Press, 1981.

Weber, Max, *Die Römische Agrargeschichte in ihrer Bedeutung für das Staats-und Privatrecht*, 1981, Amsterdam, P. Schippers NV, 1966.

—— *Roscher und Knies und die logischen Probleme der historischen Nationalökonomie*, 1903–06, in *Gesammelte Aufsätze zur Wissenschaftslehre*, Tübingen, J. C. B. Mohr, 1973, trans. *Roscher and Knies: The Logical Problems of Historical Economics*, Guy Oaks, New York, The Free Press, 1975.

—— 'R. Stammlers "Überwindung" der materialistischen Geschichtsauffasung', 1907, in *Gesammelte Aufsätze zur Wissenschaftslehre*, Tübingen, J. C. B. Mohr, 1973, trans. *Critique of Stammler*, Guy Oakes, New York, The Free Press, 1977.

—— *The Agrarian Sociology of Ancient Civilizations*, 1909 and 1896, trans. R. I. Frank, London, New Left Books, 1976.

—— *Economy and Society: An Outline of Interpretative Sociology*, 1 and 2, *Studienausgabe*, Tübingen, J. C. B. Mohr, 1976, trans. Guenther Roth and Claus Wittich (eds), Berkeley, University of California Press, 1978.

Wiek, Kurt (trans.) *The Legal Philosophy of Lask, Radbruch and Dabin*, Cambridge, Mass., Harvard University Press, 1950.

Young-Bruehl, Elisabeth, *Hannah Arendt: For Love of the World*, New Haven, Yale University Press, 1982.

Index